The Founding of Israel

The Founding of
Israel
The Journey to a Jewish Homeland
from Abraham to the Holocaust

Martin Connolly

PEN & SWORD
HISTORY

AN IMPRINT OF PEN & SWORD BOOKS LTD.
YORKSHIRE – PHILADELPHIA

First published in Great Britain in 2018 by
Pen & Sword History
An imprint of
Pen & Sword Books Ltd
Yorkshire - Philadelphia

ISBN 978 1 52673 715 1

Printed and bound in the UK by TJ International

Pen & Sword Books Ltd incorporates the Imprints of Pen & Sword
Books Archaeology, Atlas, Aviation, Battleground, Discovery,
Family History, History, Maritime, Military, Naval, Politics, Railways,
Select, Transport, True Crime, Fiction, Frontline Books, Leo Cooper,
Praetorian Press, Seaforth Publishing, Wharncliffe and White Owl.

PEN & SWORD BOOKS LIMITED
47 Church Street, Barnsley, South Yorkshire, S70 2AS, England
E-mail: enquiries@pen-and-sword.co.uk
Website: www.pen-and-sword.co.uk

or

PEN AND SWORD BOOKS
1950 Lawrence Rd, Havertown, PA 19083, USA
E-mail: Uspen-and-sword@casematepublishers.com
Website: www.penandswordbooks.com

With respect to

Dr Edward Kessler MBE

Founder Director, Woolf Institute
Fellow, St Edmund's College
Affiliated Lecturer, Faculty of Divinity, University of Cambridge

A Jew who shone new light on Christianity

'Persecutions of the Jews, which had taken place at the beginning of the reign of Edward, had little power to check the increase or destroy the prosperity of that extraordinary people. Having no country; living among strangers and enemies; deprived of all political standing – of all the legitimate objects of ambition, even of reasonable security for his life – the Jew devoted those intellectual qualities, in which he was seldom deficient, to the one agent of power within his reach. Wealth alone could not raise him from a condition of utter misery and contempt gave him a certain standing and importance among his fellow men, and offer employment for his energies. If the favour of the law was to be bought, the wealthy Jew might have hoped to buy it, while for the poor there was no mercy. If he was derided and persecuted by the haughty sons of a happier race, he returned scorn for scorn and revenged himself where he could by trading upon their necessities. If he became grovelling and avaricious, absorbed in a mean and unworthy passion, perhaps the fault should be ascribed less to him than to those unconquerable prejudices isolated him in the midst of his kind and condemned him to the fate of Ishmael.' *Cassells Illustrated History of England, Vol 1, p.314*

Contents

Acknowledgements

It is truly said that no man (or woman) is an island and even though writers lock themselves away as they create their work, they still rely on the willingness and kindness of others to assist their endeavours. Over many years I have been grateful to those Jewish people who have shared their thoughts and insights and have shown a generosity of spirit. I still remember the words of Mr Marks, a Jew, who visited my home when I was a child, and brought many gifts for our poor family. He told me, 'We enter this world to embrace life and to help make the world a better place, to fail to do so implies we have not really lived.' I later understood that he had survived the Holocaust and he had never spoken of it but showed a remarkable capacity to love and care, despite what he must have suffered and for one poor Irish family at least, he made the world a better place.

I have also had the privilege in adult life to have had Jews teach me about hope, forgiveness and understanding the other. One such man is Doctor Edward Kessler, who founded the Woolf Institute, which is devoted to the study of relations between Jews, Christians and Muslims and who shone new light for me to understand better the truth that Judaism and Christianity cannot be fully understood without reference of one to the other. It is through his and others' work at the Centre for Jewish Christian Relations (now the Woolf Institute) in Cambridge, that my knowledge of Jewish matters was broadened and deepened. For that I am very grateful and it was there the seeds of this present book were sown.

For the Jewish people, family is very important and as I have studied the history of genocide that has seen the destruction of so many families I am ever grateful and appreciative of my wife Kitty and Mark, Jonathan, Angelina, Angela, Richard, Janice and Esther and their respective husbands and wives and my grandchildren, a great family who are never slow to support and encourage my efforts.

The people at Pen & Sword, as always, prove a great resource for aid and succour and my editors never cease to improve my work. There are also the people at the National Archives, ever willing to help, as are those at archives in America and Israel. There are also those who have shared with me at synagogues and offered their wisdom and insights into the topic and commented on my own thoughts.

Whilst I have acknowledged in my notes, as far as possible, all sources I am sure there are many individual voices I have heard which are not included and to them I am also thankful. As ever, whilst I mention these things, the work, its opinions, ideas and conclusions remain my responsibility alone.

Martin Connolly, 2018

Introduction

'Here [in the State if Israel] their spiritual, religious and political identity was shaped. Here they first attained statehood, created cultural values of national and universal significance, and gave the world the Eternal Book of Books.'

David Ben-Gurion, 14 May 1948

'Let there be no more war or bloodshed between Arabs and Israelis. Let there be no more suffering or denial of rights. Let there be no more despair or loss of faith.'

Anwar Sadat, 26 March 1979

Ben-Gurion and Sadat were entrenched enemies who had been determined to see the other's ambitions thwarted to the point where Sadat expressed the determination to see that a State of Israel would never come into existence. However, the eventual recognition by him that Israel had a right to exist because of her history and of the tribulations she had been through won the day and seventy years ago, the State of Israel became a reality. This work sets out a chronological history of the journey of the Jewish people to that day in 1948 and recounts the many trials and tribulations that they experienced. It is a story of great tragedy but also of great resilience and joy and one that demonstrates that the spirit of hope within a people can never be extinguished by hate and suffering, when that hope is based on a belief that what is hoped for is right and just. It is also very true of those who hold a religious persuasion that remains fixed on their Messiah and the conviction that one day He will stand on the Mount of Zion and the deliverance of the Jewish people will be total and complete.

In setting out to write this account there is one thing I have had reinforced, that in coming to understand any issue, context is hugely important. Whether it is in Theology, Psychology, counselling clients or writing history, knowing what went before and what is happening currently allows a better and more accurate picture to be seen. So often, opinions or attitudes on many subjects are based on ill-informed views or are formed through the prism of prejudice and irrational hatred. Unfortunately, this is particularly true when the subject is Israel and the Jewish people. This book sets out to look at their journey – a terrible journey that takes them through almost every country on earth. They are a rejected people, an exploited people and a people who have to take whatever steps are necessary simply to survive and keep their Jewish identity alive. Indeed, in researching for the book I discovered so many cases of massacres, killings, property confiscation and other anti-Semitic attacks that it became impossible for one book to contain them. It may be asked why highlight the Jewish experience, when there are many other cases of ethnic cleansing and massacres and the simple answer is that there has been no other group who have been systematically attacked with a view to remove them from the face of the earth, in almost every century of human history, since they first entered the scene.

A major question on identity needs to be clarified right from the start which, in many ways, is a question that initially seems strange. Who is a Jew? The answer is not straightforward. Louis Finkelstein between 1949 and 1960 went through contortions of physical, cultural and religious aspects to try and reach a conclusion, without arrival at a satisfactory answer. The Jews are descendants of a branch of a group known as the Semites. The term Semites was first recorded in the 1770s by researchers at the Göttingen School of History, who derived the name from Shem, one of the three sons of Noah in the Book of Genesis. The existence of Semites can be traced to the earliest records of history. Archaeological research in the Middle East has found evidence of Western Semitic people from around the 4-3 millennia BCE. There is a caution that must be given in that the term 'Semite' really refers to those who speak the Semitic language and is often confused with race or ethnicity. There is a general acceptance that Babylonians, Assyrians, Hebrews, South Arabian Sabaeans, Phoenicians, Aramaeans, Abyssinians and Bedouins of northern Arabia and of Mesopotamia belong to this Semitic group.

The term 'race' is regularly used to describe human groups and the Nazis would employ it heavily in their attitudes to Jews, Gypsies and so on. Yet the word was not found in ancient literature. It was a word that appeared in the sixteenth century. From Middle French (*rasse*) and

Italian *(razza)* it was used to classify 'race, breed, lineage, family' and 'people of common descent'. There may be a connection with Latin radix *'root,'* but this may have been a means to arrive at the idea of 'tribe'. In modern times, 'race' has come to be used to debate skin colour, physical features and blood line – the latter being at the centre of the notorious Nazi Nuremberg Blood Laws. The simplistic view that any of these traits determine 'race' is erroneous and misses out a basic fact. The human being no matter where he or she originates has the same basic genetic make-up and blood types which vary in the finer DNA detail. In fact, all human beings are 99.9 percent identical in their genetic makeup. As Naomi Zack wrote, 'All human beings belong to the same species'. There is a debate between mono-origins of man and multi-origins; is man descended from one source or from multiple sources around the world? The University of Cambridge, funded by the Biotechnology and Biological Sciences Research Council, carried out a significant study, the results of which concluded, 'Our findings show that humans originated in a single area in Sub-Saharan Africa'. Therefore, because there is only one race, all who try to argue for the superiority of one racial group over another, as the Nazis did, is flawed. It is more correct to speak of one human race that has developed cultural and regional diversity from an original tribe, with each individual equal in dignity and value

Mark Dyble, an anthropologist at University College London, and many others have done a great deal of work looking at how mankind developed. There is agreement that mankind began in family groups, which expanded to clans and then to tribes. These tribes needed space to live and resources to survive with land from which to obtain them. From this, the concept of tribal lands arose. As populations grew, these tribal lands expanded and combined to create the modern ideas of countries. Often this growth was accompanied by violence and tribal conflict which even today can be seen in the Middle East, India, Africa and the Baltic regions. From this came the ideas of countries expanding into empires as one group attempted to exploit and take a greater share of the world's resources and accumulate wealth and power. Throw in religion and a powerful cocktail is developed, that breeds prejudice, violence and persecution. The Babylonians, Greeks, Romans, Ottomans, Russian and British, are all examples of such activity. Again, this was always with war.

The tribal group we will focus on is that of the 'Semitic' tribe, the Jews, who in turn had twelve sub-tribes. There will be an examination of who belongs to that group, who they were, their origins, their journey and their arrival in a homeland, not specifically focusing on the religion of the Jews and only touching on it when necessary to explain a geo-politically related idea or attitude. This is not because their religion is unimportant but to recognise that it is a matter of faith and belief and that religion in itself does not define a Jew. There are further complications in definition of a 'Jew'. In the Jewish Scriptures we find in the record that kings and patriarchs have mixed their blood in marriage. Ishmael was the son of Abraham by an Egyptian woman. Isaac and Jacob both had Aramean wives. Joseph married an Egyptian and Moses a Midianite and even king David himself was descended from Ruth the Moabite. Religious reforms over the centuries have brought about a developing awareness of what the reformers called 'purity'. This has never been truly successful and even in modern times many marry outside the faith.

That is why we can speak of religious Jews, atheistic Jews, British Jews, American Jews and Jews from every nationality. There are also those Jews who hold the belief in Jesus as the Messiah, and chose to embrace that belief and in modern times refer to themselves as Messianic Jews.

Many non-Jews may join the Jewish population through religion and identify themselves as Jews, some may even naturalise themselves in Israel and take the name Jew. More correctly nowadays, the term Israelis would apply to the citizens of that modern country; Israel. No matter what the adjective, the Jews originate from a common source. That source would be the Jewish tribe and particularly the sub-tribe of Judah, that eventually settled in Israel under King David and despite internecine wars and intermittent banishment to other lands, they have remained rooted in that region.

I will therefore concentrate on the historical facts were known and allow these to speak to the central theme of a Jewish homeland. One thing that will become apparent is that from earliest times there were many attempts to establish the Jewish people back in what has been called the Holy Land. These attempts have been inspired by the religious faith of the Jewish people wanting to return to the birthplace of their people and the promises of a land within their Scriptures. These attempts were also inspired by Christian Zionists who believed in the establishment of a Jewish state as part of their own faith's second coming of their Messiah. It is a relatively modern phenomenon that has seen this desire to establish a Jewish homeland becoming the realisation of a more secular ambition, which some religious Jews have embraced, while others treat it with suspicion.

Perhaps it may be wise to remember the words of Maya Angelou, who was a civil rights activist in America, 'Prejudice is a burden that confuses the past, threatens the future and renders the present inaccessible.' There is in the Jewish Scriptures in the Book of Proverbs a wise saying, 'Faithful are the wounds of a friend; but the kisses of an enemy are deceitful.' As a friend of the Jews, it is therefore necessary to also look at the issues of injustice, not only against the Jews, but those perpetrated by them. Only then can we arrive at a place to view the entire picture in the round and understand the founding of the State of Israel.

Chapter One

From Abraham to the Assyrian Conquest

I n setting out to describe the history of the Jewish people there is a need to clarify the dates used. There is a train of scholarly thought that would argue the present dating system is incorrect and therefore archaeological finds and dating is a matter of dispute. British scholar Pater James is among them. He argues:

> 'By re-dating the beginning of the Iron Age in Palestine from the early 12th century BCE to the late 10th, a completely new interpretation of the archaeology of Israel can be offered: One which is in perfect harmony with the biblical record.'

This argument is not particularly relevant to this particular book as it focusses on events and their relevance to the story of Israel in the Middle East. However, it has to be acknowledged that some debates as to archaeological facts mentioned do refer to dating and the reader must use their own judgement, in the light of this debate, in assessing them.

The earliest attempts to establish a Jewish homeland will begin with those, both Jewish and Christian, who hold a religious belief that the land was promised to the Jews by God. It is essential that this background belief is understood as it underpins a great many attempts to establish Israel over the centuries. Therefore, with all the qualifications already set out, a man given the name 'Abraham' began a journey from Haran. Haran's ruins are close to Harran in modern Turkey, not far from the Syrian border. It is first found in the Ebla Tablets and was a city that attracted many different people. Throughout its history, Haran has been the home of the Akkadians, Babylonians, Assyrians, Hittites, Persians, the Alexandrian Empire, Romans, Byzantines, Seljuks, Ayyubids, and many others. It is an important place in the history of the Jews, Moslems and Christians. It was here that Abraham, a worshipper of many gods, would have made a choice of a personal god as was the custom. The tradition is that he had a vision of one particular God, *Yahweh*, who Abraham would come to believe was the only God. Abraham believed that his God told him to go to a land that he did not know and, with his extended family, he set out for Canaan. The area known as Canaan in ancient times covers parts of modern-day Israel, the Gaza Strip and the West Bank. It also covered parts of the coastal regions and areas of Syria, Lebanon and Jordan. There is no record of the exact route he took to get to Canaan. There were two, one a dangerous desert crossing or a well-travelled route which was the safest route in those days. He would have chosen the latter with such a large caravan of relatives and animals. This safer, alternative route followed what is the modern International Coastal Highway that links Egypt and Mesopotamia. It led through the ancient cities of Carchemish, Aleppo, Ebla, (home of the Ebla Tablets), Qatna, and into Damascus. From Damascus, the King's Highway led into the Transjordan (now Jordan). This was a major route for nomadic people, merchants and the military; it would be the most natural choice for Abraham. The 400-mile journey took Abraham to Shechem. This city is believed to be at Tell Balata, close to the modern city of Nablus in the modern West Bank. The descriptions in the Hebrew Bible fit well with archaeological discoveries. It is mentioned in the Amarna Letters[1] (dated about 1400 to 1300 BCE) which were found in Upper Egypt. The letters, although later than Abraham, are still a source of intriguing statements about the Canaanites he would have found on his arrival. One document from a Canaanite reads:

> 'Behold this land of Jerusalem neither my father nor my mother gave it to me; the mighty hand of the king gave it to me. Behold, this deed is the deed of Milkilu, and the deed of the sons of Labaya, who have given the land of the king to the Habiru. Behold, king, my lord, I am innocent as regards the Kashi. Let the king ask the officers if the house is very mighty (f). Indeed, they have aspired to perpetrate a very wicked crime; they have taken their implements and ... sent to the land ... servant; let the king take heed to them, that they support the lands with their hand. Let the king demand for them much food, much oil, and many garments, until Pauru, the king's officer, goes up to Jerusalem.'[2]

We find the name *Habiru*, believed to a West Semitic people, the Hebrews, from which Abraham came, linked to the Canaanites and it is also interesting that the dispute is about land. The enemy of the *Habiru* acknowledges that Jerusalem and surrounding lands had been given to them. Who is entitled to the land in that area has remained the subject of contention for millennia. A recent discovery in 2016 of a papyrus that dated back 2700 years is an extra-biblical source that mentions Jerusalem and reads, 'From the king's maidservant, from Na'arat, jars of wine to Jerusalem' thus giving evidence to an organised kingdom with Jerusalem at its centre. When Abraham arrived at Shechem it was a small unfortified town and the area was populated by many different peoples as well as the nomadic wanderers who passed through. For religious Jews this is a very important point in their tradition. It is at this point they believe that Abraham was given a promise – 'To your offspring I will give this land'. This promise is something that will be returned to later. Abraham then moved towards Luz, later known as Bethel. This is also in the modern West Bank. A famine in the area caused him to move to Egypt and eventually he returned to Bethel. Tradition states that he was a very wealthy man with great possessions and animals. He and his nephew then separated and settled in different parts of Canaan. This was the beginning of the settlement of the land by the ancestors of the Jewish people. The settlement was not allowed to live in peace and Abraham found himself involved in military conflict. The Jewish tradition believes that once more the promises were given to him of the land in which he had settled. It is here that the story and indeed the future conflicts over land begin. Abraham had a servant Hagar, who was an Egyptian, who became pregnant by Abraham and had a son, Ishmael. Ishmael became an important controversy between Jews, Moslems and Christians in later years. It is believed that he was the forefather of the Arabs. In modern times, the dispute of the right to the land centres on the Jews and the Arabs. The term Arab is used historically in many sources, but it is important to point out that the term covers a variety of peoples, from different areas and cultures; for consistency, it will be used throughout this book to identify an Arabic people. For our purposes, the story moves on and Abraham had a son, Isaac, by his wife, Sarah. In terms of future disputes over land, Isaac and Ishmael became the subject of controversy between Jews and Moslems. What is of note however is that the literature of both groups agree that God would bless both men and make them leaders of great nations. However, Jewish tradition believes that it is Isaac who was brought into covenant with God and through him the promises of the land for the

Jewish people was confirmed. When Abraham died, Ishmael and Isaac were united at the tomb where they buried him. Perhaps there is a hope that two Semitic people who have become enemies may one day stand together and bury the past but still honour it as a shared tradition.

Isaac then had twin sons, Jacob and Esau. Here again both sons became fathers of great nations and both would be the source of conflict over land even in their own time Eventually Jacob came to Luz (Bethel) and there the Jewish tradition believes that God changed Jacob's name to Israel. Jacob/Israel's twelve sons were the origins of the twelve tribes of Israel who eventually settled in the land of Canaan. So far, the narrative has relied on Jewish tradition based on their Scriptures. But is there any evidence from secular research that would confirm this narrative? First of all, there is the Merneptah Stele, now in the Cairo Museum, that is dated to 1206 BCE. This is an Egyptian record and it mentions an Israelite people, 'Israel is laid waste, his seed is no more'.[3] There is other evidence emerging that will help. One of Jacob's sons, Joseph, is recorded as being taken into Egypt and becoming a high official in the Egyptian government. Archaeology has discovered evidence that would confirm the presence of a Semitic people at the right time that is contemporary with Joseph. Furthermore, there is substantial evidence that a high-ranking Semitic individual had a house and was buried in a tomb in Egypt, with his statue also found and defaced by tomb-robbers. It has been suggested that this indeed was Joseph, particularly when it was found that the body bones were missing as described in the Jewish Scriptures, where they are reported as being taken by Moses to Canaan. Because Joseph was a high official it would be expected to find this evidence of him, however, there was no immediate evidence of any of the other sons. This was the situation until 1977 when a discovery was made of a Greek/Aramaic inscription which for the first time gave the Biblical name of Dan. This discovery brought the story of Jacob and his sons into sharp focus. Further support for the tradition came with the discovery of the Mesha Inscription. This gave the name of another son, Gad. Judah, another son, has now been found in many records in which his name is mentioned. This secular evidence does much to substantiate the traditional history of the origin of the Jewish people and their having rooted themselves in this particular part of the Middle East. The intention of this narrative, as already indicated, is not to consider the religious belief of the Jewish people, except where it is necessary for the subject matter of the Jewish homeland. That belief speaks of the many tribulations suffered in Egypt and their final entry back into Canaan. Archaeology or inscription research does not help us establish many of the actual facts. However, one thing about archaeology that is certain is that nothing in its findings is certain. The interpretation of finds has a great deal to do with the motives and attitudes of the archaeologist. There is also the issue of one discovery being followed by another that casts doubt on the former. This is particularly true of Middle East and Biblical archaeology which is strewn with controversy. All that can be done is to take the general picture that all the finds present and to stand back and view them, like a great artistic masterpiece, and in this case what we see is a people springing from a religious tradition that is set in a landscape that is now the modern Middle East.

As we move to the line of the descendants of Jacob's son Judah, we find an important king, David. He and his son, Solomon, are at the centre of much controversy. There are two questions raised in the debate. Did David exist and did he have an empire? The confirmed facts are that the Jewish people of that time had internecine conflict that caused the nation to divide into Southern Judah and Northern Israel. David from the line of Judah was in the Southern area. Firstly, evidence has been found that confirms that a House of David existed. In 1993, an inscription was found at Tel Dan. It points to the Southern area and a House of David. This at least points to a leader in Judah who was named David. As to his ruling a large kingdom, the truth is that there is little extra-Biblical evidence for it. Israel Finkelstein argues that there is no evidence for a large population that could have allowed David a large army as there were no major fortress settlements. However, this has been challenged by the discovery at Khirbet Qeiyafa. This is a fortress structure discovered in the Judean area. It is unusual in having two large gates that make it impressive for that period. Whilst there are arguments about this finding, it does provide strong evidence of an organised fortress structure and an army. Professor Yosef Garfinkel of the Humanities Faculty at the Hebrew University, Jerusalem, gives a very convincing account that this is indeed a Davidic site. Despite arguments to the contrary, especially from professor Israel Finkelstein, Professor of Archaeology at Tel Aviv University, his conclusions remain forceful. Furthermore, Alan Millard, outlines a scholarly discussion on a piece of pottery with an inscription found at Khirbet Qeiyafa and concludes, 'I see no good reason to doubt the existence of a kingdom ruled by David from Jerusalem and happily associate the Khirbet Qeiyafa ostracon with that time.' However, in the modern Israel, land disputes continually cast a shadow over archaeology and none more so in the discovery of a site in Jerusalem itself – the Palace of King David.

In 2005, Eilat Mazar announced to the world that she had found David's Palace. What she had found was a large 'fortress structure' and from a Jewish Scripture verse that spoke of King David 'going down' into his fortress, then the palace must be above the area she had discovered. She gave a number of evidences of her claim that indeed supported the finding to be from the date of King David. However, the arguments began and others suggested a different interpretation of her finds. Once more the search for archaeological evidence is shrouded in controversy.

However, can we say that there is any non-Biblical evidence of a powerful Israelite nation in the Middle East? For this we can turn again to the Mishna Stone already mentioned. This was written in the Phoenician alphabet. The stone was discovered intact by Frederick Augustus Klein, at the site of ancient Dibon (in modern Jordan), in August 1868. It was later smashed during a local village dispute about ownership. However, the inscription was preserved and later the fragments put together to confirm the record. This is a very important archaeological discovery as it does much to confirm the Jewish Scriptural record and its wording is important:

> 'Omri was king of Israel, and oppressed Moab during many days, and Chemosh was angry with his aggressions. His son succeeded him, and he also said, "I will oppress Moab". In my days he said, "Let us go, and I will see my desire upon him and his house", and Israel said, "I shall destroy it for ever". Now Omri took the land of Medeba, and occupied it in his day, and in the days of his son, forty years … I took from it the vessels of Yahweh [Israel's God], and offered them before Chemosh. And the king of Israel fortified Jahaz, and occupied it.'[4]

After all the disputes about the Jewish Scriptures and the archaeological evidence we have at last an undisputed account that places Israel's king Omri into an historical context. There is a very small group who wish to deny Israel any historical foothold in the Middle East and who would claim it is a forgery or not a true historical record. Albright is clear, 'The Moabite Stone remains a corner-stone of Semitic epigraphy and Palestinian history'. Omri comes from the line of Judah/Israel, and whilst his heritage is unclear, he may have been of the tribe of Issachar or Manasseh. My own studies suggest his origin is Issachar which had tribal lands in what became Samaria. An Omri is mentioned as an earlier leader of the Issachar tribe and may well be that his descendent was King Omri and Samaria was also where king Omri based his centre of power. Here he ruled over the Northern State of Israel. The date of his reign has been dated to the mid to late eighteen hundreds BCE. At this time, the Northern Kingdom and the Southern Kingdom of Judah were at war with one another. The historical presence of the ancient Jewish people in this area is strongly confirmed with non-Biblical evidence also available.

In 1861, John G. Taylor discovered the Kurkh Monoliths (879-853 BCE) in what is now Turkey. These were an amazing find as they gave the battle boasts of Shalmaneser III over his enemies. A portion on the stone reads[5]:

'I destroyed, devastated, and set fire to Karkar, his royal city. Irhulêni brought twelve kings to his support; they came against me to offer battle and fight: 1,200 chariots, 1,200 cavalry, and 20,000 soldiers belonging to Hadad-ezer of Damascus; 700 chariots, 700 cavalry, and 10,000 [or 20,000] soldiers belonging to Irhuleni of Hama; 2,000 chariots, and 10,000 soldiers belonging to Ahab, the Israelite[A-ha-ab-bu Sir-ila-a-a].'

Here is another undisputed non-Biblical reference to a powerful Israel ruler. With such a large army he can only have had rule over a sizeable area. As Susan Ackerman says:

'The size of Ahab's contribution to the anti-Shalmaneser fighting force at Qarqar indicates, for example, that Israel was still a major military power in Syria-Palestine at the end of the first half of the ninth century B.C.E.'

The Israelite people were not able to rest easy in their lands. A major group became dominant in the Middle/Near East; the Assyrians. They are traceable as a state from the 2400s BCE. Shalmaneser III, Tiglath-Pileser III and Shalmaneser V were involved in the conquering of Israel in the mid-700s BCE, eventually occupying both the Northern and Southern Kingdoms. Sargon II and his son Sennacherib would complete their work. Lachish, a great centre of Israel was taken, burned and destroyed. Sennacherib's palace would have a room decorated with the scenes of its destruction. A great number of the Israelites were removed from the land and the Assyrians settled many people from other nations there, particularly in Samaria. The Samaritans grew from this settlement and took on the practice of a form of Judaism. Indeed, the long historic enmity between Jews and Samaritans began from here. It was Sennacherib who came and besieged Jerusalem, the Judean centre, attempting to occupy and despoil it. The historical records confirm that due to the distractions of battles with Egypt and Babylon, he had to abandon the siege, but he still extracted huge treasure from king Hezekiah and to all intent and purpose made him his vassal. The point to be made here is that the evidence demonstrates the presence in the area of the Israelite people and their forced removal and displacement by others. This denial of the right to remain in their own homeland and their deportations would not be the last they would experience.

Chapter Two

Origins – A Journey begins

Having laid this background, our journey starts with the Italian Archaeological Mission, led by Paolo Matthiae, who began a dig in 1964 at Tel Mardikh in Syria. Later in 1968, a statue of Ibbit-Lim, King of Ebla, was discovered there. This also revealed that the goddess Ishtar was the object of worship and for some time there was a hope of discovering the city of Ebla which had been referenced in ancient Near Eastern texts, but its location was unknown. However, the discovery of the statue gave a strong indication that the site of Ebla may be close. In 1974 until 1976, further work revealed the Royal Library and at last the city of Ebla had been found. The library, which dated to about 2500 BCE, included about 2,000 complete tablets from one inch to over a foot long, 4,000 fragments and over 10,000 chips and small fragments, making this the largest library ever discovered from the third millennium BCE. What was interesting about this discovery was the language on the tablets. It was a Semitic tongue that had echoes in Hebrew script. Whilst there was sharp debate about this significant find, Giovanni Pettinato commented:

'Since the discoveries at Ras Shamra beginning in 1929, many biblical scholars have shown a certain reluctance to exploit this new textual material because they felt that it was too early (circa 1375-1190) and too far away to be relevant for solving problems in texts composed in Hebrew and in Palestine in the first millennium B.C. In his review of L. Sabottka, Zephaniah, a work which attempts to apply Ugaritic data to the text of the prophet which bristles with difficulties, F. C. Fensham writes, 'One must, however, be very cautious in comparing Ugaritic material from the fourteenth to twelfth centuries BC with the Hebrew of Zephaniah (ca. 612 B.C.), with the interval of about six hundred years in which the meaning of a word or a literary device could have changed enormously. In cases where one has no choice but to compare Ugaritic and Hebrew so far apart, it would be wise to put a question mark after one's solution.' But Ugaritic and Hebrew no longer seem to be so far apart, thanks to the Ebla Tablets of 2500 B.C. which illumine the Hebrew text on point after point and which in turn are elucidated by the biblical record. Scholars are, in fact, beginning to remark facetiously that the Ugaritic texts may be much too recent to be relevant for biblical research! Not the least of Ebla's contributions will be the gradual demolition of the psychological wall that has kept the Ras Shamra discoveries out of biblical discussions in some centers of study and from committees convened to translate the Hebrew Bible into modern tongues.'[1]

It is only right to point out that Pettinato and his conclusions are a matter of debate and there is disagreement on his conclusions. The weight to put on the findings does depend on the particular views of the interpreter. Whilst the many now dismiss Pettinato's conclusion, there are a substantial number who believe the jury is still out.

One particular name was found on the tablets; Ebrium. This is the name Eber in Hebrew, the language of the Jews. James Watson wrote:

'One of the most striking correspondences is between the name of the great king of Ebla, Ebrium, which is semantically and linguistically equivalent to the name Eber in Genesis 10:26 (and other places), who is one of the ancestors of Abram (= Abraham), the name Eber gives rise to the Gentilic form Ibri (= Hebrew, the general term for Abraham and his descendants) The correlation is intriguing although there is no evidence from the tablets linking the two persons or, to be sure, from the Bible.'[2]

On its own, the name would not carry a great weight but over the various tablets there are references to other Biblical names and places. Robert Althann rightly concludes:

'J.L. Ska cautions that only long and patient work will allow us to determine the links which existed between Ebla and the biblical world. Similarity does not automatically imply dependence, and a culture can borrow certain elements from another and profoundly transform them. Ebla cannot be expected to provide "proofs" of the existence of biblical persons or of the historicity of certain facts narrated in Scripture. But Ebla does allow us to see increasingly clearly the roots of the Bible in the history of the ancient near east. The material from Tell Mardikh premises to be of the greatest value for illuminating points that are still obscure in the history and language of the Bible. On the linguistic side, we can expect a considerable reduction in the number of texts whose translation remains uncertain. On the other hand, we can hope to be able to measure more precisely the degree of historicity to lie accorded the patriarchal traditions and therefore to appreciate better the narratives of Israel's origins. Thus we may expect our knowledge of the Bible to be deepened and enriched.'[3]

Indeed, Israel Finkelstein said in a documentary, 'Abraham is beyond recovery'. However, the fact of his existence should not be dismissed. If we hold that a tribal people have a spoken tradition that is passed from generation to generation, it is no great stretch to see that the Genesis account, when written down, may indeed have the traditional history of a man called Eber noted in the tablet. Indeed, Titus Flavius Josephus, born Joseph ben Matityahu, was a first-century Romano-Jewish scholar historian. He is a reliable source for many aspects of the Hebraic history. He also records Eber as part of the oral tradition. What is important for us is that as far as the self-understanding of the Jewish people is concerned, Eber is a figure in the genealogy of their existence. From him comes the lineage that leads to Terah. This name appears in cuneiform tablets that have been found but as is very usual with such finds the significance is debated. Tad Szulc comments:

'If archaeology denies us any direct evidence of Abraham, Terah's name appears tantalizingly in cuneiform tablets. Ömer Faruk Harman of Marmara University in Istanbul cautions that "Terah" almost certainly is not a personal name. It is probably a clan name or the name of a town in extreme northern Syria or, more likely, south-eastern Turkey, not far from Haran. Still, Abraham was a son of Terah, which may establish the connection between Abraham and Haran.'

Szulc quotes Rabbi Menahem Froman who said, 'For me Abraham is philosophy, Abraham is culture. Abraham may or may not be historical. Abraham is a message of loving kindness. Abraham is an idea. Abraham is everything. I don't need flesh and blood.' Perhaps the wisdom of William Dever, Professor Emeritus at the University of Arizona is apposite:

> 'The fact is that archaeology can never prove any of the theological suppositions of the Bible. Archaeologists can often tell you what happened and when and where and how and even why. No archaeologists can tell anyone what it means, and most of us don't try.'

As the debate continues, Abraham, the son of Terah, still remains the focal point for not only the Jewish people but for Christians and Moslems. Therefore, it is a matter of faith as to the existence of an actual man called Abraham. That does not remove the idea of the beginning of a people from the Ur region that has been a part of their tradition for millennia. It is no different from the oral traditions of many diverse people who trace their origins from the mist of the past. Aborigines, Native American Indians and even the origins of Britons/English rely on the hand down of myths and legend and genetic investigations are now the popular method to attempt to trace origins. What can be accepted is that the history and understanding of a particular period can support an oral tradition that certain activities took place. Traditional historical criticism is a methodology of Biblical criticism that was developed by Hermann Gunkel an Old Testament scholar who belonged to the History of Religions School at Göttingen and whilst the oral tradition may have exaggerations it contains elements that point to a real past. Often it is true that real history becomes legend and legend becomes myth and modern sceptical minds too often dismiss the myth without intelligent investigation into its origins. In the case of Ur, we do know that many nomads moved around that area, seeking out their own futures. It is not impossible that one man did in fact make such a journey and has been given that name, Abraham. He embarked on a journey which is the beginning of the journey of the Jewish people.

It has to be stressed that Abraham was not a 'Jew' at the start of his travels. He was referred to as a 'Hebrew'. This is interesting as at Mari, one of the principal centres of Mesopotamia during the third and early second millennia BCE, archaeologists discovered tablets that had a reference to the '*Habiru*'. Abraham too originates in Mesopotamia, and belongs to a family who were polytheistic. It has to be said that the name '*Habiru*' is a matter of debate as to its meaning, but it is generally accepted that they were Western Semites active in Mesopotamia. The Jewish Scriptures tell us in Genesis 11:31:

> 'And Terah took Abram his son, and Lot the son of Haran his son's son, and Sarai his daughter in law, his son Abram's wife; and they went forth with them from Ur of the Chaldees, to go into the land of Canaan; and they came unto Haran, and dwelt there.'

In what is modern Iraq there stands, in a barren area, the remains of a ziggurat (a large structure that reached high towards the sky and had a temple built on its top) which is the site of Urim (Ur), an important Sumerian city in ancient Mesopotamia. It is located at the site of modern Tell el-Muqayyar in southern Iraq. The ziggurat was built around 2100 BCE by UrNammu. Originally a huge structure four times its current height, the Iraqi government restored the base that remains for tourists to see. The city was a centre of cultic worship and whilst many gods were honoured there, some centres were dedicated to a particular god. In Ur this was Nanna, who was intimately connected with the cattle herds that were the livelihood of the nomadic people in the marshes of the lower Euphrates River, where the cult developed. Piotr Michalowski, the George G. Cameron Professor of Ancient Near Eastern Languages and Civilizations, an expert on the area, describes a thriving urban centre, with bustling, narrow streets full of shops, where craftsmen manufactured leather goods and precious ornaments. It was a major commercial centre, a place of bustling trade and it had links to what are now modern Iran, Turkey, and Afghanistan, Syria, Israel and Egypt. It was agriculturally abundant with irrigation canals from the Euphrates and the Tigris which then flowed closer to the city. It allowed many crops such as barley, lentils, onions, garlic. The husbandry of sheep and goats supplied ghee and wool. Michalowski, also editor of the *Journal of Cuneiform Studies*, describes the wealth of information available from the period that allows us this understanding of these conditions. Terah and his sons would have prospered in such a place and developed the great skills of business and leadership that Abraham would later display. Terah and his family would have been involved in this activity as well as the cultic activity and when they travelled to Haran, they would have come into contact with the god Sin, another form of Nanna. Mesopotamia, much like the Middle East today, was a place of regular armed conflict, with marauding bands that would threaten villages and trade caravans. Terah and his sons would develop their military skills and the ability to protect and defend their families and goods and it was at Haran the path of Terah and his son Abraham would divide and the Jewish journey start.

Chapter Three

By The Rivers Of Babylon: Longing For Home

I f ever there was a piece of poetry that spoke to the longings of Jewish people to return to their homeland it is found in Psalm 137:

'By the rivers of Babylon, there we sat down, yes, we wept, when we remembered Zion.

Upon the willows in the midst we hung up our harps.

For there they that led us captive asked of us for words of song, and our tormentors asked of us mirth: 'Sing us one of the songs of Zion.'

How shall we sing the LORD'S song in a foreign land?

If I forget you, O Jerusalem, let my right hand forget her cunning.

Let my tongue cleave to the roof of my mouth, if I remember you not; if I set not Jerusalem above my chiefest joy.'

It is no surprise that the activity of the Babylonians in Israel and Judah, as to dates and what actually happened, is a matter of debate. The debate is informed by the point of view of those debating, be it political, theological or archaeological. The important point is in regard to the evidence of the occupation of the land by the Jewish people. In this there is complete agreement. Nebuchadnezzar, the king of Babylon, had a great desire to spread his kingdom across the Near and Middle East. To this end, the kingdoms of Israel and Judah were brought into his orbit. He entered their lands and the greatest tragedy of his invasion was the destruction of Jerusalem in c.597 BCE. Tablets discovered in Iraq gave the evidence of Nebuchadnezzar's actions:

The sixth year, in the month of Kislev, the king of Akkad mustered his troops and marched on Haiti. From Hatti, he dispatched his troops, and they went in the direction of the desert. They carried away astonishing riches, cattle and the gods of the many Arabs. In the month of Adar the king returned to his country.

The seventh year, in the month of Kislev, the king of Akkad mustered his troops, marched on Hatti, and set up his quarters facing the city of Yehud [Judah] in the month of Adar, the second day, lie took the city and captured the king. He installed there a king of his choice. He colle[cted] its massive tribute and went back to Babylon.

[The eighth] year [in the mon]th of Tebeth, the king of Akkad [marched] on Hatti as far as Carchemis. [...] he [...] not [...]. In the month of Sebat, [the king] we[nt back to] his own country.'[1]

This, along with the excavation of ruins in Jerusalem, gives outstanding evidence of this period. Not for the first or the last time, the Jewish people were subjected to humiliation and suffered the brutality of an oppressor, their existence and way of life threatened. There is some dispute about whether the country was completely emptied of all the inhabitants. The records would indicate that there was a deportation of a sizeable number of the citizens to Babylon and Egypt but in the rural areas many did in fact remain. This remnant of the Jewish people continued the presence of the Jewish people in the area until their fellow Israelites returned to rebuild their homeland. The great Babylonian Empire went the way of all empires as eventually a greater one and its ruler arose. This was Cyrus the Great and the Persian Empire. The Cyrus Cylinder held by the British Museum records details of his exploits. The pagan god Marduk was said to have called him to greatness:

'Marduk surveyed and looked throughout the lands, searching for a righteous king, his favourite, He called out his name: Cyrus, king of Anšan; he pronounced his name to be king all over the world.'

The Cylinder records his version of the taking of Babylon by Cyrus and his relative Gubaru the Mede, thought to be Darius the Mede mentioned in the Jewish Scriptures, incorporating it into his Empire. Cyrus was kindly disposed to other religions and the record notes:

'Agade, Ešnunna, Zamban, Me-Turnu, Der, as far as the region of Gutium, the sacred centers on the other side of the Tigris, whose sanctuaries had been abandoned for a long time, I returned the images of the gods, who had resided there, note to their places and I let them dwell in eternal abodes. I gathered all their inhabitants and returned to them their dwellings. In addition, at the command of Marduk, the great lord, I settled in their habitations, in pleasing abodes, the gods of Sumer and Akkad, whom Nabonidus, to the anger of the lord of the gods, had brought into Babylon.'

It was this generosity of spirit that allowed the exiles from Israel and Judah to return home to rebuild their Temple and once more settle in the land. The historic story and evidence accords closely to the Jews' own Scriptural accounts. Over this period, the Jewish people experienced deportation and returns to their land three times. The first return to Judah for the Jews came shortly after the Persian conquest of Babylon in 538 BCE, led by Sheshbazzar. The second came 80 years later, in the seventh year of Artaxerxes I, 458 BCE led by Ezra. And the third came thirteen years after the second, in the twentieth year of Artaxerxes I, 444 BCE, led by Nehemiah. The yearning of these exiles to return home has been the yearning of the Jewish diaspora throughout the ages. Their return to the land allowed them to reconstruct the Temple and once more to establish themselves in the land where they belonged. When one considers the size of their territory and their lack of power in the wider strategy of the vast empires and countries around them, the question of why they suffered so much has to be asked. Jacob Hoschander wrote:

'It was always the aim of intolerant rulers to compel the Jews to abandon their exclusive position, and this task could not be accomplished except by means of persecution.'

In the book of Esther found in the Jewish Scriptures, the Jewish scribe wrote of an enemy of his people:

'And Haman said unto king Ahasuerus: 'There is a certain people scattered abroad and dispersed among the peoples in all the provinces of thy kingdom; and their laws are diverse from those of every people; neither keep they the king's laws; therefore it profiteth not the king to suffer them. If it please the king, let it be written that they be destroyed; and I will pay ten thousand talents of silver into the hands of those that have the charge of the king's business, to bring it into the king's treasuries.'

The Book of Esther is not without its own controversy among scholars from all schools of thought and indeed, from the Islamic point of view, Haman belongs to a very different time, if he existed at all, they would argue. Hoschander's excellent work sets the book in its proper time and shows that the 'intention of Haman was the destruction of an idea, not the individuals who adhered to it'. Hoschander rightly sets the issue in the context of a world in which the Jews were determined to remain steadfast to their religion and refused to accept the common practice of idolatry and pagan practice. Their Scriptures made the command of their God clear:

'You shall not make idols for yourselves or erect an image or pillar, and you shall not set up a figured stone in your land to bow down to it, for I am the LORD your God.'

The historic records show that Artaxerxes had attempted to enforce the worship of the Persian goddess Anahita throughout his kingdom. This was rejected by the Jewish people and indeed it has been the case throughout history for adherents to the Jewish faith, despite the fact that there were those who strayed from it and were rebuked by the religion's prophets. Therefore, whilst the arguments about the book of Esther may rage, the book does bring out a reality. This is stated by Hoschander in his discussion on Purim, the festival that celebrates Esther:

'This is exactly what our narrative meant to indicate and to impress upon the mind of the Jews that the danger they escaped is not a matter to be forgotten that their descendants and all such as joined themselves unto them, no matter what country they might live, would be exposed to the same danger [of persecution].'

As we will see, that danger was ever present down the ages and would be experienced in a horrific way in modern times.

Historically, the Jewish people now became a settled community after their return from exile. However, the tectonic plates of world power were shifting and there arose a new power, Alexander the Great. A young Macedonian, he was an unlikely conqueror of the world. Yet incredibly, his army marched forth to great triumph across the Persian territories of Asia Minor, Syria and Egypt without suffering defeat. At the Battle of Gaugamela, in what is now northern Iraq, in 331 BCE, this youthful leader of the Greeks became master of Asia Minor and Pharaoh of Egypt and indeed King of Persia at the age of 25. Such an overwhelming crushing of his enemies could have signalled disaster for the tiny Jewish kingdom, yet he came and passed by Jerusalem and left the Jewish people untouched. He conquered across three continents and his power seemed invincible until in 323 BCE he was struck down with a fever and died aged 32. His death would be the beginning of a power struggle that would have the Jewish people at its centre until it would boil over in an attempt to destroy them.

The Empire that Alexander built was in danger of collapsing. But two generals emerged and agreed to divide it between them. The northern section of the empire was taken by Seleucus and became known as the Seleucid Dynasty. His centre of power was located in what is today Damascus. The southern section was in the hands of Ptolemy who centred himself in the city of Alexandria, which had been renamed in honour of Alexander. Judea stood on the frontier between them. For 130 years, the two new powers vied for influence over the territory. Finally, the Seleucid Empire became aggressive and invaded the Southern territory. Under Ptolemy's rule, the Jewish people had full civil rights and they lived contentedly under that rule. They continued to practice their religion and worship in their Temple and were largely unaffected by Hellenism, which was thought to pollute traditional Judaism with Greek culture. However, this was all to change after the invasion. Antiochus Epiphanes, then king of the Seleucid Empire, styled himself a demi-god and sought to impose his Greek ideas on religion upon the Jews. This included the worship of Zeus. His aim was to destroy the Jewish people's way of life and bring them more in line with Hellenism. This was complicated by a conflict between Hellenised Jews who embraced certain Greek ideas and the traditional Jews who resisted it. Antiochus was brutal and desecrated their holy Temple. Josephus captures the drama:

> 'Now Antiochus was not satisfied either with his unexpected taking the city, or with its pillage, or with the great slaughter he had made there; but being overcome with his violent passions, and remembering what he had suffered during the siege, he compelled the Jews to dissolve the laws of their country, and to keep their infants uncircumcised, and to sacrifice swine's flesh upon the altar.'

In Antiochus' absence when he went to lead the Seleucid army against the Parthian empire, which was the most enduring of the empires of the ancient Near East, centred around modern Iran, he sent his general Lysias to deal with a revolt in Judea by the Maccabees. They were a Jewish band led by Judah Maccabee and his brothers for the liberation of Judea from foreign domination and the account of their exploits are found in the canon of Scripture in the Greek Orthodox, Roman Catholic, Coptic, and Russian Orthodox churches, but they are not recognized as canon by Protestants and Jews. Judah's father, Matisyahu was the father of the Hasmonean dynasty to which the Macabees belonged. The rebels succeeded and eventually ended the oppression of Antiochus. He died in 167 BCE during his campaign and the Jewish people were left in peace to practice their religion. This allowed the victorious Hasmonean dynasty to rule semi-autonomously as an independent Jewish State. However, the Jewish people would not be left to remain in peace; another Empire would covet their territory and they once more would experience persecution and banishment from their own land.

Chapter Four

Under Rome: The Road To Freedom Blocked

Josephus sets the scene for the next tragic episode in the Jewish history:

'Now the occasions of this misery which came upon Jerusalem were Hyrcanus and Aristobulus, by raising a sedition one against the other; for now we lost our liberty, and became subject to the Romans, and were deprived of that country which we had gained by our arms from the Syrians, and were compelled to restore it to the Syrians. Moreover, the Romans exacted of us, in a little time, above ten thousand talents; and the royal authority, which was a dignity formerly bestowed on those that were high priests, by the right of their family, became the property of private men.'

The death of Queen Alexandra Salome in 67 BCE exposed the underlying tensions between her two sons, Hyrcanus and Aristobulus. The young Aristobulus rejected his elder brother's rule and a civil war ensued, that brought disturbance to the region. They both made an appeal to Pompey, the Roman general and consul, who was conducting war in Syria, enforcing law and order in the region. A dispute in Judea was not welcomed by him. Aristobulus was too strident and he was arrested by Pompey, who then ordered Jerusalem to be taken. On his arrival he found the gates locked against him. Josephus recorded the event:

'... for he saw the walls were so firm, that it would be hard to overcome them; and that the valley before the walls was terrible; and that the temple, which was within that valley, was itself encompassed with a very strong wall, insomuch that if the city were taken, that temple would be a second place of refuge for the enemy to retire to.'

Hyrcanus saw the opportunity for his own advantage and allowed entrance to Pompey into the area of the city he controlled. The result was a three-month long assault on Jerusalem that destroyed many of its precincts and allowed Pompey to even enter into the Holy of Holies of the Temple – an anathema to the Jews. Over 12,000 Jews were killed before the survivors were allowed to cleanse the Temple of this desecration. Pompey did not give Hyrcanus his expected reward and did not restore him to the kingship. Instead, he was allowed to remain as High Priest and Judea became subject to Rome and paid tribute. The outcome of these events was disastrous for the Jews. Their land was cut up and areas given away, another aspect of history that would repeat itself in modern times. In 37 BCE, the Romans appointed Herod the Great to rule as their puppet king. This was a controversial appointment because he was not considered a true Jew:

> 'But at heart Herod, an Idumaean, was more a pagan than a Jew, as his conduct throughout his reign was to show. The Idumaeans were still regarded by the Jews as semi-foreigners…'

Under Herod, the Jewish people never felt truly free and independent, as he acted more in the interests of Rome than the Jewish people. This desire to shrug off the imposition of foreign rule sowed the seeds of groups that would wish to overthrow this occupation and establish a true independent Jewish State. The Pharisees, Sadducees and the Essenes were examples of religious groups who wanted to see a pure religion within a true Jewish Theocracy. As with all groups that adhere to extreme beliefs, they spawned those who would go further and look to bring about their aims through violence and revolt. Therefore, the area suffered from continual outbursts of violence and retaliation that kept the Roman heel on the necks of the people. The hotbed of Jerusalem was a particular problem with the Temple sited there. The decision was taken by Rome to re-site their military headquarters:

> '… the Romans moved the governmental residence and military headquarters from Jerusalem to Caesarea. The centre of government was thus removed from Jerusalem, and the administration became increasingly based on inhabitants of the Hellenistic cities (Sebaste, Caesarea and others).'

This historic information allows us to place another Roman in Judea who would be involved in the harsh repression of the Jewish people – Pontius Pilate. Evidence of his presence was found in the discovery of the Pilate Stone in Caesarea in 1961. The short inscription reads:

'To the honourable gods (this) Tiberium Pontius Pilate, Prefect of Judea, had dedicated …'

Philo describes Pilate as, 'a man of a very inflexible disposition, and very merciless as well as very obstinate'. When the leaders of the people threatened to write to the Emperor about his behaviour Philo notes:

'… as he feared lest they might in reality go on an embassy to the emperor, and might impeach him with respect to other particulars of his government, in respect of his corruption, and his acts of insolence, and his rapine, and his habit of insulting people, and his cruelty, and his continual murders of people untried and un-condemned, and his never ending, and gratuitous, and most grievous inhumanity.'

This attitude towards the Jewish people fomented anger and developed a deep resentment to the Roman authority – resentment that would eventually lead to great tragedy.

In 6 BCE an event occurred that not only would shake the Jewish world but would impact on the whole of world history – the birth of *Yeshua haMashiach* as he was called by his first followers – the Jew would become known in the wider world as Jesus Christ.[1] The historical reality of the man is well attested in ancient sources outside the Bible. Tacitus, a historian of the Roman Empire, Josephus, the Jewish historian, Lucian, a Greek satirist, Celsus, a Greek philosopher and opponent of Early Christianity and Pliny the Younger, a lawyer, author, and magistrate of Ancient Rome, all refer to him.

In 6 CE, Cyrenius, a Roman consul, was sent to Judea. Josephus wrote, 'Cyrenius came himself into Judea, which was now added to the province of Syria'. Here was the first move by Romans to begin a process to remove Judea as a separate entity, grouping it with Syria for economic and administration purposes. This trend continued to provoke hostility among the Jewish community. Again, Josephus records:

'Yet was there one Judas, a Gaulonite, of a city whose name was Gamala, who, taking with him Sadduc, a Pharisee, became zealous to draw them to a revolt, who both said that this taxation was no better than an introduction to slavery, and exhorted the nation to assert their liberty; as if they could procure them happiness and security for what they possessed, and an assured enjoyment of a still greater good, which was that of the honour and glory they would thereby acquire for magnanimity.'

The Roman attitude to the Jews was becoming increasingly intolerant and in Rome, Tiberius forced 4,000 Jews into his army and called for all Jews to abjure their religion. Their refusal resulted in their expulsion from Rome in 19 CE.

In 24 CE, Jesus began his public ministry and many Jews followed him, believing him to be their Messiah. They had expectations of him not only as a religious leader but as the one who would remove the Romans from their land and establish the Jewish kingdom. The growing frictions between his followers and the rest of the Jewish community brought further causes for Roman action against the population in Judea. This would lead to the crucifixion of the leader of the Jesus community by Pilate in 27 C.E.[2] This Roman execution would become the basis of much persecution of Jews, with the false charge of Deicide, God killers. From it would come many pogroms, the Crusades, the Spanish Inquisition and ultimately the Holocaust. It was not until 1962 that Paul VI issued *Nostra Aetate*, in which the Catholic Church at last repudiated the idea.

In 37 CE, the Jews of Alexandria were treated in a way that would become familiar across the world and down the centuries. Philo records the events there:

'Since, therefore, the attempt which was being made to violate the law appeared to him to be prospering, while he was destroying the synagogues, and not leaving even their name, he proceeded onwards to another exploit, namely, the utter destruction of our constitution, that when all those things to which alone our life was anchored were cut away, namely, our national customs and our lawful political rights and social privileges, we might be exposed to the very extremity of calamity, without having any stay left to which we could cling for safety, for a few days afterwards he issued a notice in which he called us all foreigners and aliens, without giving us an opportunity of being heard in our own defence, but condemning us without a trial; and what command can be more full of tyranny than this? He himself being everything—accuser, enemy, witness, judge, and executioner, added then to the two former appellations a third also, allowing anyone who was inclined to proceed to exterminate the Jews as prisoners of war. So when the people had received this license, what did they do? There are five districts in the city, named after the first five letters of the written alphabet, of these two are called the quarters of the Jews, because the chief portion of the Jews lives in them. There are also a few scattered Jews, but only a very few, living in some of the other districts. What then did they do? They drove the Jews entirely out of four quarters, and crammed them all into a very small portion of one; and by reason of their numbers they were dispersed over the sea-shore, and desert places, and among the tombs, being deprived of all their property; while the populace, overrunning their desolate houses, turned to plunder, and divided the booty among themselves as if they had obtained it in war. And as no one hindered them, they broke open even the workshops of the Jews, which were all shut up because of their mourning for Drusilla, she was the sister of the emperor, and at her death her brother ordered that divine honours should be paid to her and carried off all that they found there, and bore it openly through the middle of the market-place as if they had only been making use of their own property. And the cessation of business to which they were compelled to submit was even a worse evil than the plunder to which they were exposed, as the consequence was that those who had lent money lost what they had lent, and as no one was permitted, neither farmer, nor captain of a ship, nor merchant, nor artisan, to employ himself in his usual manner, so that poverty was brought on them from two sides at once, both from rapine, as when license was thus given to plunder them they were stripped of everything in one day, and also from the circumstance of their no longer being able to earn money by their customary occupations.'[3]

Even allowing for hyperbole, the situation was one that would repeat itself and demonstrate why Jewish communities were forced to extreme measures simply to survive and drove them to hope for a place of safety and security. In Rome itself, the Emperor Claudius associated Christians with all Jews and banished them from Rome in 50. Vespasian, a rising Roman star who would become Emperor, was sent to wage war in Judea and Syria and it was in 66 that the first Roman-Jewish war, known as the Great Revolt, began. Ever since the Romans occupied Judea, their rule had been brutal, oppressive and intolerant of any dissent. By 66, the emerging Zealots had become more and more determined to bring liberty and freedom to their nation. A group known as the *Sicarii* massacred a troop of Romans at Masada, a hilltop fortress. At Caesarea, disputes between Greeks and Jews erupted and the Roman authorities refused to intervene. The Zealots therefore took matters into their own hands and attacked and defeated the Roman troops. The insensitive reaction by the Romans in Jerusalem led to further rebellion against the Roman forces and after their fleeing to Beth Horon, the rebel forces attacked and inflicted a devastating defeat on Rome killing 6,000 troops. The response from Rome was immediate and bloody. In 67, Vespasian was dispatched to deal with the revolt and along with his son, Titus, brought over 60,000 troops into the area. He swept through the land taking towns that surrendered and destroying those that resisted. Gradually, the Jews were forced to retreat south to Jerusalem. There civil conflict broke out and the Zealots killed leaders and citizens who had any connection or sympathy with the Romans and they fortified the city ready to resist any further Roman advance. Internal politics, murder and intrigue called Vespasian back to Rome. Titus carried on the war against the Jews driving more and more refugees to Jerusalem. It was a bloody prolonged siege of Jerusalem that followed, with Titus determined to break the will and morale of the city's defenders. One method was crucifixion of anyone trying to flee. The scene was one from hell, as Max Dimont noted:

'To make sure that no food or water supply would reach the city from the outside, Titus completely sealed off Jerusalem from the rest of the world with a wall of earth as high as the stone wall around Jerusalem itself. Anyone not a Roman soldier caught anywhere in this vast dry moat was crucified on the top of the earthen wall in sight of the Jews of the city. It was not uncommon for as many as five hundred people a day to be so executed. The air was redolent with the stench of rotting flesh and rent by the cries and agony of the crucified. But the Jews held out for still another year, the fourth year of the war, to the discomfiture of Titus.'

By 70, the siege had succeeded and Titus destroyed the city walls and more importantly destroyed the Temple, the Jews' most holy and sacred place. He took away the treasures within the Temple and proceeded back to Rome for a victory march. A victory tower was erected in the city showing his looting of the Temple. A defeated and devastated people, scarred by the atrocities of Titus, nevertheless settled back again under Roman domination. The destruction of the Temple had huge implications for the Jews and the practice of their religion, to which it was central. The hatred and resentment towards Rome burned under the surface. After the destruction, the Romans turned their attention to those who would still resist. In 73, the then governor, Flavius Silva, sent troops to Masada to deal with the *Sicarii*. He besieged the fortress with 5,000 soldiers and the 900 or so Jews were hemmed in with little food or water. To take the fortress, a huge ramp had to be built of mud and stones; this ramp can still be seen today. Before the Romans eventually entered the fortress, the remaining Jews committed suicide rather than be taken alive by them, though there is dispute about the number of those who died.

Whilst the Jews in Judea suffered the ignominy of Roman rule, their fellow Jews throughout the world were faring no better. The claims against them, that they murdered people, usually Christians, and drank their blood in rituals which became known as the Blood Libel, were surfacing more and more. These claims of drinking blood were made by the ignorant who did not understand the Jewish Law and tradition. Murder was prohibited because of the preciousness of life and secondly there was strict prohibition on the consumption of any blood, demanding all animals be drained of it before eating because the 'life was in the blood'. It was also a strange charge by Christians who themselves celebrated the sacrifice of the mass, in which they believed they drank Christ's blood. Poets like Juvenal were writing anti-Semitic pieces based on obvious ignorance of how Jews actually lived and worshipped. Josephus would take up his pen against Apion, to refute the slurs and misunderstandings against his people. Apion was not alone in the misunderstanding of the Jewish people. Tacitus was another whose polemic showed that he neither understood the Jews or their religion and he took their observances as an affront to his own culture. Commenting on the wars against them he went on to write:

'This worship, however introduced, is upheld by its antiquity; all their other customs, which are at once perverse and disgusting, owe their strength to their very badness. The most degraded out of other races, scorning their national beliefs, brought to them their contributions and presents. This augmented the wealth of the Jews, as also did the fact, that among themselves they are inflexibly honest and ever ready to shew compassion, though they regard the rest of mankind with all the hatred of enemies. They sit apart at meals, they sleep apart, and though, as a nation, they are singularly prone to lust, they abstain from intercourse with foreign women; among themselves nothing is unlawful. Circumcision was adopted by them as a mark of difference from other men. Those who come over to their religion adopt the practice, and have this lesson first instilled into them, to despise all gods, to disown their country, and set at nought parents, children, and brethren. Still they provide for the increase of their numbers. It is a crime among them to kill any newly-born infant. They hold that the souls of all who perish in battle or by the hands of the executioner are immortal. Hence a passion for propagating their race and a contempt for death. They are wont to bury rather than to burn their dead, following in this the Egyptian custom; they bestow the same care on the dead, and they hold the same belief about the lower world. Quite different is their faith about things divine. The Egyptians worship many animals and images of monstrous form; the Jews have purely mental conceptions of Deity, as one in essence. They call those profane who make representations of God in human shape out of perishable materials. They believe that Being to be supreme and eternal, neither capable of representation, nor of decay. They therefore do not allow any images to stand in their cities, much less in their temples. This flattery is not paid to their kings, nor this honour to our Emperors. From the fact, however, that their priests used to chant to the music of flutes and cymbals, and to wear garlands of ivy, and that a golden vine was found in the temple, some have thought that they worshipped father Liber, the conqueror of the

East, though their institutions do not by any means harmonize with the theory; for Liber established a festive and cheerful worship, while the Jewish religion is tasteless and mean.'[4]

This was a common theme across all the countries where the Jews resided. Their attempts to live peaceably and practice their faith was misinterpreted and they were often simply abused because of anti-Semitic prejudice.

Wherever the Romans ventured and Jews were found there was trouble. The destruction of the Temple caused a great bitterness and revolts spread across the Roman Empire. The reply from Rome was brutal and these revolts came to nothing. It was during the Emperor Trajan's reign such revolts saw the destruction of Roman temples, particularly in Cyrene and Egypt. Appian the Greek historian writes of the situation as 'war':

'Once, during a night, when I was trying to make an escape from the Jews during the war in Egypt and tried to reach Arabia Petraea across a branch of the river, where a vessel was ready to bring me to Pelusium, I had an Arab as guide.'

Trajan sent his general, Quietus, to deal with the problem and his time in Judea saw great brutality. The death of Trajan in 117 brought his cruelty to an end and the accession to power of Hadrian. He wanted to stop the disturbances in the Empire and one act in this was to remove Quietus from Judea and have him executed. Initially, it seemed that the Jews in Judea might have respite from persecution under his rule, but this was a vain hope. Rather, around 130, he conceived a plan to turn Judea into a pagan territory and establish a temple to Jupiter on the site of the ruins of the Temple. The reasons for this are mixed but they were due to Hadrian's attempt to assert himself and Rome as the final power. This was not only to the Jews but to the growing Christian influences that were being established. His actions in Jerusalem with building the Jupiter temple, banning male circumcision and renaming the area *Aelia Capitolina*, after his own family name, brought a bloody response. Both Jews and Romans died in great numbers. Dio Cassius reported, 'the whole of Judea became a desert'. Hadrian's decisions would lead to one of the great Jewish tragedies and leave a historical legacy that continues to haunt the modern era in the Middle East.

In 132, Simeon bar Kochba emerged as a leader of an organised revolt against Tinnius Rufus and the Rome he represented. He even over-struck Roman coins with the inscription, 'Year 1 of the liberty of Jerusalem'. Whilst the Jews revolted, the Christian population refused to join them and remained separate from the war. Bar Kochba waged a running guerrilla battle with the Romans from the Judean hills and also through direct attacks in towns and villages. The Romans suffered many losses. Rufus disappeared from the scene and it is not known what happened to him. Hadrian believed there was a danger that the revolt might succeed so he brought his general Severus from Britain. With this move he also brought one third of the Roman army into Judea and with these overwhelming odds, the rebels retreated to the Betar fortress to the south-west of Jerusalem. The Romans laid siege to the fortress and with their overwhelming military might the fortress fell. The Romans had a lesson to teach and on taking the city they went on a destructive rampage. Men, women and children were all put to the sword and the historic writings refer to it as a massacre. In all, the revolts caused the death of well over a half of a million Jews. Dio Cassius is graphic:

'Five hundred and eighty thousand men were slain in the various raids and battles, and the number of those that perished by famine, disease and fire was past finding out. Thus nearly the whole of Judaea was made desolate, a result of which the people had had forewarning before the war. For the tomb of Solomon, which the Jews regard as an object of veneration, fell to pieces of itself and collapsed, and many wolves and hyenas rushed howling into their cities. Many Romans, moreover, perished in this war. Therefore Hadrian in writing to the senate did not employ the opening phrase commonly affected by the emperors, 'If you and your children are in health, it is well; I and the legions are in health.'

There this no doubt that what the Romans did in Judea was genocide. It was followed by Hadrian imposing harsh rules on the Jews. He burned their sacred scrolls and erected statues of Jupiter on their sacred places. He was determined to wipe out completely any sign of Jews or Judaism. He would not let the Jews live in or enter Jerusalem except once a year and he outlawed many of their religious practices. He had felt the humiliation through the effectiveness of the revolt in its early stages and was determined that it would never happen again. J.E. Taylor wrote:

'Up until this date the Bar Kochba documents indicate that towns, villages and ports where Jews lived were busy with industry and activity. Afterwards there is an eerie silence, and the archaeological record testifies to little Jewish presence until the Byzantine era, in En Gedi. This picture coheres with what we have already determined ... that the crucial date for what can only be described as genocide, and the devastation of Jews and Judaism within central Judea, was 135 C.E. and not, as usually assumed, 70 C.E., despite the siege of Jerusalem and the Temple's destruction.'

Not only was he intent on destroying this people but went further – he renamed the area *Syria Palestina*. It is suggested that Palestine was a name used by Herodotus as early as the fifth century BCE, but it is more likely the term used by him should be *Philistia*, as the Greek word used is that for the Hebrew word for the region and connected to the Philistines.[5] It can also be suggested that it was an attempt to remove the sacred link that the rebelling Jewish people had with the land, as it was commonly called Judea by the Jews. What is clear is that since this name change, the area now becomes known as Palestine in common use in the Roman world. Hadrian died in 138; his death brought Antonius Pius to rule and his reign was a blessed relief to the Jewish people. A delegation to the Emperor by Jewish rabbis brought a repeal of many of the laws and restrictions Hadrian had imposed. They were again allowed to enter Jerusalem and many returned from other countries to live once more in their homeland. However, Antonius forbade Gentiles to join with Jews in their practices. The use of the Temple site by Rome for their gods continued but the Jewish religion was once more allowed to thrive with a new learning centre established. One minor revolt was attempted but was quickly put down and the area had relative peace throughout Antonius' reign. He died in 161 and his successor Marcus Aurelius said of him 'Remember his qualities, so that when your last hour comes your conscience may be as clear as his.'

Under Marcus Aurelius, the Jews continued to enjoy a relatively happy existence being free to enjoy their religion. However, beneath the surface there was always that tension of wanting to be free and independent as a country. Aurelius is alleged to have said when he visited the area, 'These people are even more restless than the Marcomanni, the Quadi and the Samaritans.' His visit there in 175 was during a period of violence generated by internal Roman politics in which the Jews refused to be involved. It is also during this period we find a writer using 'Palestinians' to refer to the Jews as the Roman term became more common. The subsequent centuries saw the Jewish people and their religion enjoying great freedoms and throughout the Roman Empire they flourished in religion and wealth. In the second and third centuries, the coming and goings of emperors did cause some discontent but in general there were no major revolts against Roman rule. The coming of Diocletian in the third century saw him expand the geographical area of what was known as Palestine to include Arabia. It was during Diocletian's rule that the Roman Empire was split into the Western and Eastern administrative areas, effectively creating two empires. However, from Hadrian to Diocletian, whilst proselytising by Jews was restricted by Rome, the Jewish people enjoyed liberty of religious practice and controlled governance in their homeland.

Constantine became a Christian on his deathbed and most of his successors felt they had to follow his lead, having a direct effect on the Jewish people. Their homeland now became the focus as a Christian centre with Constantine's mother Helena particularly seeking to establish places of pilgrimage. The Jewish people became those who had rejected Jesus and new laws were enacted to show Judaism as an inferior and unacceptable faith. In 321, the status of Jews began to change. From a protected people who were recognized as being citizens of Rome, new laws began to erode that status. In 329, he passed a law against joining the Jewish faith:

'We want the Jews, their principals, and their patriarchs informed, that if anyone-once this law has been given-dare attack by stoning or by other kind of fury one escaping from their deadly group and raising his eyes to God's cult [Christianity], which as we have learned is being done now, he shall be delivered immediately to the flames and burnt with his associates. But if one of the people [a Christian] shall approach their nefarious sect and join himself to their conventicles [synagogues], he shall suffer with them the deserved punishments.'[6]

In 353, he further decreed:

> 'If someone shall become Jew from Christian and shall be joined to
> sacrilegious assemblies, we decree that his property shall be vindicated
> to the fisc's [state treasury's] dominion once the accusation has been
> proven.'[7]

Constantine, in the Council of Nicaea, made the separation of Christianity
from Judaism complete, in that it took decisions to separate the practices
and doctrines and even the celebration of feasts. He gave status to the
Bishops of the Church who grew more and more anti-Semitic and stood in
opposition to the Jews. It has to be noted that ever since the time of Jesus,
there were great tensions between his followers and those that rejected him.
Constantine died in 337 and his death would bring in a turbulent period for
Rome. The Empire would go through a period of divisions and reunions
until its eventual collapse.

Julian became Emperor in 361. His abandonment of Christianity brought
him the title 'Apostate' by the Christian world. However, the Jewish people
fared well under him. His first act was to announce a religious amnesty which
would allow all religions to exist. In doing so, he also removed the heavy
burden of taxation that had been imposed on pagans and Jews, declaring that
'ye are all brothers, one of another: God is the common Father of us all'. In
Jerusalem he also established magistrates who would look after the affairs of
the people. The Talmud confirms them and refers to them as *Aristoi*.[8] Whilst
showing remarkable support for the Jewish people and their religion he wrote
polemic letters against Christianity. The historical records do show that he
had an excellent grasp of the Jewish and Christian Scriptures. The early
Church Fathers in their various dialogues also refer to an intention of Julian
to rebuild the Jewish Temple in Jerusalem. There is also some support for
the view that a start was made on the construction. A remarkable letter from
Julian to the Jewish community in Jerusalem that showed his commitment
to establish the Jews securely in their own homeland and rebuild Jerusalem:

> 'To the Community of the Jews,
>   More oppressive for you in the past than the yoke of dependence
> was the circumstance that new taxes were imposed upon you without

previous notice, and you were compelled to furnish an untold quantity of gold to the imperial treasury. Many of these hardships I myself noticed, but I learned more from the tax-rolls that were being preserved to your detriment, which I happened to light upon. I myself abolished a tax which was about to be levied upon you, and thus put a stop to the impious attempt to bring infamy upon you; with my own hands did I commit to the flames the tax-rolls against you that I found in my archives, in order that no one might ever spread such a charge of impiety against you. The real author of these calumnies was not so much my ever-to-be remembered brother Constantius, as those men who, barbarians in mind and atheists in heart were entertained at his table. With my own hands have I seized these persons and thrust them into the pit, so that not even the memory of their fall shall remain with us. Desiring to extend yet further favours to you, I have exhorted my brother, the venerable Patriarch Julos, to put a stop to henceforward no one will be able to oppress your people by the collection of such imposts, so that everywhere throughout my kingdom you may be free from care; and thus, enjoying freedom, you may address still more fervent prayers for my empire to the Almighty Creator of the Universe, who has deigned to crown me with his own undefiled right hand. It seems to be the fact that those who lead lives full of anxiety are fettered in spirit, and do not dare to raise their hands in prayer. But those who are exempt from all cares, and rejoice with their whole hearts, are better able to direct their sincere prayers for the welfare of the empire to the Mighty One, in whose power it lies to further the success of my reign, even according to my wishes. Thus should you do, in order that when I return safely from the Persian war, I may restore the Holy City of Jerusalem, and rebuild it at my own expense, even as you have for so many years desired it to be restored; and therein will I unite with you in giving praise to the Almighty.'[9]

The anti-Semitic works of the early church fathers are littered with references to Julian's attempt to raise the Temple and their invectives against it include supposed miracles that prevented it. The truth is that the letter was written six months before his death and his death alone was the reason for the Temple not being rebuilt. Julian's reign was short lived, ending in

363, and one wonders what changes there would have been to the Jewish people's future if he had succeeded in his aims?

Following Julian, the Roman Empire entered a turbulent phase and in general the main religious concerns were in disputes about Paganism and Christianity, with Christianity usually in the ascendancy. For the Jewish people in their homeland, they were left in relative peace. Laws were brought in to control the perceived disadvantages of Christian slaves with the Jews forbidden to have them. Laws on marriage banning any Jew marrying a Christian and having property rights were also framed against Jews. However, laws were also passed to prevent abuses towards Jews by Christians and there was protection offered to their Synagogues.

In the fourth century, many attempts were made to accuse the Jews of killing Christians. However, the evidence is clear that these stories were fabrications and the deaths were due to the persecutions of Diocletian. There is of course the possibility that certain Jews did harass Christians, but there are no notable records anywhere that this was widespread or common. However, there was a revolt in Diocaesarea in 351 by some Jews. This was not against Christians but due to the continued friction against the Roman occupation. The heavy Roman response destroyed the city. One major intervention on Jewish religion and their status was made by Justinian in 553. He immediately displayed his opposition to the Jews on his accession. He gave the Christian bishops magisterial authority:

'But the Jews are not even to have their own judges, and are to be subject to Roman courts; moreover the Roman princes judge the Jewish leaders, who only seem to be leaders among their own people. But this, too, is to be noted, that the Jews have no champion in law who is a qualified judge, but all their affairs are idle and collapsing and full of folly.'[10]

Justinian issued a new law that brought the use of Greek in Synagogues alongside Hebrew and also banned the Jewish Mishnah. It also brought in 'the harshest punishments' for anyone introducing 'ungodly nonsense'. In effect it was promoting Christianity over the Jewish faith. The picture across the Roman Empire was mixed, depending on the level of anti-Semitism from Christians in any given area. Everett Seaver rightly concludes:

'The fourth century was the age of the great conflict between the church and the synagogue. The church fathers from Eusebius to Augustine tried to show that the Jews were wicked and depraved monsters, fit only to be an evil and eternal example to pious Christians. 'The Jew' became a fearsome theological abstraction to suit the propaganda purposes of the victorious church. The anti-Semitic propaganda of the church leaders gradually spread to their flocks, and the Christian record was marred by atrocities against the Jews from the middle of the fourth century on: typical acts of violence were the forced conversions on Minorca, the destruction of the synagogue at Callinicum, the massacre at Edessa, and the expulsion of the Jews from Alexandria. Under pressure from Christian zealots, the imperial administration gradually succumbed to the rising tide of anti-Jewish feeling.'

Despite all this, in the Jewish homeland there was a relatively peaceful existence as the western Emperors changed. The Jewish people had a homeland but not the freedom to control their own destiny.

To a large extent, the Justinian legal codes held in the Eastern Empire, the Byzantium, into the ninth century. The Persians had always had ambitions to expand their empire and there were a number of clashes between the Byzantium and the Sasanian Empire of Persia. These conflicts spread across the Middle East. In 608, a violent persecution of Jews led to a revolt that was put down. Following internal revolts, in 610 Tyre and Acre also saw revolts. As a result, large numbers of Jews were massacred. The Christians were heavily involved and the Jews now saw Byzantium as a Christian Empire enemy. In the same year, Heraclius came to power and began to push back against the Persians. However, in 613, Shahrbaraz succeeded in conquering Antioch. Then with Jewish help he went on to occupy Jerusalem without much resistance. As Neusner wrote:

'At Tyre and Acre in 610 Jews attempted to support the invading armies. [Persians] The Jewish community at Tyre was massacred in retaliation. In Acre the Jews destroyed churches and homes and forcibly converted a priest who had been notorious for his anti-Judaism. As Iranian armies advanced on Palestine, therefore, none could have been surprised at the enthusiastic Jewish response.'

In 614, the city was in the hands of the Persians and Jews. The record after this victory does neither the Persians nor the Jews any credit. The victorious army slaughtered 60,000 Christians. The Persians also took 37,000 'skilled workmen' from among the remaining Christians back to Persia. The Jews left behind went through the city and destroyed all the Christian churches to 'sanctify the city'. The Jews were hoping that the Persians would give them their own country back. However, the very strong Christian lobby brought about a Byzantium/Persian alliance. The outcome was that because the Jewish followers of Judaism were in the minority, the Persians did not grant them their wishes. Neusner is right to conclude:

> 'My view is that the excesses of the Jews themselves, combined with the pro-Christian sympathies of Khusro II [king of the Sasanian/Persian Empire] and the influence of Yazden [A Nestorian Christian in charge of Khusro's finances], caused the Iranians to revise their Palestinian policy.'

Yazden would restore the churches in Jerusalem and punish the Jews. However, his fortunes would change and he was killed by Khusro II, as the king turned against Christians after defeats by Heraclius. He defeated the Persians at Constantinople in 626 and in the following year invaded Persian territory; his success brought the Persians to ask for a peace treaty. After Khusro II's death in 628, the Empire went into decline and would finally collapse. His reign had been a disappointment to the Jews. The real hopes they had that their support for him would result in an independent homeland were dashed and on his death they remained a people under the authority of others.

Heraclius's response to the Jews in again controlling Palestine was to renew persecution. This was to break a promise he had made to pardon them. Christians wanted revenge and they influenced the situation to massacre great numbers of Jews and began a process of forced Christian baptism. This persecution would continue across the empire, but a new power was rising and would sweep through the Middle East. It would chase Heraclius out of Syria and Palestine and would be the new overlord of the Jewish nation. Mohammed and Islam had entered the scene.

Chapter Five

Terror On The Journey: Islam and the Crusades

The area of Arabia, which bordered Syria Palestina to the south and east, had been fought over by the Persian and the Byzantine Empires. The area itself was occupied by a mixture of pagans, Christians, and a myriad other religions that were unique and who borrowed ideas from other faiths. Polytheism dominated the region and there was also a community of Jews that had moved from Palestine. Arabia was a mixture of different kingdoms and tribal areas that experienced various conflicts within and without. There was one dominant tribe, Banu Quraish of Mecca, who, from being responsible for the religious duties around the shrine there, rose to control trade and money in the region. Their dominance led to inter-tribal conflict involving one man who became prominent in the opposition to the persecutions and treatment they handed out. He was Mohammed. In 610, he declared a new religion. This was Islam, the surrender to the will of Allah, a monotheistic faith. He gathered his military forces to oppose the power at Mecca.

By 628, the politico-religious power was now under the Caliphate of Mohammed and a treaty was signed with the Banu-Quraish. This was broken and in 630, Mohammed attacked Mecca and established the Islamic rule under which all Quraish embraced the new religion. It is notable that there were Jewish and Christian settlements throughout the region which were appreciated for their superior knowledge of agriculture and irrigation. Neither Persia nor Byzantium could withstand the new military and religious power. In 636, the Islamic army besieged Jerusalem and eventually overcame the defending majority Christians in 637, signing a pact with Caliph Umar. Many Arab Moslems emigrated to Palestine under the new rulers and the Christians and Jews were able to continue their religion, paying a special tax to the Caliph. The situation for the Jews was to see their homeland dominated by the Islamic presence and various internal disputes within Islam would see different Caliphs control their destiny. Further anguish was caused when an Islamic prayer house was built on the sacred site of the Temple in Jerusalem. As the Romans had desecrated the site with their own shrines now the Jews witnessed, what was for them, further insult. In turn this would be expanded in 705 to the elaborate Al-Aqsa Mosque, marking the alleged site of Mohammed's ascent to heaven.

Despite the Islamisation of Palestine, the Jewish people were permitted to continue their occupancy of the area and practise their religion as second class citizens, as they were respected as 'People of the Book'. There were some conflicts in Arabia between Jewish groups and the Moslems and eventually the decree was made that all Jews had to leave that area. Many Jews would come from this and other areas where they experienced persecution, to settle in Palestine. For example, the Visigoth king Erwig in 681 enacted laws that were both harsh and punitive, with forced conversions and heavy penalties for apostasy, alongside expulsion for those who refused. The Jewish people were put under the strict control of Christian bishops and anyone being circumcised according to Jewish religious tradition would be castrated. The seizure of Jewish property was also sanctioned by law. Along with these Spanish Jews, many also left Constantinople after the Quinisext Council in 681 which also contained anti-Semitic injunctions such as:

'Let no one in the priestly order nor any layman eat the unleavened bread of the Jews, nor have any familiar intercourse with them, nor summon them in illness, nor receive medicines from them, nor bathe with them; but if anyone shall take in hand to do so, if he is a cleric, let him be deposed, but if a layman let him be cut off.'[1]

Furthermore, the Visigoth king Egica continued to persecute the Jews in Spain just as his predecessors did. It is no wonder that many sought the relative safety of Moslem rule even though they had to accept the status of second class citizenship. Indeed Reuven Firestone wrote:

'Most Jews living in the Muslim world during this early period lived in the Land of Israel/Palestine, Bavel/Mesopotamia, and Egypt, though communities were spread from Morocco to Khurasan (today's northeastern Iran, western Afghanistan, and southern Turkmenistan)'

Many historians, such as Mark Cohen, describe this period as a 'Golden Age', but it may not be the complete picture. It is true that the Jews did have a great deal of protection and were allowed to practise their religion, but they had to accept restrictions on what they could do. Under the surface there were many tensions as both Jews and Christians were often consigned to menial tasks. There was also the issue of orphaned Jewish children who would be given to Moslem families to be brought up in the Islamic faith. These tensions would erupt, not because Mohammed and his followers were specifically anti-Jewish, but due to the Jewish people not being able to accept certain religious ideas that were being promulgated. This was because the Islamic religion had taken many concepts from Jewish and Christian thought and brought a different understanding to them through Mohammed as a prophet. They therefore considered him a false prophet and could not recognise him as the new religion required. Again Firestone:

'The Jews of Medina had no choice but to oppose Muhammad as a false prophet who, from their perspective, was distorting the truth of God's revelation that had already been fully disclosed and codified in the Torah. But from the perspective of Muhammad and his followers, the Medinan Jews were unequivocally trying to oppose God by resisting and delegitimizing his prophecy and the authentic redemptive message that he brought. Parallel scenarios are easily found with the emergence of Christianity and its revelation in relation to Judaism, the emergence of Islam and its revelation in relation to Christianity, and the emergence of post-Qur'anic religion and its revelation such as Bahaism in relation to Islam. The aggrieved parties observe the conflict from radically different perspectives and each constructs a narrative to explain the conflict that favours its own particular point of view.'

Although most Jews accepted these conditions, there was a remnant who maintained a hope of a Messiah who would deliver them to freedom in the land of Israel. If he was not appearing, then some would try to speed him along. One such sect of Judaism in Persia, the Isawites, led by Abu Isa al-Isfahani, saw him as that Messiah and revolted against Islamic rule, hoping for a victory that would sweep them on into Judea and the Messianic age. A decisive battle at Rai, during which their leader was killed, brought an end to their vain hope. Such sporadic incidents were happening across the Islamic world, but none were of any great consequence. The situation in Palestine under Islamic rule continued in relative peace until the ninth century when divisions began to creep into Islam. Rival dynasties fought over political and religious issues. The Fatimid Caliphate, a Shi'ite branch of Islam, dominated the North African region and based its headquarters in Egypt. Byzantium tried to take advantage of the divisions in Islam and once more cast its eyes on the Middle East. Palestine became a battleground for the great powers seeking domination in the area. As Mann noted:

'Palestine was swept into the maelstrom of fiercely contending factions. It became frequently the battle-ground of the Egyptian armies coming from the south and the northern invaders.'

Initially the Fatimid rule was good for both Jews and Christians, as under it they were able to have prominent roles and Islamic laws were not so rigorously enforced. This was due to the main branch of Islam – Sunni – refusing to support the Fatimid regime and the willingness of non-Moslems to cooperate with it. However, the third caliph, al-Ḥakim who ruled from 996–1020 took a harsher line and returned to enforcing the laws against non-Moslems. This in turn caused many Jews to embrace Islam but a great many also chose to leave Palestine. Documents discovered in the Ezra Synagogue in Cairo *Genizah* (Hebrew for hiding place) show that Christians also turned against Jews out of jealousy and added to Jewish woes by having them dismissed from government posts. The arrival of al-Ḥakim's successor al-Ẓāhir, who ruled from 1020–34, again brought a more tolerable state of affairs for the Jews, although some local Christian officials continued to harass them. Overall, there is no doubt that the Jews were able to thrive, especially in trade, under this rule, yet there remained a desire to have their own land, to control their own destiny. This was continually reinforced in places like Spain which had always been a difficult place for Jews whether it was under Moor or Christian control and it was there in 1066 in Granada, 1,500 families, about 4,000 Jews, were massacred. At a later time, Poet Yehudah HaLevi, a Spanish Jew wrote of his longing to return to his natural home:

'My heart is in the east, and I myself am on the western edge.
How can I enjoy drink and food! Could I ever enjoy it?
Alas, how do I fulfil my promise? My sacred vow? since
Zion is still in Roman bondage, and I in Arabic bonds,
A light thing would it seem to me
All goods of Spain are chaff to my eye, but
The dust on which once stood the tabernacle is gold to my eye!'

He called on all Jews to return home and he himself went to Israel in 1141 but died in Jerusalem a few months after his arrival. However, these Jewish hopes were not recognised by the Christian world and they had other ideas as they saw Jerusalem and Palestine as their 'holy' property and the Jews as religious heretics. Throughout the Christian world the Christians continued their allegations of the Blood Libel and in Blois, France in 1171 thirty-one Jews were burned at the stake for it. These persecutions and continued anti-Semitism were about to be followed by events that would bring slaughter on a greater scale – the Crusades.

The Byzantine Emperor Alexios I Komnenos held great ambitions to see his Empire once again flourish. He believed that through uniting himself with the Pope he might advance his cause. Urban II responded and preached a Crusade against the Islamic world and the recapture of the Holy Land. Urban had his own ambition which was to unite the Eastern and Western branches of Christendom. Men like Peter the Hermit would respond by raising armies to carry out the Pope's wishes. He gathered over 40,000 men and women into a paupers' army who marched forth believing they were protected by the Holy Ghost. It is not surprising that the first target of the Crusade was the Jews in Germany, throughout which the Jewish communities were massacred and their properties destroyed or confiscated. Forced conversion and expulsion was once again rife, which had not been seen on such a scale since the seventh century. One unofficial Crusade leader, Count Emicho, decided to attack Jewish communities, in the Rhineland. The Solomon bar Samson Chronicle written c.1140 noted of the period:

'Look now, we are going a long way to seek out the profane shrine and to avenge ourselves on the Ishmaelites, when here in our very midst, are the Jews – they whose forefathers murdered and crucified him for no reason. Let us avenge ourselves on them from among our nations so that the name of Israel will no longer be remembered'.

Whilst many claimed to be acting for Christ, a great number of Crusaders saw their debts to their Jewish lenders wiped out in the massacres. One French knight, Godefroy de Bouillon, was plain in his thoughts:

'… to go on this journey only after avenging the blood of the crucified one by shedding Jewish blood and completely eradicating any trace of those bearing the name 'Jew,' thus assuaging his own burning wrath.'

It is true that some Christian bishops were appalled at the bloody slaughter and forced conversions but their attempts to stem the blood-lust were generally in vain. The Crusaders would move on from Europe, heading for Jerusalem, and cut a bloody path through the countries they passed, massacring Jews along the way. This was despite the appeals of many bishops and indeed Henry IV, the Holy Roman Emperor, specifically instructed de Bouillon not to take part in them. By 1099, the Crusaders had reached Jerusalem and after a short siege, with the Jews and Moslems fighting together against them, the city was taken and the inhabitants were massacred and the city looted. Jews who took refuge in their synagogues found themselves locked in the buildings and burned alive. Many Jews were also taken alive to Europe and sold as slaves. Palestine was once more a conquered land with both Moslems and Jews murdered, expelled or running from the marauding Christian knights. Godefroy de Bouillon was left as the ruler of what became known as the Kingdom of Jerusalem – although he refused the crown himself – and after his death, his brother Baldwin was proclaimed king. Thomas F Madden wrote of Baldwin, that he was:

'..the true founder of the kingdom of Jerusalem,' and 'had transformed a tenuous arrangement into a solid feudal state. With brilliance and diligence, he established a strong monarchy, conquered the Palestinian coast, reconciled the crusader barons, and built strong frontiers against the kingdom's Muslim neighbours.'

It was estimated that only '1,000 poor Jewish families' remained in Palestine. The massacre of the Jews particularly, was seen as a pious Catholic fury and Pope Urban's 'schismatic' Orthodox Christians did not escape lightly, as they too suffered at the hands of the violent knights. The situation in Palestine did not cause much consternation across the Islamic world as they did not perceive it as a religious conflagration but rather more a Byzantine attack by mercenaries and soldiers of fortune.

Within the Islamic world there were divisions and the focus was diverted from Palestine. These divisions meant that for some areas under certain Caliphates, Jews were forced to convert or die. Many, with good reason, would flee from these persecutions to Egypt and Palestine, where more tolerant Caliphates gave them relative safety. Men like Peter the Venerable, abbot of Cluny, made it their business to destroy Jews wherever they were found. In 1146 he wrote:

'But why should we pursue the enemies of the Christian faith in far and distant lands while the vile blasphemers, far worse than any Saracens, namely the Jews, who are not far away from us, but who live in our midst, blaspheme and trample on Christ and the Christian sacraments so freely, insolently and with impunity.'

Once more the need for a safe independent homeland for the Jewish people was being made clear by the actions of those who would seek to destroy them.

In 1147, a second Crusade was launched against Islam and had some success but it had no real impact and after a huge defeat in Turkey a remnant fought its way through to Jerusalem. After a disastrous attack on Damascus, the Crusaders retreated to Jerusalem, divided and discouraged. From this point onwards, the tenure of the Kingdom of Jerusalem began to slip from the Crusader's grasp. One outcome of the great tribulation caused by the mixture of Crusade massacres and Moslem reactions was the idea of an imminent coming of the Messiah. The revived belief was that the Messiah would come and establish the Jewish homeland and free them from all oppressors. Therefore, a number of men arose across the Islamic and Byzantine worlds claiming to be the new Messiah and called on their followers to prepare to march on Palestine and re-establish the glorious messianic kingdom in their homeland, Judea. One such man was David El-Roy who was a scholar of the Jewish and Islamic religions as well as a magus. Benjamin of Tudela wrote of him in his travel journal:

'Ten years ago [1155] there rose a man of the name of David El-Roy, of the city of Amaria, who had studied under the prince of the captivity, Chisdai, and under Eli, the president of the college of Geon Jacob in the city of Baghdad, and who became an excellent scholar, being well versed in the Mosaic law, in the decisions of the rabbis, and in the Talmud; understanding also the profane sciences, the language and the writings of the Mohammedans, and the scriptures of the magicians and enchanters. He made up his mind to rise in rebellion against the King of Persia, to unite and collect the Jews who live in the mountains of Chaphton, and with them to engage in war with all Gentiles, making the conquest of Jerusalem his final object. He gave signs to the Jews by false miracles, and assured them, 'the Lord has sent me to conquer Jerusalem, and to deliver you from the yoke of the Gentiles.' Some of the Jews did believe in him, and called him Messiah.'

It is unclear what eventually happened to El-Roy but Benjamin recorded that he was killed by his father-in-law, it was said to protect the Jewish people, although 'ten thousand florins' he was alleged to have received from the king of Persia, may have also been an incentive. These and many so-called Messiahs failed to bring an independent homeland to the Jews and so their unhappy lot continued across the Christian world with men like Philip Augustus of France in 1180, imprisoning all Jews and demanding ransom for their release. The following year he would annul all loans from Jews to Christians and take a cut for himself, eventually expelling all Jews from Paris. The Crusader rule in Palestine had lasted for a century and in in 1187 the Islamic general Salah ad-Din Yusuf ibn Ayyub (Saladin), who came from Cairo, once more, conquered most of Palestine and took Jerusalem from the Christians. One irony of this situation was that the reports of the lot of the defeated Christians reached England and a cry for financial support went out. Henry II raised £70,000 (£1.5m, 2017) but decided this was not enough and turned to extort money from the Jews to assist the continued subjection of their own people. In Cassells' 1865 Illustrated History of England we find this account:

'The sum of £70,000, which was raised by this means, proving insufficient, Henry extorted large sums of money from the Jews and the people of that unhappy race were compelled, by imprisonment and other severe measures, to yield up their hoards. One-fourth of their whole property was thus extorted from the Jews, and probably, in many cases, a much larger sum.'

Saladin had removed Crusader rule from a number of towns and cities in the Palestinian area and as he moved to take Jerusalem he was met with an attempt by a small Christian remnant who tried to hold the city. His overwhelming army did not take long to bring the city under his control and he proved a merciful conqueror with an agreement to allow the Christians to leave unharmed and no mass slaughter occurred.

Whilst the removal of the Crusaders meant the Jews continued as second-class citizens in their own land under Islamic rule, they were treated better by Saladin than they were by the Christians. Indeed, Saladin had Jews around him and appeared to show a great tolerance to non-Moslems. One prominent Jew, Maimonides, who lived in Cairo and acted as a doctor to Saladin, wrote:

'My duties to the Sultan [Saladin's son] are very heavy. I am obliged to visit him every day, early in the morning, and when he or any of his children or concubines are indisposed, I cannot leave Cairo but must stay during most of the day in the palace. It also frequently happens that one or two of the officers fall sick and I must attend to their healing. Hence, as a rule, every day, early in the morning, I go to Cairo and, even if nothing unusual happens there, I do not return to Fostat until the afternoon. Then I am famished but I find the antechambers filled with people, both Jews and Gentiles, nobles and common people, judges and policemen, friends and enemies – a mixed multitude who await the time of my return.'

Saladin demonstrated his tolerance when he called on all Jews to return to their homeland. Many responded and came to live, work and practice their religion in peace, untroubled by the anti-Semitism that still swept across Christian Europe not yet conquered by Islam. The Jewish poet Judah Ben Solomon Harizi, wrote twenty-five years later:

'But why didn't the Jews settle here [in Jerusalem] when the city was in the hands of the Christians? Because they [the Christians] said that we killed their God, and that we offended them; and if they would have caught us here, they would have eaten us alive. But God raised the spirit of the Ishmaelite King Saladin, in the year 4950 from the creation of the world [1190 Christian era], Imbuing him with wisdom and courage. He marched with an army from Egypt, besieged Jerusalem, and God handed over the city into his hands. Then he sent out a call through all the cities: let each one of the decedents of Ephraim return there [from Ashur and Mitzraim] Mesopotamia and Egypt – and from all the localities where they are dispersed.'

Despite the situation in Palestine there were still a few pockets in the Islamic world where Jews did not fare well, being made to wear distinctive clothing that ridiculed them and made them stand out, much like the Nazis would do centuries later.

The victory of Saladin caused deep anger and passion in Christendom because of the loss of the Holy City. Henry II of England and Philip II of France, who had been in conflict, buried their differences and called for a third Crusade to retake Jerusalem. On Henry's death Richard I, the Lionheart, became king of England and his beginnings as king demonstrated what could be expected by Jews during his reign. William H. Rule, writing in 1854, from Latin and Syrian sources, gave an account of the king's coronation that amply demonstrates why the Jews needed a country of their own. The king banned all Jews from entering the place of his coronation because he had religious superstitions about what harm they might do him. However, the Jews of England wanted to express their loyalty to the king and to honour him and attempted to deliver gifts at the event. A knight called Brompton attacked the Jews to be then joined by others whilst 'there sat Richard. At the time he said not a word to still the tumult, but left the sufferers to their fate'. Later he would take action against the Pudsey and Percy families, who were involved in the anti-Jewish attacks and concerned about the finances the Jews supplied, took steps to protect them This lack of immediate action acted as a signal to the crowds who then began what was described as a massacre of the Jews throughout London. The record notes, 'the Priests and Monks enjoyed the sport to well to interrupt it'. Jews of both sexes and of all ages were murdered and some who took refuge in home or synagogue found themselves surrounded and the building set on fire and left them to burn to death. Richard of Devizes wrote chillingly in terms that would echo under the Nazis in the Second World War with the first use of 'holocaust' to describe the treatment of the Jews:

> 'On the very day of the coronation, about that solemn hour in which the Son of God was immolated to the Father, a sacrifice of Jews to their father the devil was commenced in the city of London; and so long was the duration of this mystery, that the holocaust could scarcely be accomplished the ensuing day. The other cities and towns of the kingdom emulated the faith of the Londoners, and with a like devotion dispatched their bloodsuckers with blood to hell'

Indeed in York in 1190 Crusaders preparing to set out for Palestine, could not wait to satisfy their bloodlust, carrying out a massacre of Jews and taking others to the continent to be sold as slaves. Local residents, owing money to their Jewish lenders, joined the horror to remove their debts. This graphic account of Ephraim of Bonn who recorded the incident demonstrates the horror and degradation of the Jewish people:

> 'The number of those slain and burned was one hundred and fifty souls, men and women, all holy bodies. Their houses moreover they destroyed, and they despoiled their gold and silver and the splendid books which they had written in great number, precious as gold and as much fine gold, there being none like them for their beauty and splendour. These they brought to Cologne and to other places, where they sold them the Jews.'

In the same year at Norwich, the Jews were also targeted in another Blood Libel charge when all Jews who had not taken shelter in the castle were slaughtered and after the event only eight Jewish tax-payers were found registered.

Richard left behind this bloody business and led the Crusade against both Moslem and Jew and had much success in Palestine but could not take the city of Jerusalem. Finally, after battles at Jaffa, Saladin realised that compromise had to be made and negotiations were entered into with the English king - there was no point in further warfare. Moslem control of the city was agreed and Christians could visit as long as they remained unarmed. At least for those Jews left in Jerusalem this was good news. With this Richard returned home in 1192 and following his departure the Kingdom of Jerusalem was no more than a remnant of knights who withdrew to centre themselves in Acre where the Crusaders intended to have a foothold in Palestine and future hope of once more conquering Jerusalem.

The Christian world was frustrated with the continued occupation of Palestine by the Moslems, particularly Jerusalem, which in their minds was *their* 'Holy City'. However, they had much more on their plate than they could handle with heresies breaking out all over territory where the Pope's authority ran. In 1184 in France as a response to the Catharist heresy the Medieval Inquisition was the first of these to take place in Europe. There was also the continued resentment against the Jews who refused to acknowledge Jesus as their Messiah and who were still held accountable for deicide by the popes. The Jews too would be brought into the witch-hunts of the Inquisition, with torture, forced conversion or expulsion. In 1202, under the inspiration of Pope Innocent III, a fourth Crusade was launched through Venice. The plan was to attack the heart of the Moslem Empire through Egypt as it was thought that this tactic would lead to the eventual taking of Jerusalem from the Islamic grip. First though with Byzantine collusion their sights were sat on Constantinople. From here the Crusade would march on to reclaim the Holy Land and once more the Christian world would establish its authority over 'the sacred ground where Christ walked'. However, the sacking of Constantinople would go down in history as one of the most shameful acts of rape, plunder and pillage by the Christian Crusaders. Indeed it was noted that they were 'madmen raging against the sacred' who refused to 'spare pious maidens'. In a moving address in 2001, Pope John Paul II rightly expressed sorrow for what the Crusaders had done and stated:

'It is tragic that the assailants, who set out to secure free access for Christians to the Holy Land, turned against their brothers in the faith. That they were Latin Christians fills Catholics with deep regret.'

By the end of this bloody period, the fourth Crusade would come to an end, finally splitting Eastern and Western Christianity without achieving its initial goal set by Innocent – the retaking of Palestine and Jerusalem.

Pope Innocent III and his successor Honorius III would spend eight more years (1213-1221) in a fifth Crusade to occupy Palestine and reclaim Jerusalem. Even though the Crusade was to attack the Islamic occupiers of Jerusalem, Honorius in his pronouncements would bring into the matter the papal views against the Jews, using a passage of Scripture (Matt 23:37) that was often the basis of charges against them:

'Repetition of Jerusalem is like a complaint or objurgations [in the mouth of the Apostle]. It is as if he said: 'O Jerusalem, I have promoted you to the rank of master of the nations and first of the provinces, but because you kill the prophets and the Lord of the prophets, I condemn you to hell. Jerusalem, I honoured you by granting you a temple, a clergy and the royal dignity, but because you stone those who are sent to you, I will not leave any stone standing within your walls, as you did not recognise the time of my visit.'

Once more a huge army was raised initially from Hungary and Austria. The Hungarian army under King Andrew II was the largest ever Crusader army to attempt to retake Jerusalem, but they failed.

There was a sixth Crusade in 1299 led by Frederick II of Germany, who did not join in the previous Crusade. For what looked like political reasons he married Isabella (Yolanda), who was the daughter of John of Brienne, king of Jerusalem. On marriage he claimed the title for himself. As an Arabic speaker, Frederick decided on a more peaceful approach to Al-Kamil and he entered negotiations with him which resulted in the gaining of Jerusalem, Nazareth and Bethlehem, along with a route giving access to the sea. He entered Jerusalem on 18 February 1229, where he was crowned King of Jerusalem and considered himself to be a messiah, a second David. With his diplomatic skills he achieved more than all the bloody Crusades attempted previously. His attitude to the Jewish people was favourable as in 1236 he issued a refutation of the allegations of the Blood Libel. In this document he made clear that Jews were entitled to be treated fairly:

'Providing then for the security and peaceful status of the Jews of Germany, we cause this special grace to be extended to all Jews who belong directly to our court. That is to say, copying and adhering to the edicts of our aforesaid grandfather, we confirm for the Jews by our natural mercy the above privilege and those stipulations contained in it, in the same manner as our divine and august grandfather granted to the Jews of Worms and their associates.'

As to the specific charge of the Blood Libel he had made investigations and stated:

'When their findings were published on this matter, then it was clear that it was not indicated in the Old Testament or in the New that Jews lust for the drinking of human blood. Rather, precisely the opposite, they guard against the intake of all blood, as we find expressly in the biblical book which is called in Hebrew, '*Bereshit*' [Genesis], in the laws given by Moses and in the Jewish decrees which are called in Hebrew, 'Talmud.' We can surely assume that for those to whom even the blood of permitted animals is forbidden, the desire for human blood cannot exist, as a result of the horror of the matter, the prohibition of nature, and the common bond of the human species in which they also join Christians. Moreover, they would not expose to danger their substance and persons for that which they might have freely when taken from animals. By this sentence of the princes, we pronounce the Jews of the aforesaid place and the rest of the Jews of Germany completely absolved of this imputed crime. Therefore, we decree by the authority of the present privilege that no one, whether cleric or layman, proud or humble, whether under the pretext of preaching or otherwise, judges, lawyers, citizens, or others, shall attack the aforesaid Jews individually or as a group as a result of the aforesaid charge. Nor shall anyone cause them notoriety or harm in this regard. Let all know that, since a lord is honoured through his servants, whoever shows himself favourable and helpful to our serfs the Jews will surely please us. However, whoever presumes to contravene the edict of this present confirmation and of our absolution bears the offense of our majesty.'

With this attitude from Frederick, the Jews in Jerusalem were able to co-exist with Christians and Moslems in peace. It is to be noted that Frederick was a highly intellectual man and held views that were agnostic about Moses,

Jesus and Mohammed and it was these views that continued to cause conflict with papal authorities. Crusaders acting on behalf of these papal authorities continued their slaughter across Europe and in France in 1236 the Crusaders attacked the Jews at Anjou, Poitou, Bordeaux and Angouleme, and gave them the choice of Christian baptism or death. Five hundred Jews feigned baptism to avoid death but more than three thousand would not yield and were slaughtered with men, women, many pregnant, and children included, some being trampled under the horses of their killers.

Jerusalem and its environs remained peaceful until a Crusader baron, Peter of Brittany, attacked a caravan belonging to An-Nasir Dawud, a Kurdish sultan, in 1239. He in turned attacked Jerusalem which was weakly defended and destroyed all the fortifications of the city. He had no intention to continue occupation of Jerusalem and so it was returned after a few months to Christian control. However, there were conflicts within the Moslem/Kurdish groupings and alliances were formed with Crusaders which caused various movements of power in the region. The ripples of the papal Crusade against Jews continued to reverberate and in 1240, Duke Jean le Roux expelled the Jews from Brittany, in order to wipe out the debts owed to Jews, debts that were taken on to help fund the Crusade. Eventually in 1244 Jerusalem itself came under siege by the Khwarezmians, a Moslem group originating in Turkey but also consisting of many mercenaries. On taking the city, they completely destroyed it and all Christians were expelled. This signalled the beginning of the end of all Crusader influences in the region with the triumphant Ayyubids, a Kurdish Sunni Moslem grouping, gaining the upper hand and once more brought Palestine and the Transjordan under Islamic control. However, there would be more Crusades that would make final attempts to bring Christian rule back to the Holy Land but as we will see they were in the main pathetic and unsuccessful.

Chapter Six

Devastation In Judea, Persecution In Europe

In 1244, the Mongols, under Möngke Khan's rule, invaded Syria and after savage progress, Egypt and Syria became vassal states under the authority of the Mongol forces but without full occupation. The Mongols were initially tolerant of all religions and they themselves followed Buddhism, Shamanism and Tenriism and many followers of different religions were found as officials within the empire; it was only later that some Mongol leaders embraced Islam. Meanwhile, in Palestine by 1250, it was estimated that only 200 Jews remained within Jerusalem. As to the Jews under the Mongols, we need to set the situation in the context of what was happening in Christian Europe and other places before we turn to consider the long reign of the Ottomans.

In 1253 in England, Henry III introduced a statute of Jewry which reflected what was happening elsewhere in Europe after the Seventh Crusade. One reaction to Henry's statute and abuse was men like Elias l'Eveske, the arch-presbyter of England's Jews, applied to leave the country but was refused. In 1254, Simon de Montfort revolted against Henry. In his charter, De Montfort's stated, 'No Jew or Jewess in my time, or in the time of any of my heirs to the end of the world, shall inhabit or remain, or obtain a residence in Leicester.' Such a mood prevailed in England and subsequently, in 1263, a slaughter of Jews ensued:

'In the week before Palm Sunday, the Jewry in London was wantonly destroyed, and more than five hundred Jews "murdered by night in sections" – none escaping, seemingly, except those whom the mayor and the justiciars had sent to the Tower before the massacre began'

In 1254, Louis IX expelled the Jews from France, stealing their property and confiscating their synagogues. Matthew Parish wrote of the Jews of that time, 'See how the king of France hates you and persecutes you.'

A severe blow to the Islamic hold in the Middle East was inflicted by the Mongols in 1258, when Genghis Khan's grandson, Hulegu, laid siege to and captured the Islamic centre of Baghdad. The city's population was massacred along with caliph Al-Mustasim but the Mongols showed favour to Christians and the Shia Moslems but were hostile to the Sunni Moslems who they considered their enemies. This was the beginning of the end for the Ayyubids who were finally destroyed in 1260, when Syria was conquered by the Mongols who now numbered some Christians within their ranks. In the same year, they were carrying out raids into Palestine beginning to threaten the hold of the Islamic power but they came to a halt when the Islamic Mamluks met them in battle at Ain Jalut in Galilee and there defeated a depleted Mongol army. Eventually, the Mongols would lose Syria and Mamluk's rule dominated the region including the city of Jerusalem. The tragedy of the Jewish people throughout all this was recorded by Nahmanides, a noted Jewish scholar, who arrived in Jerusalem in 1267. He found a 'Judea devastated' with the buildings of many cities in ruins. He himself found only 'two self-supporting Jews' in Jerusalem itself. The continual wars over Palestine and the bloody conflict the Jews had experienced once more stirred in them the belief that the troubles were the fore-runner of the Messiah. Unfortunately, that was not to be.

In Vienna, in 1267, the Jews were forced to wear a distinctive coned shaped headdress as well as the yellow badge they were already compelled to wear, whilst in Poland, not for the last time, the Jews were ordered to be separated into ghettos by the church Synod of Breslau and ordered to also wear a pointed hat. Fortunately, on this occasion the orders were not enforced but they reinforced the deep anti-Semitism of the time. Edward I of England, son of Henry III, also was opposed to the advancement of Jews, considering them and their property as his own. One of his first acts as king was to insist that any property held by a Jew should be restored into Christian hands and the original loan be repaid to the Jews and he would then extract money from them. The Jews also had to wear the distinctive yellow badge and their loathing by the populace saw many petitions to the king to expel them from the country. Following the expulsion of Jews, he received substantial sums from the clergy and laity to show their favour. In France, Louis IX may have been cured of an illness but the experience had not cured him of his desire to continue the Crusade and he made another attempt in 1270, but his death in Tunis brought it to nothing. Jerusalem and most of Palestine were still under Islamic control. Before he was crowned, Edward I was the last to lead a Crusade to Palestine, in 1271. Initially he had some success in his campaign, but he never had enough resources to attempt to take Jerusalem from the Moslems. There was also the background of divisions within the Christian kingdoms and after retiring to Acre, Edward returned home to England. In 1276, in Fez, a massacre of Jews occurred that would have wiped out the entire community but for the intervention of the emir. In Germany, in 1283 and 1285, there were more Blood Libel allegations leading to the death of hundreds of Jews. Edward I of England had allowed the Jews to remain until he had no longer need of their money and in 1287 imprisoned them all and demanded a ransom of £12,000 (£14.25m, 2017) for their release. When this was paid, they were banished from the country in 1298. In the same year in Germany, another massacre began that is estimated to have killed up to 100,000 Jews over a few years.

In the Middle East in 1300, the Mongols made a brief re-appearance in an attempt to extend power in the region, but this lasted only a few months and the Mamluks successfully repelled them. Acre would finally be taken by the Mamluks and by 1303 the Crusaders had finally been driven out of the Holy Land. The territory was now fully under Islamic control and after 208 years, the Christian world had failed to gain authority over the Jewish homeland. The Mamluks would retain their hold until the sixteenth century and under their reign, the condition of the Jews was no different from the other non-Moslem religions. All such religions were treated as inferior and experienced different attitudes depending on the ruler of the day. Taxation and distinctive clothing and various restrictions on what was permitted were enforced and on many occasions the Moslems' specific actions against Christians were clouded and Jews were included in the punishments. The attitude to both were summed up by the comment, 'Jews and Christians are no better than dogs'. So whilst both Christians and Jews laboured under the Mamluks, they often were involved in conflict with one another as both tried to live out their religious practice under Mamluk rule. Palestine also suffered greatly from earthquakes over that period and the plague that had afflicted Europe also reached the area and devastated not only the population but hit all aspects of life including trade and commerce. The ongoing conflicts with Mongols and internecine intrigues necessitated harsher taxes which fell heavily on non–Moslems. Savage conflict of another raid into Syria by the Mongols rocked the Mamluks' hold in the region.

As the fourteenth century began, the persecutions of the Jews continued with Philip IV of France seizing Jewish property and expelling them from his country in 1305. Louis X would revoke this order and re-admitted the Jews in 1315 but when Philip V had come to power, a shepherd boy in 1320 claimed he had a religious vision that told him to go on crusade and fight the Moors. Philip refused to accept the shepherd's invitation to join him and the result was the shepherd's army went through France and Spain killing along the way, attacking particularly Jews as well as others who opposed them. The kings of France and Aragon, along with the Pope, tried to stop the slaughter but were ignored and the communities where the Jews were attacked were fined but this in turn resulted in more attacks on Jews. David Nirenberg, commented:

'The shepherds came to focus most spectacularly on the Jews, converting or killing Jews at Saintes, Verdun on the Garonne, and in the dioceses and cities of Cahors, Toulouse, and Albi (the massacre in Toulouse occurred on June 12). Massacres are also recorded at Castelsarrasin, Grenade, Lezat, Auch, Rabastens, Montguyard and Gaillac. In many places townsfolk and municipal officials may have been sympathetic to the pastoureaux, even complicit in their atrocities.'

In 1325, Charles IV sought to raise finance because of wars and imposed taxation which fell heavily on Jews who had begun to flee France but in 1327, he expelled all remaining Jews. Jews had lived in Spain from earliest Biblical times and indeed the history of Toledo has them residing there 500 years before Christianity arrived. This country stands with many others in Europe with a terrible history of persecution against the Jews which can be traced back to 418, when a Christian bishop confiscated two synagogues and in the Council of Toledo canons were passed to impose discrimination against the Jews as early as the fifth century. Whilst it is true that Catholic Spain often brought sanctions and penalties against the Jews, it is also true that there were periods when Jewish learning flourished there and many great Jewish scholars came from Spain. In the thirteenth century, laws came into force that gave some protection to Jews but were also very proscriptive in places and included the death penalty for any Christian who became a Jew. The council of Zamora in 1313 brought in a fresh wave of anti-Semitism including the order to wear a mark of clothing that showed their separation from Christians. The council of Salamanca in 1322 brought further proscription against the Jews, including a ban from holding public office. Christians were forbidden to use Jewish doctors; these orders also applied to the Moors. It has to be said that despite these laws, attempts were made to protect the Jews and allow them the right to earn a living but there remained a general public animosity towards them. In 1332, an attempt was made by a Spanish general who offered money to the king to expel the Jews from Spain but the king, although desperate for such help to fight a war, refused. The growth of the Jewish population in areas of Spain was alarming to local bishops and they began to impose heavy fines for the smallest infringements of the law. There was also a growing resentment in the area of finance and loans, with the king having to intervene to maintain justice for the Jews, causing further anger among the bishops and populace. The arrival of Peter (the Cruel) – despite his nickname – was particularly favourable to the Jews and they flourished under him. Rivalry within the Spanish kingdom led to many attempts to have the king turn against the Jews, and petitions often made to persecute them. E H Lindo in 1845 wrote:

'… the said Jews, as a wicked and daring people, the enemies of God and all Christendom, with great insolence commit many wrongs and extortions in such manner that everyone in our kingdoms, or the greater part of them are ruined and driven to despair by the said Jews, which they do in contempt of Christians and our Catholic faith. And since it is our will that this evil company may live in our kingdoms, and our pleasure was, that they, as well as Moors, should wear a badge, and that they may live marked and apart from Christians, as God commands, and justice and the laws ordain; beside that they should not hold any posts in our household, nor those of the grandees, knights and squires of our kingdoms.'

The king rejected these false allegations and refused to implement their suggestions declaring the Jews should have justice and be allowed to live in peace, but daily life for Jews remained pressured because of those with whom they lived. This contradiction in the attitude of the governing authority and action against Jews from the population, was also prevalent in Germany, where, in 1336, Arnold von Uissigheim, a German knight and convicted felon, slaughtered Jews. Eventually, he would be arrested and executed but persecution still persisted with sixty-five Jewish communities being entirely wiped out. Two years later in Bavaria, the onslaught continued with local government officials introducing laws to justify it. The ugly reasons for those in power opposing the persecutions was not from any sense of humanity, but because the Jews provided a ready source of financial exploitation through heavy taxation.

The Black Death ravaged Europe and caused a huge loss of life as country after country was devastated by the disease. The ignorance of its cause added to the woes of the Jews, when in many places they were alleged to be that cause. For example, 900 Jews were burnt in Strasbourg, 40 in Toulon and in Germany these suspicions added to the already brutal attacks and in 1349 a pogrom against Jews resulted in deaths and a huge amount of property being claimed by the authorities with Charles IV of Germany taking every advantage for himself. In the same year in Basel, 600 Jews were burned at the stake, 140 children forcibly baptized, and the remainder of the city's Jews expelled. The city synagogue was turned into a church and the Jewish cemetery was destroyed. In a massacre at Erfurt, 3,000 Jews were murdered and right across Europe the picture was repeated as the underlying hostility towards Jews found excuse for release. After the plague had passed, there seemed to be no further need for excuses, as the hostility continued. A massacre in Brussels in 1370 saw the last of the Jewish community in that city and Wenceslaus, the Holy Roman Emperor, expelled the Jews from the Swabian League and Strasbourg in 1386, stealing their property. Prague was the setting for another outrage when some Jewish children at play were charged with insults against a Catholic priest and 3,000 Jews were killed, with the mobs destroying the Jewish cemetery and the city's synagogues. The desecration of Jewish places of worship and the senseless barbarity of the mob was compounded by the remarkable comments of Wenceslaus, who blamed the whole matter on the Jews for daring to go into the streets during Holy week – a picture far removed from our carol of Good King Wenceslaus. Spain, once more, was also the scene of anti-Jewish violence, incited by the Archdeacon of Ecija, Ferrand Martinez. The Jewish quarter in Barcelona was destroyed. His campaign quickly spread throughout Spain (except for Granada) and destroyed Jewish communities in Valencia and Palma De Majorca. Thousands of Jews are murdered or forced to accept baptism and the Spanish historian Amador de los Ríos wrote:

'The cause of this attack was something else: the tinder was already at hand, only awaiting the application of fire. The sermons of the archdeacon of Ecija,..caused this horrible firestorm.'

France 1394 saw further expulsions of Jews and in 1399 in Posen, another Blood Libel case began when an archbishop charged Jews with stealing three pieces of the Host and stabbing it, so that blood spurted from it. The verdict of the trial was certain and led to the burning alive of the rabbi and thirteen elders, with an 'eternal fine' being imposed on the Jews which had to be paid to the Dominican order. Incredibly, this fine was technically still in place in the eighteenth century.

The coming of the fifteenth century did not auger well for German Jews, as in 1400 the *Judensau* (German for 'Jews' sow' or 'Jewish sow'), a folk art image of Jews in obscene contact with a large sow, in Judaism an unclean animal, began to appear in churches, sanctioned by Church and State authorities. These grotesque images, often accompanied with scenes of Blood Libel, were seen as an 'exclusively German phenomena' and provided a reminder and stimulus to Germans for anti-Jewish sentiments. In Spain, despite the presence of a king favourable to Jews, the Christian church continued its anti-Semitism with forced conversions, especially through the preaching of the Dominican friar Vicente Ferrer. Even though he spoke against the forced conversions, he did nothing to prevent them and in 1412 demanded the excommunication of anyone associating with Jews. His ideas were formulated into laws by Benedict XIII in 1415, which in effect reduced the Jews to impoverished pariahs, forcing many to convert or die. Duke Albrecht V turned against the Jews and imposed punitive taxes on them; in cases of non-payment, he ordered the torture of Jews, to discover their supposed hidden wealth. In Vienna, a pogrom climaxed in the Vienna Edict of 1421, which continued to pour more tribulation on their heads, when more Jewish property was confiscated. When the children of Jews were forcibly converted and baptised, many Jews barricaded themselves in their Synagogue and committed suicide rather than betray their faith. Furthermore, to impress their claims, 212 Jews (92 men and 120 women), who refused baptism, were burned alive at the stake and across Germany, France and England many other terrors were inflicted on the Jewish community. Many expulsions were carried out as Austrian Christianity continued to assert its 'right' to destroy the Jewish people and their religion. For thirty years there was no community in Austria and the Jews now referred to Austria as *Erez Hadimin*, 'Land of Blood'. Perhaps as a response to this, a year later, Pope Martin V issued a Papal Bull, reminding Christians of their Jewish roots and warned friars not to incite against the Jews, but the following year it was withdrawn. These persecutions continually fanned the flames of passion of Jews who yearned for a homeland and many sailed from Italy as it was close to the sacred places of their desire, but in 1427, the Pope banned sea captains from taking Jewish passengers and the hopes of many were dashed.

In Switzerland, Majorca and Poland the pressure remained on the Jewish people but in 1447, Casimir IV renewed all the rights of the Jews of Poland and marked his charter one of the most liberal in Europe. This encouraged many Jews to move across borders to safety, but the charter was revoked in 1454 after a defeat of the Polish army and at the insistence of Bishop Zbigniew, a powerful Cardinal at Cracow. Expulsions, confiscations, exploitations and heavy taxation remained throughout Europe alongside the continuing attempts to gain forced conversions; this was despite many attempts by some kings and princes to intervene, often for financial reasons. Such interventions had only a short-term effect as the general Christian populations maintained their anti–Jewish attitudes. However, it was not only in Europe where Jews continued to be the object of terrible atrocities. In 1465, in Fez, Morocco, another attack on the Jewish quarter almost wiped out the entire population of the district – an Arabic letter of the time gave the details:

'On the eleventh of Shawwal 869 [7th June 1465], the news arrived in Tlemcen from Fez that the great mass of people of Fez had risen up against the Jews there and had killed them almost to the last man'

The reason given for the attack was that the ruler Abd al-Haqq had appointed Jews to high rank over the Moslem population and those Jews had not changed their religion. As in many other places, the Jews were often opposed when they received any favour or power from a ruler. There was also the issue for those Jews who had converted, either willingly or otherwise, that did not escape the madness when it arose. In Cordoba, Spain, in 1473, the mobs attacked, murdered and robbed both Jews and converts, with the Catholic Cathedral records showing that the greatest concern of the church authorities was the loss of their rental income. Such was the picture for Jews in the wider world; back in Palestine, in Jerusalem the situation had also deteriorated. There was a rise of conflict between Mamluk rulers in different areas, which in turn was exploited by the indigenous Bedouins who even attacked Jerusalem and put the city's Governor to flight. In 1481, Ramla, in the centre of Palestine, was sacked and a Mamluk army sent to deal with it was annihilated. Obadiah ben Abraham di Bertinoro, an Italian Jew, had longed to live in his homeland, as did many of the persecuted who had fled. They believed there would be found a paradise but in 1488, when Obadiah arrived in Jerusalem, he found a quite different situation.

'Jerusalem is for the most part desolate and in ruins ... As for Jews about seventy families of the poorest classes have remained ... One who has bread for a year is called rich ... In my opinion an intelligent man versed in political science might easily raise himself to be chief of the Jews as well as Arabs, for among all the inhabitants there is not a sensible man who knows how to deal kindly with his fellow-men.. Among the population there are many aged, forsaken widows from Germany, Spain, Portugal, and other countries. It is impossible to gain a living ... except that of shoemaker, weaver, or goldsmith.'

He also found the Mamluk and Jewish agents both dishonest, with the Jewish elders wickedly placing heavy taxation on incoming refugees. Not only this, but they had also sold off synagogue furnishings and Torah scroll ornaments to fill their own pockets and please their Moslem rulers.

Throughout Syria and Palestine, because of the heavy taxation and the conscription of youth into the army, citizens looked outward to the Ottoman power which was growing and believed that life under them would be better. Therefore, with a growing dissatisfaction among its people, internal conflict and Bedouin pressure, it was only a matter of time before a collapse would come.

Chapter Seven

Sheltering Under The Ottomans

The Ottoman Empire arose out of Turkish tribes in Anatolia, Asia Minor, and it grew into one of the most powerful Empires in the world at its height during the fifteenth and sixteenth centuries. They ruled their territory from 1299 and it came to an end in 1922 after 600 years, when it was replaced by the Turkish Republic and other states in South Eastern Europe and the Middle East. Their area of control covered present-day Hungary, the Balkan region, Greece and parts of Ukraine, along with portions of the Middle East including the present Iraq, Syria, Israel, and Egypt. It also included North Africa as far west as Algeria and large parts of the Arabian Peninsula. The Empire took its name from its first ruler Osman I (Arabic: ʿUthmān), who was a nomadic Turkmen chief who founded the empire about 1300. The many powers in the conquered areas tried to resist but because of internal conflicts and expediency for alliances with the Turks, they proved too weak to stop the Ottoman advance. Except for a brief period in the fifteenth century, the Empire settled and began to institute means of Government and military power that facilitated its continued growth. Whilst the Empire was basically Islamic, it did tolerate all the older religions with some Christians and Jews converting to enjoy the full benefits of the Empire; the greater number continued to practice their faith without hindrance. This was still not the case in countries outside the Ottoman control.

In Neubrandenburg, Germany, in 1492, an allegation of desecrating the host caused a massacre that brought the Jewish community there to an end with 65 Jews being tortured, 27 of them being burned alive and the remainder expelled. It was in that same year that the Catholic authorities in Spain became concerned about Jewish influence on their members. The allegation was made that they were converting Christians and circumcising their children and that the Jews had not stayed within the quarters of the cities to which they were confined. The penalty for non-compliance with the order was death and seizure of property. The result was that Ferdinand reluctantly expelled over 150,000 Jews who were still in Spain and they made their way into the Ottoman Empire, after Bayezid II issued an invitation to the Jews expelled from Spain and Portugal and even sent out ships to safely bring them to their new home. Some decided to go to Holland and Portugal and settled among a Jewish community established there. Sicily in the same year was experiencing the Italian Inquisition, and an edict of Ferdinand against the Jews was also applied there, despite the local population's petitions and protests, with even the Inquisitor testifying that they were of righteous behaviour. The Jews were there in great numbers and were prosperous, contributing to the overall wealth through taxation so that their departure was a major blow to the island. Many of them resettled in other parts of the Italian mainland but many also moved into the relative safety of the Ottomans. Manuel I of Portugal, with an eye to political advancement and the approval of the papacy, began the process of removing both Jews and Moslems from Portugal in 1496. Around 30,000 Jews had gone there from Spain and many argue that it was this pressure that brought about Manuel's decision, but this does not appear to be so, as the Jews paid huge 'entrance fees' to the Portuguese Exchequer and had resources to look after themselves. It is therefore likely that Manuel was following the line of all other European states and ensuring that his country remained Christian through and through, as it became, after the expulsions. With this background, the Jews were faced with an Odyssean choice; to remain in the countries where they lived and accept the risk of death, exploitation and forced conversion or to move to the shelter of the Ottomans and accept the second class status of a non–Moslem. Many choose the latter. However, some went to Palestine and took passage to the land their hearts had always longed for, even though it was under Mamluk control, though that was soon to change. When Salim I came to power in 1512, he was intent on increasing the Ottoman Empire and marched on Syria with great military firepower. Both Mamluk and Egyptian armies were crushed and before long the Ottomans had taken full control of Syria and Palestine and both these areas would once more be joined as one, just as the Romans had done many years earlier. In its greatest period or power, the empire included most of South Eastern Europe right up to the gates of Vienna.

For the Jewish people, Europe remained a dangerous place and in Venice the authorities needed the Jews as money lenders, but at the same time the Catholic authorities were in conflict over the treatment of Jews. On one hand, the papacy ordered that Jews should not be interfered with but locally, the clergy preached vehemently against them, often inciting riots and expulsions. There was also the introduction of *Monte di Pietà*,[1] a system of charitable lending that would harm the Jewish trade in finance. Further restrictions on Jewish pawnshops and papacy concerns led to an order that the Jews were only allowed to sell second-hand clothing, but the industrious Jews were able to make their own new clothing and with subtle deliberate 'marks' sewn into obscure places, they could sell the new clothes as used and thus avoid the magistrates. Eventually expulsion of Jews from Venice was carried out but not with great success as the Jews found ways to return to the city and maintain trade. Increasing pressure was then brought to bear and more restrictions ensued. However, Venice was reaching its own crisis with banks failing; the great Venetian dream was beginning to crumble and once more it was realised that Venice needed the Jews. In 1508, war between the Venetian republic and a confederation of Pope Julius II, Emperor Maximilian and King Ferdinand of Spain, saw Venice lose mainland cities and Venice itself threatened. The Jews fled the areas of conflict and took shelter in Venice and began to experience a relaxation of the distinctive clothing laws and were even allowed to be armed in certain areas. The money the Jews brought with them was much needed by the Venetian government and they did all they could to make them welcome. The Church authorities were not so gracious and as the city fell into great moral corruption, religious fervour was whipped up and the Jews became the object of fiery sermons and an explosive situation was developing. By 1514, the military situation was improving with the moral climate still deteriorating but the Jews remained relatively free of legal burdens. However, tensions were growing with the Venetian senate demanding huge sums from the Jews who in turn resisted. The Ottoman Empire stood on the boundaries of the Venetian territory and the Jews used their presence as a bargaining chip: if the Venetian state did not want the Jews and their money, then the Ottoman Empire would welcome them. Eventually a settlement was reached, but the troubles of the Jews were not over. In 1515, the idea of a ghetto was raised, with pressure being put on the authorities to hem the Jews in and restrict their movements and abilities to trade. On 29 March 1516, a decree was issued by the Venetian Senate:

'The Jews must all live together in the Corte de Case, which are in the Ghetto near San Girolamo: and in order to prevent their roaming about at night: Let there be built two gates on the side of the Old Ghetto where there is a little Bridge, and likewise on the other side of the Bridge, that is one for each of said two places. Which Gates shall be opened in the morning at the sound of the Marangona, and shall be closed at midnight by four Christian guards appointed and paid for by the Jews at a rate deemed suitable by Our Cabinet'

Not only this, but the Jews had to pay for two patrol boats that would make sure they could not use any waterway to leave the ghetto. Anyone familiar with Shakespeare's *Merchant of Venice* will appreciate how he portrayed Shylock with all the prejudice of the Elizabethan era against Jews which reflected the same virulent anti–Semitism that marked Venice. Once more, we see the great need that existed for a country the Jews could call their own and where they could live and practice their religion in peace and safety.

This would be further reinforced in Germany when Martin Luther became increasingly angry with the established Roman Church and was reinforced when Pope Leo X introduced a new set of indulgences to raise money to help build St. Peter's Basilica. On October 31, 1517, Luther nailed a parchment with his 95 Theses on the University of Wittenberg's chapel door. The printing press enabled copies of the Theses to spread throughout Germany within two weeks and throughout Europe within two months. The actions of Martin Luther would eventually irrevocably split the universal church in two; Protestantism and Romanism would now compete for adherents in the arena of Christian faith. Whilst Luther had admirable aims of reformation and was seeking genuinely to improve the lot of Christians, especially the poor, there was a horrific side effect the later Nazis would embrace in their genocide attempt on the Jewish people. The long–held ambition of the Catholic Church to bring the Jews to the Christian faith was totally accepted by Luther, who initially believed the Jews were the people of God. In *That Jesus Christ Was Born a Jew*, he was clear on his views at that time (1523):

'Therefore, I will cite from Scripture the reasons that move me to believe that Christ was a Jew born of a virgin, that I might perhaps also win some Jews to the Christian faith. Our fools, the popes, bishops, sophists, and monks – the crude asses' heads – have hitherto so treated the Jews that anyone who wished to be a good Christian would almost have had to become a Jew. If I had been a Jew and had seen such dolts and blockheads govern and teach the Christian faith, I would sooner have become a hog than a Christian. They have dealt with the Jews as if they were dogs rather than human beings; they have done little else than deride them and seize their property. When they baptize them they show them nothing of Christian doctrine or life, but only subject them to popishness and monkery.'[2]

Luther's wish was that the Jews would become Christian and he held a sincere belief that if treated properly by Christians, they would convert. However, earlier, in a letter to George Spalatin in 1517, he seemed to believe that the Jews would not abandon their faith and had written:

'But what am I doing? My heart is fuller of these thoughts than my tongue can tell. I have come to the conclusion that the Jews will always curse and blaspheme God and his King Christ, as all the prophets have predicted. He who neither reads nor understands this, as yet knows no theology, in my opinion. And so I presume the men of Cologne cannot understand the Scripture, because it is necessary that such things take place to fulfil prophecy. If they are trying to stop the Jews blaspheming, they are working to prove the Bible and God liars.'

Gradually, Luther became increasingly frustrated that the Jews were not converting and his attitude became more strident in his opposition to them and reached the point where he decided that they never would:

'It is not my purpose to quarrel with the Jews, nor to learn from them how they interpret or understand Scripture; I know all of that very well already. Much less do I propose to convert the Jews, for that is impossible.'

His increasing anger was displayed in his book, *The Jews and Their Lies*, which was a long theological discourse in which he set out his interpretation of Scripture and saw himself in the tradition of the Jewish Prophets who had invoked curses on the Jewish people when they had strayed from the Laws of God. The modern mind will recoil at what he wrote, but it must be seen in the light of medieval anti-Semitism to which Luther had succumbed:

'First to set fire to their synagogues or schools and to bury and cover with dirt whatever will not burn, so that no man will ever again see a stone or cinder of them. This is to be done in honour of our Lord and of Christendom, ... But if we, now that we are informed, were to protect and shield such a house for the Jews, existing right before our very nose, in which they lie about, blaspheme, curse, vilify, and defame Christ and us (as was heard above), it would be the same as if we were doing all this and even worse ourselves, as we very well know. ... I advise that their houses also be razed and destroyed. ... I advise that all their prayer books and Talmudic writings, in which such idolatry, lies, cursing and blasphemy are taught, be taken from them. ... I advise that their rabbis be forbidden to teach henceforth on pain of loss of life and limb. ... I advise that safe-conduct on the highways be abolished completely for the Jews. For they have no business in the countryside, since they are not lords, officials, tradesmen, or the like. Let they stay at home. ... I advise that usury be prohibited to them, and that all cash and treasure of silver and gold be taken from them and put aside for safekeeping ... I commend putting a flail, an axe, a hoe, a spade, a distaff, or a spindle into the hands of young, strong Jews and Jewesses and letting them earn their bread in the sweat of their brow, as was imposed on the children of Adam (Gen 3[:19].) ... all who are able toss in sulphur and pitch; it would be good if someone could also throw in some hellfire. ... Burn down their synagogues, forbid all that I enumerated earlier, force them to work, and deal harshly with them ... we must drive them out like mad dogs, ... Now let everyone see to his. I am exonerated.'

There is no defence for Luther in this terrible venom and it was an unwise decision to write as he did. It could be argued that Luther had no intention that the Jewish people should be actually destroyed, but his foolish diatribe, which included the account of the killing of the 3,000 by Moses, led to a misunderstanding by many anti-Semites and became rooted in the Lutheran German psyche. The Nazis would later embrace it in their barbaric plans, using Luther's own phrase that they 'were doing their duty', although Luther would have been horrified to see anyone use his theological arguments as a pretext for genocide on an almost industrial scale. Thus, the Jewish people were now the object of hate from many in the reformed Protestant and Catholic traditions and throughout Europe. The old medieval institutions and attitudes were disappearing as the Catholic Church was challenged with nationalism and humanism beginning to flower. Men and women everywhere had begun to seek to throw of bondage and serfdom as the Renaissance threw light on the practices and powers of the Ecclesiastic establishment and exposed their wickedness and manipulations. Though for the Jews this was not the case, as they continued to be the object of persecution and hate and their lives, property and freedom to follow their faith, remained at hazard. In Palestine in 1520, an internal revolt was attempted by Mamluks, joined by Bedouins, but this was savagely put down and new governors were appointed. However, these steps were very inadequate and the Bedouins, although also Moslem, continued to harass and disrupt the governance of the region, making even the collection of taxes impossible in some areas.

In 1524, the pope, Clement VII, was under great pressure with the reformation in Germany, the European Renaissance and the opposition of the Holy Roman Emperor, Charles V. He had devastated Italy and brought it into servile dependency and now held power over German, Spain and areas of France. The Pope, in the centre of all of this, also saw the Ottoman expansion, conquering Belgrade and Rhodes with Hungary and Austria being the objects of its military might. Clement cast his eyes around for anything that might help relieve his problems, especially the growing threat of the Moslem Ottomans. His Inquisition was continuing its purges of Christendom and it did not mind if its net fell over the Jews, even though they were not supposed to be their concern. However, many Jews who had converted to Christianity for expedient reasons and the many who converted but continued to practice Judaism, called Marranos, were considered fair game for the Inquisitor's torture, if any signs of relapse were detected. Once more the Ottoman Empire became a place of refuge for many Jews and Marranos who fled the Inquisition's onslaught.

It was therefore a surprise when a Jew, David Reubeni, came into Rome riding on a white stallion for an audience with the pope, to offer him a solution to his Moslem problem. He presented Clement with the strangest letter:

'I am David the son of King Solomon (may the memory of the righteous be blessed), and my brother is King Joseph, who is older than I, and who sits on the throne of his kingdom in the wilderness of Habor [Chalabar], and rules over thirty myriads of the tribe of Gad and of the tribe of Reuben and of the half-tribe of Manasseh. I have journeyed from before the king, my brother, and his counsellors, the seventy elders. They charged me to go first to Rome to the presence of the pope, may his glory be exalted.'

The desperate pope allowed Reubeni to continue and he went on to inform the pope that he had a plan to drive the Ottomans out of Europe and Palestine and establish a homeland for the Jews. Despite the incredible claims being made the pope did enquire about Reubeni and granted him letters to take to Portugal and Ethiopia to gather more support for the plan. Portugal proved a difficult place for Reubeni as many of the Jews who had converted for one reason or another decided he was a true man from God and deserted Christianity to return to their Jewish faith. This stirred up the animosity of the Inquisitors and the Portuguese Catholics, who put pressure on the pope to reconsider his support for Reubeni and institute the Inquisition in Portugal. Reubeni was captured by the Spanish after being shipwrecked near Spain and was only released on the intervention of Charles V, after which he fled to papal protection in Avignon. Pressure grew from both Spain and Portugal who saw the activities of one of his early 'disciples', Molcho, disturb their countries, particularly the Jews who had converted to Christianity. Molcho (aka Diogo Pires), born into Christianity, became a follower of Judaism and saw himself as a prophetic fore-runner of the Messiah, was associated in minds as connected to Reubeni and indeed did make some plans with him in northern Italy to help the plight of the Marranos. However, both men eventually were imprisoned by the authorities in Italy with Molcho being tried by the Inquisition and refusing to recant his Jewish 'conversion'. He was burned at the stake. Reubeni, not ever being a Christian of any sort, could not be touched by the Inquisition but he was returned to prison in Spain, where he died, probably being poisoned. The dream of a Jewish homeland therefore remained just that and the Jews continued under persecution in Europe and in the Ottoman Empire continued to have the protection of their Moslem overlords.

Some of the Marranos sought to flee to Mexico to evade the Inquisition but even there they were pursued and in 1528, in the first *auto-da-fé* ,[3] three Jews were burned at the stake. This would not be the last of these public punishments, which grew into great occasions for the crowds and would spread to other countries under Spanish rule. The Spanish were also active against the Ottomans and in 1535 they captured Tunis from them after the Ottomans had taken it the year before. The attempt to flee by Tunisian Jews to another area of the Empire was prevented and many were sold into slavery by the conquering Spaniards, with 150 being rescued by Italian Jews paying a ransom. The European pursuit of Jews continued in Prague and in 1540 they were expelled, whilst in Russia, the Jews had been living and promoting their faith, even into the higher circles of royalty and the nobility, causing rivalry between Poland and Moscow. The church authorities were also becoming concerned and agitation against the Jews increased. The arrival of Ivan IV (the Terrible) brought harsh pressure on them and in 1550, when a request was made to allow Polish Jews to come to Moscow to trade, his reply was ominous for the future of the Jews:

> 'We have more than once written and noted the evil deeds of the Jews, who have led our people astray from Christianity, who have brought poisonous weeds into our land and also wrought much wickedness among our people'

These were not empty words; they turned to physical hatred and he began a campaign of forced conversions, with those not accepting his offer being drowned in the river at Polotsk. It was also in 1550 that Genoa expelled all Jews residing there following a decree by the Dominican friar Bonifazio da Casale. This was despite the Jews having had a very good relationship with many Christians in the city, who managed to get some exceptions, but the few that were able to remain had to wear the yellow badge to identify them as Jews. Genoa was not the only city in Italy to continue the hatred of the Jews and in 1554, a Franciscan friar, Cornelio da Montalcino, who had converted to Judaism, was burned alive at the stake. The following year more invectives came from the papal authorities with Pope Paul IV issuing a papal bull against the Jews:

'Since it is completely senseless and inappropriate to be in a situation where Christian piety allows the Jews (whose guilt-all of their own doing-has condemned them to eternal slavery) access to our society and even to live among us; indeed, they are without gratitude to Christians, as, instead of thanks for gracious treatment, they return invective, and among themselves, instead of the slavery, which they deserve, they manage to claim superiority: we, who recently learned that these very Jews have insolently invaded Rome from a number of the Papal States, territories and domains, to the extent that not only have they mingled with Christians (even when close to their churches) and wearing no identifying garments, but to dwell in homes, indeed, even in the more noble [dwellings] of the states, territories and domains in which they lingered, conducting business from their houses and in the streets and dealing in real estate; they even have nurses and housemaids and other Christians as hired servants. And they would dare to perpetrate a wide variety of other dishonourable things, contemptuous of the name Christian. Considering that the Church of Rome tolerates these very Jews (evidence of the true Christian faith) and to this end [we declare]: that they, won over by the piety and kindness of the See, should at long last recognize their erroneous ways, and should lose no time in seeing the true light of the catholic faith, and thus to agree that while they persist in their errors, realizing that they are slaves because of their deeds, whereas Christians have been freed through our Lord God *Yeshua* Christ, and that it is unwarranted for it to appear that the sons of free women serve the sons of maids.'

He went on to order that states within the papal authority should create controlled locked ghettos for Jews and they were only allowed one synagogue in a city, all others to be destroyed. He put restraint on their ability to socialise and to use any Christians as servants or to allow them to treat Christians medically. They were also restricted in their ability to lend money and only allowed the job of 'rag-picking'. The persecution of the Jews continued with the pope only allowing Talmuds that were censored and printed by Christians. In Venice, Spain and Portugal, the situation was becoming more and more dangerous, so much so that many Jews decided they wanted to go to Palestine and the shelter of the Ottomans.

One prominent Jew, Donna Gracia Mendes Nasi, from the Mendes family, who were among the Marranos in Portugal, left with her own family and went to Antwerp, where she became the head of a large banking concern. One of her nephews, Joao Miquez, abandoned the Marrano class and returned to his Jewish roots, taking the name Joseph Nasi. In 1561, he gained the support of Sultan Suleiman the Magnificent in Turkey and was able to get land in Tiberius, Palestine, where Jews could be settled and live free from persecution. He was so angered by the treatment of his people that he encouraged the Sultan to invade Venice, which in turn resulted in the capturing of Cyprus from Venice by the Ottomans. There were also stirrings within certain Christian circles that the fate of the Jews was linked to the return of Christ and the idea of the restoration of the Jewish people to their homeland. Indeed, it was thought by some that the Jews would be the ones who would deal with the Moslems. One English Protestant preacher, Thomas Brightman, was particularly stirred with this notion and regularly preached for every encouragement to be given to the Jews to fulfil their destiny. In a work published after his death in 1607 he wrote in an exegesis of Revelations dealing with the enemies of the Jews:

'Then, and there, he comes to the last enemies of the Jews, the Romans, which had clipped the wings of Antiochus, in the 30th verse, till at the end, their own eagles wings were also clipped by the Saracens, and Turks, in verse 40, the one like a tossing beast, does push forth at him; the other coming against him, like a whirlwind that cannot be resisted, overflows, bears down all before it, enters Judea, the Glorious Land, which has been then a long time, the cockpit of the world, in the midst of their enemies, Babylonians, Persians, Greeks, Egyptians, Seleucids, and now at this day by the Turks, the last though not the least, of their adversaries, which shall be troubled with the tidings of the Eastern and Northern Jews conversion, which shall make him march out furiously against them, like another Jehu ...

Then follow the joyful return, and resurrection of the Jews: who lay dead for almost seventeen hundred years.'

Therefore, whilst the Roman church maintained its opposition to the Jews, the Protestant church was hearing the stirrings of some voices calling for a different approach to them, although it has to be noted that the concern for the Jews was more to do with the Christian hope of redemption and the notion of the conversion of the Jews.

While the Jews of Rome experienced a relaxation of pressure, the arrival of Pope Pius V saw the re-imposition of the harsh orders of Paul IV and in 1569, he expelled Jews dwelling outside of the ghettos of Rome, Ancona, and Avignon from the Papal States, pushing more Jews to flee to the Ottoman's security. There was no let-up in action against the Jewish people, particularly in Spain and Mexico with more *autos-da-fé*, which saw many Marranos, suspected of false conversion, burned at the stake after torture by the Inquisition, such as Francisca Nuñez de Carabajal, in 1596 and Frei Diogo da Assumpcão, in Lisbon in 1603. The animosity of the Roman church was further seen when the Jesuits banned admission to anyone descended from Jews to the fifth generation in 1608. It is incredible that this was not rescinded until late in the twentieth century. There was also the problem of state authority decreeing one thing and the anti-Semitic reactions of local citizens. In Frankfurt, the Jews had protection under the Emperor, but local Guild craftsmen had a dispute with the patrician families and the council over high taxation. They also had taken umbrage at the large Jewish population. In 1614, this led to an attack on the city hall and the forced resignation of the council, after which they plundered the Jewish ghetto and violently expelled the Jews. The ring leader, Vincenz Fettmilch, and his associates were eventually arrested, tried and executed and their families flogged and banished. Fettmilch was called the 'Haman' of Frankfurt, echoing the Haman in the Biblical Esther story. In Worms, a leader in the Guild organisation led by Dr Chemnitz, had learned from the Frankfurt experience and as a lawyer he looked for 'tricks' that could remove the Jews without violence. They chose chicanery and insults of every sort and sought to wear the Jewish people down by closing the outlets of the city to them, hindered them from purchasing food, drove their cattle from the meadows and prevented milk deliveries for Jewish children being brought to the Jewish quarter. Eventually, their continued activity forced the Jews to emigrate in 1615, after which their synagogue was demolished, the cemetery laid waste, and the tombstones destroyed. It was the same year that Louis XIII re-issued the edict of 1394 for the expulsion of all Jews and they were to leave all French soil under pain of death for refusal. However, it seems that despite Louis' anti-Semitism, the edict never seemed to be enforced, although there were anti-Jewish riots in Provence which forced them to move to the northern part of France.

Despite the Ottoman protection in Palestine, in other Moslem areas there were still those who would persecute the Jews. In 1619, Shah Abbasi of the Persian Sufi dynasty, forced Jews to publicly practice Islam and he instituted harsh rules to govern their behaviour. Under him, the Jews were classed as unclean heretics and experienced the worst treatment from any Moslem ruler. This led to many Jews deciding to leave Persia and to go to the Ottoman Empire's other territory, rather than continue to suffer the indignities inflicted on them and for those that remained the situation grew gradually even more severe. There was one European country that did try to help the Jews at this time by introducing laws to stop anti-Semitism and that was Poland. By 1648, the Jewish population there was 450,000 (4 per cent of the population as a whole) whilst the worldwide Jewish population was estimated at 750,000.[4] However, not all was well within the Polish commonwealth and in the area now known as Ukraine, a Cossack leader, Bohdan Chmielnicki, carried out a hate campaign with brutal pogroms, attacks and massacres that destroyed hundreds of Jewish communities and murdered around 20,000 men out of estimated 40,000 in the region. In 1648, they turned their anger towards others they saw as their enemies; Poles, Catholics and Jews. In an attack on the town of Nemerov in Poland, anyone who refused to convert to the Orthodox faith was slaughtered and between 3,000 and 6,000 Jews were massacred and a further 1,500 in Tulczyn were also killed a few weeks later. The atrocities continued until the Polish authorities defeated him and he was forced to sign a treaty that ended his horrific onslaught.

In England in 1642, the first Civil War began followed by a second in 1648 and by January 30 1649 the English had executed their king – Oliver Cromwell was now securely in charge of England. His early religious life is not too clear, but he did come to a 'conversion' somewhere around 1638 when he wrote to his cousin and gave the account of his experience and the statement, 'My soul is with the congregation of the first born'. This was good news for the Jews who had been expelled from the country, because the Puritan Protestant was sympathetic to the plight of the Jews. It was in 1656 that, Menasseh ben Israel, the son of a Marrano and a notable Jew from Amsterdam, wrote, 'The communication and correspondence I have held for some years since, with eminent persons of England.' This indicated that Jews would like to return to England and held a dream for their future liberty set out in a pamphlet *The Hope Of Israel*. The idea of religious liberty was well held by the puritans and there was also the idea of Christian millennialism similar to Thomas Brightman's and Sergeant Finch who wrote a book in 1621, *The Calling of The Jews*, which was a call for a 'national existence in Palestine' of the Jews. Such early Zionism was not welcomed in royal circles and the publisher was put into gaol by James I. All this did was to fan the flames of millennialism, seeing the persecution as part of the end time prophecies and the restoration of the Jews. The belief was held that if England were to become enthusiastic about Jewish liberty and welcome them back with open arms, then other countries around the world would follow. Therefore, in Cromwell's England, a bill was to be presented to parliament repealing Edward's edict of expulsion but the new government was cautious and the beheading of the king led to a delay. However, there can be no doubt that Cromwell was supportive and desired toleration, writing in a letter to Lawrence Crawford, a Scottish Presbyterian general in the parliamentary army:

'The State, in choosing men to serve it, takes no notice of their opinions; if they be willing faithfully to serve it, that satisfies ... bear with men of different minds from yourself'.'[5]

Indeed, the difficulties between England and Holland and issues around trade, caused many Jewish traders to seek to move to London and ben Israel was not slow to capitalise on this, writing:

'Hence it may be seen that God hath not left us; for if one persecutes us, another receives us civilly and courteously; and if this prince treats us ill, another treats us well; if one banisheth us out of his country, another invites us with a thousand privileges; as divers princes of

Italy have done, the most eminent King of Denmark, and the mighty Duke of Savoy in Nissa. And do we not see that those Republiques do flourish and much increase in trade who admit the Israelites?" The idea of this prosperous benefit to England was not lost on Cromwell and he sanctioned petitions to allow the Jews to return. He even acted on behalf of Jews to gain back property taken from them in Portugal and thus his religious tolerance coincided with his desire for the improvement of the country's financial welfare.'

Ben Israel was invited to London on Cromwell's personal invitation to promote the Jewish case and a tract *De Fidelitate et Utilate Judaica Gentis*, (Loyalty to the Jewish People) described as *Libellus Anglicus* (the English Petition) was prepared. Cromwell wanted the Jews to be fully admitted but the Council of State was cautious about a decision and threw the matter back to Cromwell, who in turn decided that a conference be called of notables to give advice on the issue. This conference turned into a division between supporters and opponents until eventually a proposal was formed to admit Jews but to severely restrict them and to tax them heavily. Cromwell was totally opposed to this and intervened to bring the conference to a close and once more tried the Council of State route. This was proving a struggle but by now Jews were entering England and a note in the state papers shows that Cromwell was turning a blind eye to their arrival. 'The Jews we hear, will be admitted by way of connivancy [connivance], though the generality oppose.' Whilst this allowed Marranos, and openly Jewish adherents to begin to enter England, it was not without opposition from anti-Semites who continually sought to prevent Jewish immigration. War with Spain provided such an opportunity, with anti-Semitic royalists seeking out Spanish Jews and using legislation that allowed the seizure of Spanish property in England, and obtaining warrants for the arrest of Spanish Marrano/Jews. Cromwell himself intervened and with clever political skill thwarted their efforts and eventually the cause of Jews entering the country was established and the roots of Jews in England steadily deepened. The ending of the Commonwealth and the restitution of the Monarchy under Charles II was another opportunity for the anti-Semites, but Charles, who had been supported financially by Jews when in exile, refused to comply with petitions to reintroduce the expulsions of Jews and so, though Edward

I's edict was never formally revoked, the legacy of Cromwell was a thriving Jewish community that once more flowered in England. However, whilst this was positive, the original dream expressed by ben Israel for the Jewish people, 'that they keep their true religion, as hoping to returne againe into the Holy Land in due time' was not achieved.

At Safed in the Ottoman Empire, in the mid-seventeenth century, an incident took place that has been the subject of debate on the historical record. Safed had been a very active centre for Judaism and mystic studies but by the early 1600s it had become less important as a centre of Judaism and 'Safed thus ceases to be a centre of attraction. It decays slowly.' The Druze community there were involved in a struggle for power with the Ottomans and there followed the destruction of Safed and Tiberius. Some reports suggested that the Jews were utterly massacred, but this has been disputed. As with most things concerning such matters, the truth lies somewhere in between. There is no doubt that there was the destruction of the two cities and indeed Jews were killed and displaced in the event, but the evidence suggests that there still was a community of Jews in the area in 1667, who continued to benefit from the shelter of the Ottoman Empire. One man, Sabbatai Sevi, was a Jewish mystic connected with Safed and he became the focus of Jewish Messianic attention. A Jerusalem Jew, Nathan Benjamin, was sent to Africa and Europe to collect funds for Jews settling in Jerusalem. He became involved in the Jewish community in Gaza and announced that he had a vision in which he had a 'message from an angel, "now is the time of the last end meant by Scripture, for the day of vengeance is in my heart".' The persecution of the Jews over many years and his experiences in travelling, seeing the plight of Jews, would have weighed heavily upon him. In 1665, Benjamin went into a mystic state and issued a prophesy:

'Heed ye Nathan my beloved, to do according to his word. Heed ye Sabbatai Sevi, my beloved. For if ye knew the praise of Rabbi Hamnuna the Ancient, "and the man Moses was very weak".'

When asked to explain this, after his mystical state, Benjamin proclaimed Sevi as the Messiah and that he was 'worthy to be king over Israel'. The reference to 'very weak' reflected the illnesses Sevi is reported to have suffered and result of the proclamation was that Sevi's reputation as the

Messiah spread across Europe and the realisation of the Messiah's return was taken seriously. Even ben Israel in his communications to Cromwell cited Sevi and set the return of Jews to England in that context. In Baghdad, many Jews gave away property to the poor and removed the roofs of their houses.[6] In Poland, Crimea, Jerusalem, Moldovia, France and London there arose a real desire to make pilgrimage to Jerusalem, and these Jews saw their suffering as the necessary preparation for the coming of the Messiah. Indeed, there was a real movement towards repentance, fasting and holiness of great numbers of Jews. Whatever the explanation or belief in this vision, it demonstrates the heart of yearning with the Jewish people for that day of redemption when they would be free from their oppressors and under their own king, in their own kingdom. Köprülü Fazıl Ahmed Paşa, the Turkish Vizier, became concerned about the disturbance being caused and Sevi was imprisoned in the fortress at Gallipoli. This did not stop growing messianic expectation and the suffering was added to the mysticism of the Messiah, but eventually Sevi come to a point where he was made by the then ruler of the Ottoman Empire, Mohammed IV, to convert to Islam or die and, for reasons that are not truly clear, he chose to embrace Islam. After the news of the apostasy spread across the Jewish world many deserted Sevi and the dream of redemption was shattered. Sevi, continued to live a double life, sometimes following Islam and other times taking part in Jewish rituals and thus retained a following. He was eventually caught in the act of Jewish worship by Moslems and he was banished. On his death, Benjamin, faithful to the bitter end, tried to make a mystic point that it was merely an 'occultation' but by now another movement for a Jewish homeland vanished into disappointment. This episode, whilst ending in the disappointment, did have the effect of many Jews returning to a greater passion for their faith and many who had converted to Christianity now returned to openly profess their Jewish roots. This in turn meant that in many countries they once more stood out as different and in turn brought on the unwelcomed attention of the anti-Semites. Therefore, in 1667, in Vienna, more expulsions took place and in the Yemen forced conversions were followed by expulsions in 1679 of those who remained faithful to their religion.

The persecution by non-Jews was not the only issue in the Jewish world because of the residue of the disciples of Sevi, who maintained their belief that he was indeed the Messiah, and became known as Shabbetaians. One

Shabbetaian preacher who came to Lithuania was heard by a Kabbala teacher, Judah Hassid ha-Levi (aka Judah the Saint), who was so impressed by the preacher that he was swept up in the idea of a return to the land of Israel. He went throughout Poland and Lithuania passionately preaching his message of repentance, mortification and good deeds. He was now in conflict with the traditional Orthodox rabbis, who became alarmed at their renewed activity which called for a return of the Jews to the Holy Land. In 1700, the group decided to begin the process of returning to Palestine and as their journey progressed, Judah was joined by another teacher, Hayyim Malakh, a radical Shabbetaian, who helped establish the group – he would become known as Malakh, the Angel. Malakh preached his radical message and began to hold secret meetings, where he taught that Sevi was indeed the Messiah and was a type of Moses who would lead the people to the Promised Land. He went further and declared that in 1707, Sevi would rise from the dead and redeem the Jewish people. The two preachers went separately to different countries in Europe, raising funds and gaining followers with their passionate preaching. By the time they arranged the final leg of the journey to the Holy Land, the group numbered 1500, travelling in two groups under Malakh and Judah and using different routes. On 14 October 1700, around 1,000 reached their destination; the remainder had perished on the journey and Judah himself died within days of his arrival, with Malakh assuming leadership of the group. Unfortunately, when they arrived they did not find the paradise they expected but found a Jewish community in poverty and misery with internal corruption and division. Malakh himself and some of his followers also were expelled from Jerusalem because of his unorthodox views and behaviour. The desperation of the situation led some to return to Europe, some to embrace the Moslem religion and some fell under the preaching of Christians and were baptised into that faith. Whilst this expedition was a disaster it entered the lore of the Jewish people as the first organised *Aliyah*[7] of the Jews to their homeland and would remain an aspiration for many throughout the Jewish world.

One publication in 1700 which would have a huge impact on the relationship of Jews with their non-Jewish communities was an anti-Semitic publication by Johann Andreas Eisenmenger, from Mannheim. He had spent many years with Jewish scholars investigating Judaism and studying the Scriptures and literature of the Jews and his interaction with Christians who had converted to Judaism developed in him an irrational hatred of Jews. His publication, *Entdecktes Judenthum* (Judaism Unmasked), was a compilation of slander and misinterpretation of the Jewish religion and way of life. The Jews around him tried to encourage him to withhold publication, even offering him a sum of money, and though he asked for more, it did nothing to prevent his attempts at publication. The work poisoned the minds of many and indeed ever since he is uncritically quoted by many anti-Semites seeking to blacken the Jewish people. Carl Gustav Adolf Siegfried, a German theologian, wrote of Eisenmenger's work:

'Taken as a whole, it is a collection of scandals. Some passages are misinterpreted; others are insinuations based on one-sided inferences; and even if this were not the case, a work which has for its object the presentation of the dark side of Jewish literature cannot give us a proper understanding of Judaism.'

The continuing journey of the Jewish people was one marked by such prejudicial views and opinions, based on misunderstanding, envy, ignorance and often an irrational hatred, fuelled by anti-Semitic preaching from religious pulpits. Thus, Blood Libel accusations continued in such places as Sandomierz in Poland in 1710, where the Cathedral has a depiction of the event, and the result was another expulsion of Jews from the city.

Chapter Eight

Assistance On The Journey Home

The plight of the Jews and their need for a homeland was recognised among some thinkers, such as John Toland, an Irish-born rationalist philosopher and freethinker. In 1718, he wrote a wise summary of the journey of the Jews:

'Whether without having recourse to miracles, or to promises drawn from the Old Testament (which is the same thing, if you don't take those promises for wise foresight) it can be demonstrated by the intrinsic constitution of the Government of Religion of the Jews, how, after the total subversion of their State for almost seventeen hundred years and after the dispersion of their nation across the whole habitable earth; being neither favoured nor supported by any potentate, but rather exposed to the contempt and hatred of all the world: they have nevertheless preserved themselves a distinct people with all their ancient rites.'

His solution was obvious to him and he advocated it to other thinkers around him; the Jews needed to return to their homeland and have an independent state:

'Now if you will suppose with me (till my proofs appear) the preeminence and immortality of the MOSAIC REPUBLIC in its original purity, it will follow: that, as the Jews known at this day, and who are dispersed over Europe, Asia, Africa, with some few in America, are found by good calculation to be more numerous that either the Spaniards (for example) or the French: so if they ever happen to be resettled in Palestine upon their original foundation, which is not at all impossible: they will then by reason of their excellent constitution, be much more populous, rich and powerful than any other nation now in the world. I would have you consider, whether it be not both the interest and duty of Christians to assist them in regaining their country'

This was an amazing prophetic insight into the reality that the Jews had been uplifted from their roots over the centuries and should be assisted to return to their own State. However, Toland was a voice crying in the wilderness and the grotesque religious persecution of the Jews continued, showing no respect for age. In 1721, in a Spanish Inquisition *auto-da-fé* at Madrid, Maria Barbara Carillo, aged 95, was executed for heresy for reverting to her original faith of Judaism. Peter the Great of Russia had welcomed Jews and the money they could bring, but that welcome was not extended by others. Borukh Leibov, a Jew who had prospered and was a customs and excise officer, built a synagogue in Zverovich in 1727, which raised the anger of the local Greek Orthodox priest, and began a series of rumours and slander about the Jews trying to convert Christians, ultimately leading to protests to the Holy Synod in St Petersburg. Subsequently, Catherine of Russia, on coming to the throne, issued a *ukase* (decree) through the Supreme Secret Council, that removed Borukh from his employment and expelled him from Russia. This was followed later by the expulsion of all Jews, who were forbidden to take any gold or silver coins out of the country. Simon Dubnow noted:

'The Jews, both of the male and the female sex, who have settled in the Ukraina and in other Russian cities, be deported immediately from Russia beyond the border, and in no circumstances be admitted into Russia, of which fact they shall in all places be strictly forewarned.'

Many of these Russian Jews had moved out of the Russian borders proper into Poland, but even there they were not allowed to settle peacefully. In 1737, bands of *haidamacks* (rebels), who were peasants from the Greek Orthodox Church led and organised by Cossacks, devastated many towns and villages, killing and robbing many Jews. This continuing narrative of suffering was further seen in the activities of the Inquisition even as far away as Peru, where *autos-da-fé*, often illegal, sought out Jews and those who were alleged to have reverted from Christianity to Judaism. The idea of *Aliyah* was once more raised in the consciousness of Jews, as was the concern for the physical and spiritual condition of their brethren in Palestine, and a group of around thirty of them led by Hayyim ben Moses Attar, a Moroccan Jewish teacher made their way there. They eventually, after delays, reached Jerusalem in 1742 and Hayyim established a *Yeshiva* (Jewish learning academy), that became the prodigious, *Midrash Keneset Israel Yeshivah*. His greatest hope was to see the *Aliyah* of as many Jews as possible come to the Holy Land and re-establish the Jewish people in their homeland. He was not alone in his hopes. Dr. Arie Morgenstern, a senior fellow at the Shalem Center in Jerusalem, noted:

'Recently discovered historical sources from the period indicate that the messianic expectations that preceded the year 1740 sparked a mass immigration to Palestine lasting many years. These immigrants, whose numbers reached several thousand within a decade, arrived in Palestine from all over the diaspora, and particularly from within the Ottoman Empire and Italy. They settled mostly in Tiberius and Jerusalem, two cities that the Talmudic tradition had singled out for a central role in the redemption.'

There is no doubt that this caused two things to happen in Palestine: The lot of the Jews themselves improved but their Arab neighbours became alarmed at the rising number of Jews around them. Encouragement to the Jews was also given when Ottoman authorities invited Rabbi Haim Abulafia, the renowned Kabbalist and Rabbi of Izmir, to rebuild the city of Tiberius, after 70 years of ruin. Amidst the Messianic fervour this was one more sign of the coming of the Messiah and restoration of Israel. Elsewhere, there was also a change of attitude towards Jews (and others) in England in 1740 with the Naturalisation Act for the American colonies. This allowed Jews to become naturalised English without taking specifically Christian oaths:

'The law provided that any person born out of allegiance of the king of England who had resided in the colonies for seven years, and during that period had not been out of them at any one time for more than two months, could be naturalised by taking the oaths and subscribing to the declaration. Then act permitted Quakers to affirm and in the administrating oaths to Jews the words "upon the true faith of a Christian" were to be omitted.'

A small step and which still left a long way to go for Jews in England but at least it was recognition of the rights of a Jew to be part of a country without forsaking the Jewish religion. Yet in England, a law had been passed to force Catholics and Jews to have their children taught in Protestant schools and the Naturalisation Act would run into difficulty later when it was attempted to introduce it on English soil.

In 1472, Elizabeth of Russia turned once more against the Jews stating, 'they [the Jews] will not be admitted to Our Empire for any purpose'. Despite protests from some quarters, the expulsion was approved and a note from Elizabeth was adamant, 'from the enemies of Christ, I desire no profit'. In 1744, Frederick the Great, of whom the German associate of Hitler, Hanfstangl, noted, 'For years the great Frederick was his [Hitler's] hero and he never tired of quoting examples of the king's success in building up Prussia in the face of overwhelming odds.' The 'king's success' was in increasing civic disabilities and imposing severe laws, restrictions and taxes on the Jewish people, and only tolerating and protecting them for their financial benefit to Prussia. Frederick issued an edict, *Revidiertes General Privilegium und Reglement vor die Judenschaft*, (Revised General Privileges and Regulations on the Jews) which declared the 'protected' Jews had an alternative to 'either abstain from marriage or leave Berlin'. In Austria, the Archduchess Maria Theresa made funds available for an anti-Semitic newspaper, *Oesterreichischer Volksfreund* (Friend of the People); this would be used to spread the anti-Jew message in Austria. She also believed that Jews were the embodiment of the Antichrist and in 1744 expelled them from Bohemia and Moravia, although after pressure from abroad she changed her mind but made them pay a tax to re-enter the country. Her bitterness towards the Jewish people even extended to Jewish family life when she introduced a law in 1752 limiting each Jewish family to one son.

England also was the scene of struggle for the Jews, when two acts of parliament were introduced in 1753, one for Naturalisation of Jews and one on the prevention of clandestine marriage. The occasion brought out much anti-Semitic views with strong arguments against the Jewish people and the uttering of many slanders in parliament. Speaking in favour of the Jews, Lord Lyttleton declared, 'he who hated another man for not being a Christian, was not a Christian himself'. Others argued, 'that it was flying directly in the face of God and of prophecy which had declared that they should be scattered over the face of the earth, without any country or fixed abode'. The passing of the bills was irrelevant as outside parliament, a crowd created a disturbance against the Jews, so much so that a repeal bill was passed within days. It is therefore no wonder that *Aliyah* to the improving situation in Palestine under the Ottomans became more and more attractive to many Jews.

However, there was the interruption of peace in Palestine as a Bedouin chieftain rose up against the Ottomans and established an independent state under Arab control. Zahir al-Omar, held a prominent position in the Bedouin community and had seized territory in Upper Galilee. The Pasha of Sidon, responsible for the area under the Ottomans, allowed him to collect taxes, hoping this would prevent any expansion by al-Omar. This was not to be as instead he used the taxes to extend his military might and took control of more areas even up to Haifa with access to the sea routes. Despite attempts to defeat him, al-Omar continued his drive for independence, which was improved when the Ottomans were diverted by the war against Russia in 1768. Further encouragement was given when an Egyptian Mameluke Governor of Cairo, Mohammed Ali Bey, also rebelled against Ottoman rule and allied with al-Omar. At one point the whole of Palestine, with the exception of Jerusalem, was under al-Omar's control. Eventually the defeat of his ally, Ali Bey, and the overwhelming might of the Ottomans defeated him and the area returned to Ottoman control. One intriguing event at this time occurred at Leghorn in Italy. Ali Bey met with the Jewish community there and made them an amazing offer; to sell them Jerusalem. Apparently at that time, around 1771/2, he did control areas of Jerusalem. A group of German officers, allied with the Russians, conducted the negotiations; the price was exorbitant and also included a demand that Russia assist Ali Bey in his ambitions. The latter was agreed, and the Jews of Leghorn approached other European Jews to assist in raising the money. The purchase would not have allowed an independent state for the Jews, but they had controversial plans to rebuild the Temple with Messianic hopes underlining their actions. The defeat of Ali Bey in 1772 brought an end to his ambitions and to the negotiations and once more Jewish hopes of a return to their roots met with disappointment.

In Palestine, many Jews relied heavily on their fellows in the Diaspora and life was not always easy. There were also outbreaks of hostility in some areas, like Hebron, where in 1775 a case of Blood Libel was made and the Jews were falsely accused of murdering the son of a local sheikh. Despite there being no grounds for the charges, the community was made to pay a heavy fine, which depleted their meagre resources. Despite these occasional outbursts, the Palestinian Jewish community still preferred to live in the Holy Land rather than in the European hot bed of persecution. This was reinforced when Pius VI issued an edict concerning the Jews, an edict that set back the Jewish situation by two centuries and would last twenty-five years. The edict was harsh; a Jew found outside the ghetto at night would be condemned to death and the humiliating 'yellow sign' was now to be carried within the town-walls of the ghetto whereas, until the edict, it had to be carried only outside the ghetto. Their religion was also attacked as the study of the Talmud was forbidden and the funeral *cortei* was no longer allowed when burying the dead. The employment of domestic Christians, women who went in into Jewish homes to light fire on Shabbat, was prohibited as was the making of the Menorah (lamps of seven arms for ritual use) by Christian silversmiths. This, along with the inability to work other than in rag collecting and other measures to restrict trade made life very difficult. The Jewish people could not even maintain good relations with their Christian neighbours as all relationships with them came under the ban. These were some of the forty-four clauses that were intended to humiliate and destroy the Jewish religion and traditions. It did not succeed but only increased the longing for the Messiah in the hearts and minds of the Jews in Catholic dominated countries.

This Messianic passion for the Holy Land was also found in a sect of Judaism that emerged and they were great enthusiasts for moving to Palestine. The *Hassidim* (pious ones), was founded by Rabbi Israel ben Eliezer, known as the *Ba'al Shem Tov*, (Master of the Good Name). They especially would spread their message across Europe. Their existence had come about because of the terrible conditions of Jews in Ukraine and Poland and spurred on by the constant pogroms and heavy penalties imposed by the authorities. One of their parables explained the situation and why spiritual reform was needed:

'An apprentice blacksmith, after he had learned his trade from the master, made a list for himself of how he must go about his craft. How he should pump the bellows, secure the anvil, and wield the hammer. He omitted nothing. When he went to work at the king's palace, however, he discovered to his dismay that he could not perform his duties, and was dismissed. He had forgotten to note one thing – perhaps because it was so obvious – that first he must ignite a spark to kindle the fire. He had to return to the master, who reminded him of the first principle which he had forgotten.'

The Jewish people, it was believed, needed the spark of revival to flourish and this led to a flowering of piety and spiritual renewal and also an awakening of Messianic fervour. However, such religious enthusiasm was not well received by Orthodox Jews, particularly in White Russia (Belarus), who vigorously opposed the movement. Over the next twenty years many groups made plans to make *Aliyah* and sought to settle in the Holy Land and continued to look to the return of the Messiah. In 1777, a group of 300 made the journey and reached Safed, where there was great joy and excitement at their success of standing on holy ground and the possibilities of a settled future. The adjustment to life in Palestine was not easy as they experienced changes in culture and religious practice of the Jews there and the continuing need for employment. In Safed another problem arose from the opponents in White Russia, who sent letters to the older traditional Jews causing a campaign of resentment against the *Hassidim*, and the necessity to move to other areas, such as Tiberius. The *Hassidim* still put down deep roots and the group flourished, with the ongoing persecution in the Diaspora, causing many more to join them in *Aliyah*.

Despite the relative security provided by the Ottomans there were still some Moslems who did not have the same outlook. In Morocco, the situation was tragic for the Jews, as it had been on a number of occasions over the centuries, and they were required to live in walled ghettoes. In the time of the emperor, Sidi Mahomet, heavy taxation was imposed on the Jews, who Sidi believed were 'not being in the road to salvation' and he demanded that his son, Muley Ali, impose it. Muley Ali was in many ways a benevolent man, and tried to persuade his father not to impose any further burdens on the Jews:

'Sire, the Jews are so poor that they are incapable of supporting their present taxes, and it is impossible I should exact from them new ones. Should you so please, you may dispose of the revenues of my government for the benefit of my brothers; but I earnestly supplicate you will not require me to oppress these people, and thus oblige me to increase wretchedness already too great.'

The plea did not change the heart of the man as the conditions of the Jews were difficult, as one traveller through Morocco noted:

'... the Moors hold them [Christians] not in the least respect, and the Jews in still less, had they have power freely to make their aversion known. ... The Jews possess neither lands nor gardens, nor can they enjoy their fruits in tranquillity; they must wear only black, and are obliged, when they pass near mosques, or through streets in which there are sanctuaries, to walk barefoot. The lowest among the Moors imagines he has a right to ill-treat a Jew, nor dares the latter defend himself, because the Koran and the Judge are always in favour of the Mahometan.'

In 1789, after the death of Sidi, the Sultan Moulay el Yazid carried out a massacre against the Jews, in the course of which there was the torture and rape of many women. It is remarkable that despite all the suffering and persecution the Jews endured, they continued passionately in their religion and some even prospered in service to more considerate Moroccan sultans.

The Ottomans continued to be the object of opposition from Christian Europe and the Jews became the centre of attention from both sides; on one hand, Christian Messianists, still seeking the return of the Messiah, saw the establishment of a strong Jewish state leading to the defeat of the Ottomans, whilst the Ottomans believed the building up of a strong Jewish community in Palestine would strengthen their rule in the area. Anti-Moslem politicians were also keen to exploit the situation as was an emerging leader of France, Napoleon Bonaparte. His agenda was the defeat of the British by first conquering Egypt, Syria and Palestine and from there to attack India, and he looked to the Jews to assist his plans. The Jews of France numbered around 36,000 before the revolution, which brought in the concept of the rights of man and equality of all people. This of course had an immediate impact on the Jews who now expected to have full liberation as citizens of France.

There were two communities within the Jewish population, the community at Avignon, around 3,000, and the Sephardim, who were not assimilated into the French culture and language. The Avignonnais Jews on the other hand were not as observant as the Sephardim and had adopted most of the French way of life. They gained their equal status immediately, but the Sephardim had to fight for nearly a year to gain the same freedoms, which came in 1791. Freedom was a two-edged sword and came with the Socialist Republican attitude of a secular France, which sought even to restrict the Jewish right of circumcision. Churches and synagogues were closed down as the terror of the revolution spread and even though there was a measure of freedom for Jews, there were the concerns for the loss of identity as a distinct people. Napoleon's arrival deepened their anxiety, as they were concerned that another Empire would bring them further suffering. However, Napoleon's ambitions initially brought a French desire to keep the Jews on the French side and a newspaper article appeared in the *Décade* newspaper in 1798, known to favour the government. It began the discussion of the Jews as a nation and the possibility of the establishment of a State in Palestine as a base to threaten England using emotional pulls, 'We know how much they long for their ancient fatherland and the city of Jerusalem'. It continued to reveal the true purpose of the article that the French, 'can scarcely doubt that they will be strongly attached to the nation which will have restored them'. Shortly after this, an anonymous letter appeared in the *Aim des Lois*, entitled 'A Jew's Letter to his brethren' in which the arguments of the history of Jewish suffering supported the right of the Jews to their own State. Many historians have taken the letter as a genuine Jewish cry for independence, but recent research has thrown doubt on that and points to the whole thing being a manipulation of the Jews for French purposes. Napoleon did proceed with his invasions of Egypt and Syria but his attempt to conquer Palestine failed, with the British assisting the defence of Acre with a shipping blockade and supply of cannon to the Acre defenders. Another letter surfaced from, 'General Headquarters, Jerusalem 1st Floreal, April 20th, 1799, in the year 7 of the French Republic', purporting to come from Napoleon. It included:

'Israelites, unique nation, whom, in thousands of years, lust of conquest and tyranny have been able to be deprived of their ancestral lands, but not of name and national existence!

Arise then, with gladness, ye exiled! A war unexampled In the annals of history, waged in self-defence by a nation whose hereditary lands were regarded by its enemies as plunder to be divided, arbitrarily and at their convenience, by a stroke of the pen of Cabinets, avenges its own shame and the shame of the remotest nations, long forgotten under the yoke of slavery, and also, the almost two-thousand-year-old ignominy put upon you; and, while time and circumstances would seem to be least favourable to a restatement of your claims or even to their expression ,and indeed to be compelling their complete abandonment, it offers to you at this very time, and contrary to all expectations, Israel's patrimony!'

Whilst many have referred to this letter as an expression of Napoleon's attitude towards the Jews and an independent State, it has been demonstrated that the letter is in fact not genuine and an attempt to find the original of the letter failed when a collection of Napoleon's papers were bought. Indeed, Napoleon seems to have had an indifferent approach to Jews and only became involved in Jewish issues when claims against them arose in France There is no support for his wanting to establish a Jewish State in Palestine, however, the various documents discussed does reflect the continuing Messianic desires of both Christian and Jews that was now increasing as the persecution of the Jews continued in places such as Algeria, within the Franco-Ottoman Alliance; in 1808, Ahmed Khodja massacred hundreds of Jews.

One clergyman, James Bicheno, saw the French revolution as one of the signs of the return of the Messiah in his book published in 1808. In the work, *The Signs of the Times*, apart from his religious interpretations, he reprises the experience of the Jews and the turmoil across the various countries and looked to a 'political resurrection' of the Jews in Palestine. In 1810, a prominent member of the Belgian/Spanish aristocracy, Prince Charles Joseph de Ligne, published his ideas of a Jewish State. An opponent of Napoleon, de Ligne came from a very different point of view than Bicheno, seeing the establishment of a Jewish State as a support of the Ottoman Empire. As a soldier and well-travelled man, he outlined great plans for the return of the Jews to a homeland, including technological and agricultural revolutions and the restoration of Jerusalem into a great city. He was not alone in his ambitious thoughts on the Jews and many Frenchmen – Laharanne, Salvador, Dunant and Dumas amongst others – began to advocate similar ideas. In England, their voices were echoed by Lord Shaftesbury, who would become a great advocate for the Jewish people and their rights to be re-established in their 'ancient country'. He had written an anonymous article in the *Quarterly Review*, advocating a 'National Home for the Jews, with Jerusalem as its capital'. Shaftesbury was naïve as it did not address the protection of Jews in Europe and that it was suspect in that it had the conversion of the Jews to Christianity as a motive. The *Hebrew Review* would later carry an article in which it posed such questions:

'His Lordship is extremely kind in advocating our nationality, but is this consistent with the efforts of the London Society to convert us to Christianity, and destroy our nationality? Again, we are at a loss to understand how our return to the Holy Land will be conducive to the safety and peace of Europe. Does he think that the Jews in Europe endanger its safety and peace, or that the return to the East can have any influence upon that safety and peace? Is not, besides, his Lordship aware of the impracticalities of the plan so long as there is no political protection whatever for the life and property of the Jews?'

These concerns were legitimate as in 1815 Pope Pius VII re-established the ghetto in Rome after Napoleon's defeat. His defeat also was the occasion for further trouble in Germany, trouble that would spread into Denmark, Latvia and Bohemia. These outbursts would become known as the Hep-Hep riots, after the cries made by the rioters (It is believed that this cry was from the initials of the Latin phrase, *Hieroslyma est perdita*, which means 'Jerusalem is fallen' first used by the Crusaders), who following a claim or ritual murder by Jews, went on a campaign of destruction against Jews. Anti-Semitic tracts, newspaper articles and plays, were produced that fired up the riots that saw Jews, their houses and businesses attacked. Further confirmation of Jewish concerns was seen in a dispute between two British politicians, Daniel O'Connor and Benjamin Disraeli – descended from a Jewish family – in 1832, in which O'Connor, whilst attacking Disraeli, wanted to make sure he was not seen as anti-Semitic and wrote:

'There is a habit of underrating that great and oppressed nation the Jews. They are cruelly persecuted by persons calling themselves Christians — but no person ever yet was a Christian who persecuted. The crudest persecution they suffer is upon their character, by the foul names their calumniators bestowed upon them before they carried their atrocities into effect. They feel the persecution of calumny severer upon them than the persecution of actual force, and the tyranny of actual torture.'

While anti-Jewish outbursts sporadically continued throughout Europe, the situation in Palestine was also deteriorating for many Jews. In 1834, there was an uprising against the Ottomans by Arabs and Bedouins, in what became known as the 'peasant war'. This resulted in the deaths and destruction of Jewish property and the Jews were only saved by the intervention of the Ottoman forces. Indeed, even Jerusalem was entered for a short period by the rebels and one eye-witness records that only the actions of a rebel chief prevented mass bloodshed and the eventual retaking of the city relieved the fears of the Jewish people.

The following year, Russia also became difficult for the Jewish people when Czar Nicholas I of Russia introduced an oppressive constitution for the Jews. The Jews had been paying an annual sum that excused them from military service for Russia, however, Nicholas continued to take the money but forced Jews into army service. Boys as young as 12 and under (given the name 'cantonists') were herded like cattle to various parts of Russia into the hands of peasants to be made ready for an army unit. Many died en route or during resistance to forced conversions. Jewish communities were moved to remote parts of Russia and still they continued to refuse to be downtrodden and increased their numbers. By 1838, an Expatriation Law came into force witch deprived 50,000 families of their homes and means of living. Protests from within and without were raised to little effect.

Sir Moses Montefiore, a British financier and banker, activist, philanthropist and Sheriff of London, was a tireless supporter of the Jewish cause, arguing their case for justice across the world. Indeed, he was very keen to have Jews move to Palestine and create an agricultural revolution. His diary notes his ambition:

'By degrees I hope to induce the return of thousands of our brethren to the Land of Israel. I am sure they would be happy in the enjoyment of the observance of our holy religion, in a manner which is impossible in Europe'

He negotiated with Mehemet Ali, who ruled Palestine, and his efforts had the support of many in England. In May of that year, *The Times* had printed an article giving an enthusiastic backing to the Jewish people and their homeland:

'… public attention to the claims which the Jewish people still have upon the land of Israel as their rightful inheritance, and their consequent political importance in the progress of that great struggle ... The subject may be new to many of our readers, but it is one deserving the solemn consideration of a people possessing an oriental empire of such vast extent ... No people on the face of the earth has been so little understood and so grossly misrepresented as the Jewish people.'[1]

The Times also reported the following year on a conference in London concerning the protests at the treatment of Jews in Europe:

'A memorandum has been addressed to the Protestant monarchs of Europe on the subject of the restoration of the Jewish people to the land of Palestine. The document in question, dictated by the peculiar conjuncture of affairs in the East, and the other striking " signs of the times," reverts to the original covenant which secures that land to the descendants of Abraham and urges upon the consideration of the Powers addressed what may be the probable line of duty on the part of Protestant Christendom to the people in the present controversy in the East.'[2]

Lord Shaftesbury approached Lord Palmerston, a leading political figure in England, to assist in the restoration of the Jewish people to their homeland. Shaftesbury noted in his diary, 'Everything seems ripe for their return to Palestine'.

Colonel Charles Henry Churchill, an officer in the British army, born in India to British parents, rose to distinction in many military campaigns, which eventually would bring him to Syria. He had contact with Sir Moses Montefiore, who sought his views on the Jewish question. When he was marching into Damascus in 1841, he had in his possession various documents from Montefiore for the Jewish community there, who welcomed his arrival with great enthusiasm because they had endured great distress under the Ottoman Pasha who governed the city. The Hebrew Elders of the city had written to the Rothschild family and Lady Montefiore noted in her diary, the letter (dated 27 March 1840), which described their anxieties about a false Blood Libel (the Damascus Affair) that became notorious throughout the world:

'Upon this the Governor replied that, as he had accused other persons [Jews] of killing them, he must know who the murderers were; and in order that he should confess, he was beaten to such an extent that he expired under the blows. After this, the Governor, with a body of six hundred men, proceeded to demolish the houses of his Jewish subjects, hoping to find the bodies of the dead, but not finding anything, he returned, and again inflicted on his victims further castigations and torments, some of them too cruel and disgusting to be described. At last, being incapable of bearing further anguish, they said that the charge was true!' [Sir Moses noted in his own diary that he raised this matter with the Sultan in October of the same year and this brought about the release of the imprisoned Jews and a *firman* [edict] that gave protection to Jews throughout the Turkish world.]'

In this climate of fear and concern, Churchill gave an emotional address to a gathering of Jews, in which he expressed his support for the hopes of Jews being restored to Palestine. He was not an advocate of Jews for religious conversion purposes but rather as a humane reality he felt they needed this in such a terrible existence of persecution. However, he was a realist and knew that any move to establish the Jews again in their homeland needed the leadership from Jews themselves. He wrote to Sir Moses Montefiore from Damascus and this letter is worthy of attention as here was a man who was passionate about a Jewish homeland and was in a position to influence events:

'June 14th, 1841.

My dear Sir Moses, — I have not yet had the pleasure of hearing from you, but I would fain hope that my letters have reached you safe. I enclose you a petition which has been drawn by the Brothers Harari, in which they state their claims and their earnest desire to be immediately under British protection. I am sorry to say that such a measure is much required even now, not only for them, but also for all the Jews in Damascus. They are still liable to persecutions similar to those from which, through your active and generous intervention, they have so lately escaped. The Christians still regard them with malevolence, and the statement in the petition enclosed is perfectly correct.'

This petition setting out the issues facing Jews was rightly appreciated by Churchill who was unashamed in his passion:

'I cannot conceal from you my most anxious desire to see your countrymen endeavour once more to resume their existence as a people.'

Not a man who took to flights of fancy but a down to earth worldly-wise character, he had made an assessment of the possibility of a Jewish State in Palestine. However, there were conditions needed for success:

'I consider the object to be perfectly attainable. But, two things are indispensably necessary. Firstly, that the Jews will themselves take up the matter universally and unanimously. Secondly, that the European Powers will aid them in their views. It is for the Jews to make a commencement. Let the principal persons of their community place themselves at the head of the movement.'

He believed that the Jewish community had the necessary resources:

'Were the resources which you all possess steadily directed towards the regeneration of Syria and Palestine, there cannot be a doubt but that, under the blessing of the Most High, those countries would amply repay the undertaking, and that you would end by obtaining the sovereignty of at least Palestine.'

Foreshadowing the British Mandate that would come later he wrote:

'Syria and Palestine, in a word, must be taken under European protection and governed in the sense and according to the spirit of European administration.'

His own enthusiasm was not enough; he looked to the Jews:

'… to be ready and prepared to say: "Behold us here all waiting, burning to return to that land which you seek to remould and regenerate. Already we feel ourselves a people. The sentiment has gone forth amongst us and has been agitated and has become to us a second nature; that Palestine demands back again her sons. We only ask a summons from these Powers on whose counsels the fate of the East depends to enter upon the glorious task of rescuing our beloved country from the withering influence of centuries of desolation and of crowning her plains and valleys and mountain-tops once more, with all the beauty and freshness and abundance of her pristine greatness."'

He knew the task was not an easy one:

'but a beginning must be made – a resolution must be taken, an agitation must be commenced, and where the stake is "Country and Home" where is the heart that will not leap and bound to the appeal?

I am the Resident Officer at Damascus until further order.

Believe me to be, Dear Sir Moses,

Yours very faithfully,

Chas. H. Churchill.'

He added a postscript to his letter, calling on Montefiore to secure the backing of the 'Five Great Powers', (Great Britain, France, Austria, Prussia and Russia) to secure self-rule for the Jews in Palestine and that they should be exempt from military service to any power 'except on their own account as a measure of defence against the incursions of the Bedouin Arabs'. He cautioned Montefiore:

'In all enterprises men must be prepared to make great sacrifices, whether of time, health or resources. To reflect calmly before commencing an undertaking and once begun to carry it through, vanquishing, surmounting, triumphing over every obstacle, this is worthy of man's existence and carries with it its own reward, if the judgment is sound, the head clear and the heart honest. I humbly venture to give my opinion upon a subject, which no doubt has already occupied your thought - and the bare mention of which, I know, makes every Jewish heart vibrate. The only question is - when and how.'

He ended with a reinforcement of the Jews own efforts being necessary:

'Political events seem to warrant the conclusion that the hour is nigh at hand when the Jewish people may justly and with every reasonable prospect of success put their hands to the glorious work of National Regeneration.'

Once more history offered a resolution for the trials and tribulations of the Jews on their terrible journey, but incredibly, Montefiore did not support Churchill and passed the matter to the Jewish Board of Deputies in London to make their own response which was to procrastinate; Churchill's plans failed and the area returned to Ottoman control. Despite Churchill continuing to prompt Montefiore towards a Palestine state for the Jews, his efforts were wasted and the Jewish leaders of the day lost an opportunity that possibly could have changed the course of history and the tragic ongoing journey of the Jewish people.

The failure to grasp this opportunity did not deter the ongoing concern of many in Britain, who still held the ambition to see the Jews restored to their rightful home. Many continued to press for the government to take action on their behalf. One such man was George Gawler, a former governor of South Australia, who looked to the Jews to return to Palestine and colonise it under the authority of the British. In a book arguing for the emancipation of Jews, he wrote:

'First, it would be part payment of a heavy debt of retribution that England owes to the Hebrew race, for bye-gone centuries of cruelty and oppression. Westminster Abbey itself, was rebuilt by money extorted from the Jews and secondly, *it would be taking a part*, WHICH IT IS TO THE HONOUR AND INTEREST OF THE BRITISH NATION TO PERFORM, *in assisting in the great movement of deliverance from oppression and bondage that for many years past has been in operation throughout the whole civilised world, in behalf of the* ANCIENT PEOPLE OF GOD.' [Styling as in the original book]

Gawler had travelled with Montefiore through Syria and Palestine and had earlier written a tract, *Tranquilisation of Syria and the East*, in which he set out his ideas. He was not alone in his aspirations and was joined with other clergy and respected British military leaders and eventually politicians like Disraeli would also join in advocating a home for the Jewish people. Included among these men was Edward Ledwich Mitford, of the British Colonial Office, who argued that it was in Britain's interests to support the Jewish re-settlement in Palestine. In 1845 he wrote:

'The re-establishment of the Jewish nation in Palestine under British protection would retrieve our affairs in the Levant, and place us in a commanding position from whence to check the progress of encroachment, to over-awe open enemies, and if necessary, to repel their advance, at the same time that it would place the management of our steam communication entirely in our own hands.'

Mark Twain, writing in 1869 about his experiences travelling through Palestine, found a desolate place:

'Of all the lands there are for dismal scenery, I think Palestine must be the prince. The hills are barren, they are dull of color, they are un-picturesque in shape. The valets are unsightly deserts fringed with a feeble vegetation that has an expression about it of being sorrowful and despondent.'

There are criticisms of this interpretation of Twain's views but there was also a later survey by the Palestine Royal Commission (in 1913):

'The road leading from Gaza to the north was only a summer track suitable for transport by camels and carts ... no orange groves, orchards or vineyards were to be seen until one reached [the Jewish village of] Yabna [Yavne]... Houses were all of mud. No windows were anywhere to be seen....The ploughs used were of wood....The yields were very poor....The sanitary conditions in the village were horrible. Schools did not exist.... The western part, towards the sea, was almost a desert.... The villages in this area were few and thinly populated. Many ruins of villages were scattered over the area, as owing to the prevalence of malaria, many villages were deserted by their inhabitants.'3

Mitford, a colonial man, was certain that the Ottoman Empire, with its own troubles with Egyptians, Arabs and Bedouins, could be persuaded to agree to his plan. He, like Montefiore, saw the agricultural revolution in the desolate Palestine that Twain had found, would result. Although unsuccessful in his arguments, he was part of a growing swell that would one day reach a response along similar lines from the British government.

Whilst these attempts to assist the Jewish journey were proceeding, elsewhere in Europe the anti-Semitic attitudes were still abroad. In Germany, under the guise of discussing art, Richard Wagner wrote a repulsive work in which he displayed his anti-Semitism:

'The Jew - who, as everyone knows, has a God all to himself - in ordinary life strikes us primarily by his outward appearance, which, no matter to what European nationality we belong, has something disagreeably foreign to that nationality: instinctively we wish to have nothing in common with a man who looks like that. [....] the peculiarity of the Jewish nature attains for us its climax of distastefulness. ... Who has not been seized with a feeling of the greatest revulsion, of horror mingled with the absurd, at hearing that sense-and-sound-confounding gurgle, yodel and cackle, which no intentional caricature can make more repugnant than as offered here in full, in naive seriousness?'

These obnoxious views were rightly condemned in newspapers of the time and indeed the revulsion they caused brought many to consider the sanity of Wagner, though he was not the only one around Europe who still held these views. Many later commentators saw his writings as a basis for German anti-Semitism and indeed the Nazis would embrace him as a German hero. It was therefore a time of great contrasts, with ideas such as Wagner's being espoused, persecutions in Russia; on the other hand, Norway opened its doors to Jews, and England began their emancipation. The first real shoots of Jewish Zionism also began to emerge with men like Rabbi Yehuda Aryeh Leon Bibas, a Gibraltar-born Sephardic Rabbi from Corfu, who cooperated with Montefiore and travelled around Europe, He advocated the creation of a Jewish assembly and the purchase of land in Palestine to which all Jews should make *Aliyah* and begin to colonise the area. Like many, he saw the writing on the wall for the Ottoman Empire and its approaching collapse and believed that the spiritual renewal of the Jewish people was linked to a return to their homeland. Whilst his writings and insights would be picked up later by other Zionists, at the time they did not make a great impact. His ideas of a return to *Eretz Israel* found resonance in a different form with a Jewish philosopher Zvi Hirsch Kalischer who approached life in a more modern way. He had talked with Muhammed Ali, when the Egyptian ruler governed Palestine, and in 1862 produced an important work that would bear fruit, *Derishat Tzion* (Zion's Call). In this work he wrote:

'The Redemption of Israel, for which we yearn, is not to be thought of as a sudden miracle. The Almighty, blessed be His Name, will not suddenly descend from on high and command his people to go forth. He will not send the Messiah from heaven in a twinkling of an eye, to sound the great Shofar [Trumpet] for the scattered of Israel and gather them into Jerusalem. He will not surround the Holy City with a wall of fire or cause the Holy Temple to come down from the heavens. The bliss and miracles that were promised by his servants, the prophets, will certainly come to pass – everything will be fulfilled – but we will not flee in terror and flight, for the Redemption of Israel will come by slow degrees and the ray of deliverance will shine forth gradually.'

He foresaw an agricultural settlement in which the Jews who supervised the actual labourers would be participating in religious duties and that 'Jewish farming would be a spur to the ultimate Messianic Redemption'. His vision began to take shape in 1870 when the *Alliance Israélite Universelle*, a Paris-based international Jewish organization founded in 1860 by the French statesman Adolphe Crémieux, established an agricultural school, *Mikeh Israel* (Hope of Israel) under Charles Netter. Kalischer's vision was enthusiastically supported by the German Jewish philosopher, Moses Hess, who wrote at a time when Germany in the midst of enlightenment that was causing a struggle within German minds as to identity and the conflict with an alien presence, the Jews. In turn, the Jews were also struggling with religion and humanism and their role and destiny. Hess moved between Socialism and Individualism and struggled to define his own view of the world and concluded that Judaism was a humanitarian religion and that Jews had taught humanity true religion. He arrived at the conclusion that it was necessary for Jews to be a nation in Palestine and also held to the idea of love as a motivational force that would one day unite humanity. Hess looked to a day when the Jews would lead the world of science and reconciliation between nations and in his book, *Rome and Jerusalem – A Study in Jewish Nationalism*, published in 1862, he set out his ideas. His work opens with a preface that directly addresses anti-Semitism:

'From the time that Innocent III[4] evolved the diabolical plan to destroy the moral stamina of the Jews, the bearers of Spanish culture to the world of Christendom, by forcing them to wear a badge of shame on their garments, until the audacious kidnapping of a Jewish child from the house of his parents,[5] which occurred under the government of Cardinal Antonelli, Papal Rome symbolizes to the Jews an inexhaustible well of poison. It is only with the drying up of this source that Christian German anti-Semitism will die from lack of nourishment'

Hess was clear that the journey of Israel over 2000 through years of suffering did not mean the nation did not exist:

'Among the nations believed to be dead and which, when they become conscious of their historic mission, will struggle for their national rights, is also Israel – the nation which for two thousand years has defied the storms of time, and in spite of having been tossed by the currents of history to every part of the globe, has always cast yearning glances towards Jerusalem and is still directing its gaze thither.'

His argument was that Palestine was the 'ancestral home' of the Jewish people and for any country to deny them that right was for that country to deny its own right to exist. Furthermore, the reason for the denial of a Jewish right to a homeland, particularly in Germany, was to avoid recognising civil rights for Jews in the countries in which they lived. He admits with a heartfelt passion that he had drifted from his religion but now he had returned with a new and illuminated understanding, an understanding that he now realised meant that there was a need to move from a selfish individualism and look to a common understanding of mutual responsibility one for another. The Jewish religion centred in its own land would be a teacher to the world and would transform it just as the Jew *Yeshua* (Jesus) looked to do. In a prophetic insight he recognised the struggle for a 'pure German race' was in conflict with the existence of a Jewish people and therefore 'Jewish national aspirations are antagonistic because of his [the German] racial antipathy'. This understanding was brought to him by a German publisher who would not publish a book on Jewish aspirations saying it 'is contrary to my pure human nature'. Hess wrote of the then Jewish practice of righteous Jews being buried with a pouch of soil from Palestine, noting it was not just a pious religious tradition but an acknowledgement of the importance of the soil of Palestine to the Jews. He recounts the Biblical reference of Jeremiah:

'When the children of Israel were led into captivity by the soldiers of Nebuchadnezzar, their road lay past the grave of our Mother Rachel. As they approached the grave, a bitter wailing was heard. It was the voice of Rachel, weeping for her children.'

Rachel's wailing had a cause and Hess recalling the Damascus affair in a footnote, quotes from a German newspaper, *Allgemeine Zeitung des Judenthums*, 'Europe has spared the followers of the religion of Israel neither pain, nor tears, nor bitterness'. After a reprise of the struggles of the Jewish people and a call for the reform of the minds of Jews about their religion and purpose in the world, Hess again with prophetic insight states:

'..the organisation of a Jewish State … will express itself in the founding of Jewish colonies in the land of their ancestors … in spite of its having been torn from its own soil and left to wither in foreign lands. So will Israel bloom again in youthful splendour; and the spark, at present smouldering under the ashes, will burst once more into a bright flame.'

Hess noted the 'tottering' Ottoman Empire and rightly forewarned of the outcome of the advancing world wars:

'But if they continue to conjure themselves, as well as the German people with the might and glory of the "German Sword" they [German Patriots] will only add to the old unpardonable mistakes, grave new ones: they will only play into the hands of the reaction, and drag all Germany along with them'

Hess was an important voice, again not greatly recognised at the time but who gave a cogent view of the Jewish issues and rightly argued for the restoration of the Jewish people in their homeland. He was able to see the beginnings of his vision with the agricultural developments of *Mikeh Israel* but it would be many years before his aspirations reached fulfilment through others.

The ideas of Jewish autonomy in Palestine was also raised in 1876 by General Sir Charles Warren, associated with the Palestine Exploration Fund. The fund ostensibly was for the archaeological exploration in Palestine, but it passed information to the British Intelligence community. Warren was struck by the need for the development of Palestine, as it was becoming a desolate country. Lord Palmerston in 1875, addressing a meeting of the fund, said, 'We have there a land teeming with fertility and rich in history, but almost without an inhabitant – a country without a people, and look! Scattered over the world, a people without a country!' To this end, Warren issued a book, *The Land of Promise or Turkey's Guarantee*. In it, he proposed a scheme similar to the British Empire's East India Company. The Jews would eventually grow into the government of the country and Turkey would be paid revenues from the productivity created. He was aware of issues that could cause conflict and very much like today he cited the Moslem Arab population, but his experience suggested they were a small minority with a greater population composed of Canaanites, Greeks, Romans and Crusaders who had become Moslem or Christian. His military view was that the greater conflict would come from Christians, but he also noted, as is the case today, that there may be problems between Russia and the United States over any proposals for Palestine. His belief was that because so much of the land was desolate, the Jews and Arabs, who had a harmonious relationship, could make good use of the land for production. He cited small developments he had seen (possibly the *Mikeh Israel* project) which were showing success and indeed the soundings he had taken suggested that the people of the land would welcome such developments and Palestine should be given back to 'whom it belongs by inheritance – viz., the present natives of Palestine and the Jews scattered throughout the world'.

These promising signs sat alongside the ongoing struggles of the Jewish diaspora. A German Lutheran pastor, Adolf Stoecker, founded a political party on 3 January 1878, the Christian Social Party. He declared his aims were peaceful, but his rhetoric was deep anti-Semitism. In 1880, Stoecker instigated an Anti-Semitic Petition which contained a tirade of accusations and abuses against the Jews declaring, 'the Jewish hypertrophy conceals within itself the most serious dangers to our national way of life'. As with many anti-Semites, they tried to argue that the Jew does not labour and exploits the Christians, which was not the case. A straw man argument was proposed:

> 'What future is left our fatherland if the Semitic element is allowed to make a conquest of our home ground for another generation as it has been allowed to do in the last two decades?'[6]

The ideas raised, were of an 'Aryan world' that was threatened by the Jews. The echoes of Nazism are also heard in the cry that, 'the Germanic ideals of honour, loyalty, and genuine piety begin to be displaced to make room for a cosmopolitan pseudo-ideal'. He was not a lone voice in Germany. Heinrich von Treitschke, a German historian, whilst distancing himself from the 'filth and savagery' of certain types of anti-Semitism, nonetheless wanted to see the Jews moved out of Germany. He declared, 'There is only one way to satisfy our wishes: emigration, creation of a Jewish State somewhere overseas, after which we will see if it will earn the acceptance of the other nations of the world'. Indeed, the Nazis would also look to this idea of sending the Jews to Madagascar.

In Russia, the death in 1881 of Nicholas' successor, Alexander II by a bomb thrown by members of a socialist political revolutionary party, brought Alexander III to power and under his reign began a repression of the Jews and a wave of pogroms swept across Russia. The barbaric horror and the wave of Jews fleeing from Russia sent tremors of concern and revulsion across Europe and once more, in England, Lord Shaftesbury took up the cause of the Jews, demanding approaches be made to the Czar on their behalf. He denounced the brutal acts of terror and again saw the need for a homeland for the Jews as over 100,000 Jews swelled the population of the East End of London and in the United States a law was passed to stop immigration from the East and Russia. As a result of these persecutions in Russia, which were spreading to Romania, and the threats of immigration being blocked in the USA and Britain, a congress for the colonization of Palestine was held in Romania and became known as the Focsani Zionist Congress. Zionism was not really at its heart. More concern was expressed about *Aliyah* to Palestine and indeed a group was organized in 1882 when the *Thetis* carried 228 Jews from Moinesti, a city in Bacău County, Romania. On arrival in Palestine they founded two settlements, *Rosh Pinah* and *Zikron Ya'akob*. The Jews were not the only ones holding congresses and in September 1882 in Dresden, the First International Anti-Jewish Congress was held. Sir Moses Montefiore was cited in their literature and wrongly accused of a critical address at a Rabbinical Assembly at Krakau in 1840. They published a manifesto to 'Governments and peoples of Christian States endangered by Judaism', which demanded an end to Jewish immigration from Russia into Germany and that all Jewish emancipation should end. They wanted to take control of the press using terms that the Nazis would also employ, stating that 'Christian Aryan natives' should reconquer the press. This continued hatred towards Jews brought more Blood Libel allegations in Europe and in 1892 Russia once more expelled 20,000 Jews, creating more tensions in other countries as they sought sanctuary. The need now for a permanent Jewish homeland in Palestine was becoming more and more apparent to those who wanted to see.

1894 witnessed an incident in France that would once and for all set the course for the founding of a Jewish State. The Roman Catholic newspaper, *La Croix*, described the Jewish soldier involved, 'the Jewish enemy betraying France'.[7] The cause of the remark was the discovery of a spy giving French secrets to Germany. The French army intelligence had seen a handwritten note, in which the handwriting was claimed to be that of a French Jewish army officer, Alfred Dreyfus. The fact that he was a Jew made him a target of fellow French anti-Semitic members of the French army such as Colonel Sandherr, who, when challenged that there were loyal and patriotic Jewish officers in the French army, replied 'I distrust them all'. Dreyfus protested his innocence but he was brought before a military court and in a secret trial was convicted after the judges were given a secret file that the defence were not allowed to see. Crowds ran through Paris, shouting, 'death to the Jews!' His dismissal from the army in a secret 'drumming out' ceremony saw him then exiled to Devil's Island in French Guiana off the coast of South America. Jewish lawyer Theodor Herzl was present at that ceremony, which convinced him that society would never allow the Jews to assimilate successfully into any country – a Jewish State was the only answer. Herzl was born in Budapest and was heavily influenced by his mother, who impressed upon him all things German and he considered himself a liberal and an Austrian patriot. He was a lawyer but also a poet and dramatist and throughout his education and early life had experienced and seen anti-Semitism affect the lives of Jews. Herzl may have been considered by many as a dreamer and visionary, but he was also a passionate man who knew the realities of the Jewish existence and the desperate need for a State of their own in order to survive. The Dreyfus affair was one more of many incidents which reinforced in him the need to do something.

As to the Dreyfus affair, in 1898, Georges Picquart, head of the army intelligence, uncovered evidence of Dreyfus' innocence and the guilt of a Major Esterhazy who was tried and acquitted. There was clear evidence of forgery of documents against Dreyfus and Émile Zola, the French writer, took up the case and wrote *J'Accuse*, which laid out the charges and evidence against the French officers involved in the forgeries and mistreatment of Dreyfus that showed his innocence. It was a damning document which sent shockwaves around the world and landed Zola in court charged with defaming the military. He was sentenced to jail so he fled to England. He wrote:

'I shall not chronicle these doubts and the subsequent conclusion reached by Mr. Scheurer-Kestner. But, while he was conducting his own investigation, major events were occurring at headquarters. Colonel Sandherr had died and Lt. Colonel Picquart had succeeded him as Head of the Intelligence Office. It was in this capacity, in the exercise of his office, that Lt. Colonel Picquart came into possession of a telegram addressed to Major Esterhazy by an agent of a foreign power. His express duty was to open an inquiry. What is certain is that he never once acted against the will of his superiors. He thus submitted his suspicions to his hierarchical senior officers, first General Gonse, then General de Boisdeffre, and finally General Billot, who had succeeded General Mercier as Minister of War. That famous much discussed Picquart file was none other than the Billot file, by which I mean the file created by a subordinate for his minister, which can still probably be found at the War Office. The investigation lasted from May to September 1896, and what must be said loud and clear is that General Gonse was at that time convinced that Esterhazy was guilty and that Generals de Boisdeffre and Billot had no doubt that the handwriting on the famous bordereau was Esterhazy's. This was the definitive conclusion of Lt. Colonel Picquart's investigation. But feelings were running high, for the conviction of Esterhazy would inevitably lead to a retrial of Dreyfus, an eventuality that the General Staff wanted at all cost to avoid.'

Following the publication, Esterhazy, later when living in England, confessed to be the spy for money to pay off debts, and many argued for a quashing of Dreyfus' conviction, which happened but he was returned to France for another trial in 1889 and in the presence of 400 journalists from around the world, he was dramatically convicted again and given ten years imprisonment. This was despite the French politician Jacques Godefroy having forced the army officer, Lieutenant Colonel Henry, to confess that certain letters bearing on the Dreyfus case were indeed forgeries, and Godefroy still refused to believe Dreyfus innocent. The French President had to intervene and pardon him ten days later. In 1906, he was completely exonerated and promoted and given the *Legion D' Honour* award. On the Dreyfus affair, Herzl concluded:

'The Dreyfus case embodies more than a judicial error; it embodies the desire of the vast majority of the French to condemn a Jew, and to condemn all Jews in this one Jew. Death to the Jews!, howled the mob, as the decorations were being ripped from the Captain's coat.. Where? In France? In republican, modern, civilized France, a hundred years after the Declaration of the Rights of Man? The French people, or at any rate the greater part of the French people, does not want to extend the rights of man to Jews. The edict of the great Revolution had been revoked.'

Herzl subsequently wrote *The Jewish State*, which laid out his views on the future for the Jewish people. This was one of the most important milestones on the Jewish journey to a homeland. In this work, he describes his vision, which was breath-taking in its scope. It involved the setting up of a Jewish Society and a Jewish Company, both of which would oversee the moving of Jews from all over the world to the new State. He outlined in great detail his plans for agriculture, infra-structure, housing, even going into the working hours and wages of workers. He gave his ideas for the styles of housing and how the State would develop business and science ventures that would benefit the whole world. The groups that would travel would all have their own rabbi and the Jewish Society would take care of them and their assets and their land and housing to provide for them when they arrived in their new homeland. He detailed how the judicial system would be set up and how the State would be run. In turning to the idea of a Jewish State he made very clear that:

'It [the idea of a Jewish homeland] is no longer - and it has not been for a long time - a theological matter. It has nothing whatsoever to do with religion and conscience. What is more, everyone knows it. The Jewish question is neither nationalistic nor religious. It is a social question'

His concern was now simply for his people, not a religion, and in his diary, he noted a conversation with Count Goluchowski, an Austrian statesman who was foreign minister of the Austro-Hungarian Empire from 1895 to 1906, in which the count expressed surprise at the number of Jews not being reflected in the natural population growth that should be expected. Herzl replied, 'We have sustained grievous losses in the course of our history, especially during the Middle Ages.'

The social and political aspects were also addressed by Herzl, who saw the State having a constitution that would safeguard the rights of its citizens and there would be no allowing what had happened to the Jews, because of their religion, happening to anyone else who was not a Jew and lived in the new State:

'Every man will be as free and undisturbed in his faith or his disbelief as he is in his nationality. And if it should occur that men of other creeds and different nationalities come to live amongst us, we should accord them honourable protection and equality before the law.'

These lofty ideals, for Herzl, could not be maintained in a fully democratic State and he envisaged an 'aristocratic republic'. His concern was the experience of Jews down the ages and the anti-Semitism that had occurred had to give lessons to the new adventure.

One book that Herzl read particularly alarmed him and confirmed the urgency of a place of refuge for his people was *The Jewish Problem as a Problem of Race, Morals and Culture* by Eugen Dühring. He wrote, 'The Jews are, on the other hand, the most vicious minting of the entire Semitic race into a nationality especially dangerous to nations'. He was a virulent anti-Semite and his words were 'a blow between the eyes' to Herzl and he realised that if such attitudes were to persist, the very lives of Jews were at risk with Dühring's comments such as, 'It is, in the meanwhile, easier to drive out the Jews than to invite these guests once again to one's table'. For Dühring, the issue was worldwide but he emphasised that for him the problem was greatest in Germany and he even saw the Jews as 'hostile to the human race'. The work goes on to slander and disparage the Jews and their religion in a tirade of false accusations and misunderstandings, giving no credit for any good thing the Jewish people have done. The book ends chillingly:

'Precisely this situation must however urge the determined component of better humanity only so much more to act in order to create communities and communal life whose principles extend over the earth and thereby also, obviously, do not leave any room for Hebrew life'

Every Nazi who was to come would willingly and heartily embrace Dühring's poisoned views and whilst not directly the cause, they have an echo in the Nazi 'Blood and Soil' mentality and the forming of the notorious Nuremberg '*Law for the Protection of the Hereditary Health of the German People*' which sought to exclude Jews from inter-racial marriage and any role in German life and eventually attempts at their total extermination. The Thule Society formed after the First World War embraced these ideas and in turn influenced many prominent Nazis. Even today, there is a Thule Society, influenced by his ideas, which claims to be religious, with Adolf Hitler as their object of veneration. The Society's website carries much anti-Jewish rhetoric and images and in one section there can be read that they aspire, 'to follow the policies of Adolf Hitler unless new information available to us in the 21st century, indicates they it would be wisest to do otherwise.'[8] Herzl noted in his diary about Dühring's book:

'An infamous book … If Dühring, who unites so much undeniable intelligence with so much universality of knowledge, can write like this, what are we to expect from the ignorant masses?'

When Herzl thought of anti-Semitism he believed that the elements in it were 'of vulgar sport, of common trade jealousy, of inherited prejudice, of religious intolerance, and also of pretended self-defence'. He argued that no one could deny the gravity of the situation of the Jews, wherever they were found in groups they were persecuted and even when countries granted some concessions and protection in law, these were ignored and were 'dead letters'. Jews had been barred from high office, in the various armies they suffered discrimination and their businesses were boycotted with cries of, 'Don't buy from Jews!' He had seen all of these in one form or another throughout his life and he had also seen:

'..attacks in Parliaments, in assemblies, in the press, in the pulpit, in the street, on journeys - for example, their exclusion from certain hotels - even in places of recreation, become daily more numerous. The forms of persecutions varying according to the countries and social circles in which they occur. In Russia, imposts are levied on Jewish villages; in Rumania, a few persons are put to death; in Germany, they get a good beating occasionally; in Austria, Anti-Semites exercise terrorism over all public life; in Algeria, there are travelling agitators; in Paris, the Jews are shut out of the so-called best social circles and excluded from clubs. Shades of anti-Jewish feeling are innumerable.'

Herzl was aware that anti-Semitism was changing its face, no longer being mainly about religion. Rather there was now a jealousy against the Jews who were prospering and against their attempts to be considered as equals within society. He believed that this anti-Semitism would never cease until the Jews had their own State. Therefore, the urgency for a homeland burned within him. Herzl was convinced this was the only way the Jewish people could ever be secure and free. To this end he turned to a fresh idea of Zionism which he presented at the Zionist conference in Basle in 1897 and in his diary he noted:

'Were I to sum up the Basel Congress in a word – which I shall guard against pronouncing publicly – it would be this: At Basle I founded the Jewish State. If I said this out loud today, I would be answered by universal laughter. Perhaps in five years, and certainly fifty, everyone will know it.'

He was not the only one to have such a prophetic view, Adolph Dessauer, an Austrian Jewish banker, when walking with Herzl in the park, remarked, 'In fifty years' time, [I] believe the Jewish State will already be in existence'. They were both one year out. The Congress adopted the motion, 'Zionism seeks to secure for the Jewish people a publicly recognized, legally secured home (or homeland) in Palestine'. In the opening to his work, Herzl was clear:

'Everything depends on our propelling force. And what is that force? The misery of the Jews I shall therefore clearly and emphatically state that I believe in the practical outcome of my scheme, though without professing to have discovered the shape it may ultimately take. The Jewish State is essential to the world; it will therefore be created.'

This set in motion a ripple throughout the Jewish world. Not all Jews received the idea with enthusiasm with some fearing the uprooting of their lives was too much whilst others feared the implications for Jews who did not go to the new State. Herzl tried to reassure their anxieties:

> 'The idea which I have developed in this pamphlet is a very old one: it is the restoration of the Jewish State. The world resounds with outcries against the Jews, and these outcries have awakened the slumbering idea. Am I stating what is not yet the case? Am I before my time? Are the sufferings of the Jews not yet grave enough? We shall see.'

Unfortunately, Herzl was wrong, worse was to come but many just did not grasp the whole idea of his arguments about the Jewish question within the world and the anti-Semitism that he had described:

> The Jewish question exists wherever Jews live in perceptible numbers. Where it does not exist, it is carried by Jews in the course of their migrations. We naturally move to those places where we are not persecuted, and there our presence produces persecution. This is the case in every country, and will remain so, even in those highly civilized - for instance, France - until the Jewish question finds a solution on a political basis.'

He declared to them, 'If the present generation is too dull to understand it rightly, a future, finer and a better generation will arise to understand it'.[9] Herzl also had another problem, as there were countries that had other plans for a Jewish State that did not include Palestine but suggested Argentina and Uganda as options. When Argentina was proposed, Herzl found himself with the political reality and had to deal with the Turks, Egypt, France and Britain. He noted:

> 'Here two territories come under consideration, Palestine and Argentine. Shall we choose Palestine or Argentine? We shall take what is given us, and what is selected by Jewish public opinion. The Society will determine both these points.'

Aware that the Zionist Congress had passed a resolution for Palestine, he was wise enough to acknowledge:

'Palestine is our ever-memorable historic home. The very name of
Palestine would attract our people with a force of marvellous potency.
If His Majesty the Sultan were to give us Palestine, we could in return
undertake to regulate the whole finances of Turkey.'

Herzl made play of the new State being good for Turkey and good for
Europe as it would make a border against any threats from Asia. After all, the
Jewish State would be an 'outpost of civilisation as opposed to barbarism'.
Then there were the British, still Empire-minded and offering their own
imperialistic solutions. Joseph Chamberlain, the Colonial Secretary,
met with Herzl in England to discuss his ideas, with Chamberlain being
questioned as to Syria/Palestine and Cyprus. Both were discounted by him
as he believed the Turks would object in Sinai and the Moslems and Greeks
would oppose in Cyprus. He also suggested that Lord Lansdowne of the
Foreign Office and Lord Cromer, British Consul General in Egypt, would
need to be consulted regarding Syria.

Eventually both gentlemen would be consulted and a survey carried out
on Herzl's proposals and a reply was received on December 18, 1902 which
was the usual diplomatic fudge:

'Lord Lansdowne had heard from Lord Cromer, who favoured the
sending of a small commission to the Sinai Peninsula to report on
conditions and prospects, but Lord Cromer feared that no sanguine
hopes of success should be entertained, but if the report of the
Commission turned out favourable, the Egyptian Government would
certainly offer liberal terms for Jewish colonization.'

The British Government had recognized Herzl as the Zionist leader, and
the person they could negotiate with, but Chamberlain was still to be heard.
He had been on his travels and had passed through Uganda, 'I thought to
myself, that is just the country for Dr. Herzl. But he must have Palestine,
and will move only into its vicinity'. He was still determined to try a colonial
solution and spoke glowingly of the potential of Uganda, even being prepared
to give the new British controlled area the name 'New Palestine'. Two
problems arose, the first being that the English colonists in East Africa made
their opposition to scheme well known and it became less attractive to the

British government and secondly the Zionists, led by a Russian, Menahem Ussishkin, were vociferous in their opposition, threatening to withhold finances from Herzl. He was stung by the opposition, who were now making demands that the Uganda plan be abandoned and only Palestine considered. Herzl had to use all his political skills to hold things together and the matter was resolved because he had one abiding vision:

> 'We shall give a home to our people. And we shall give it, not by dragging them ruthlessly out of their sustaining soil, but rather by transplanting them carefully to a better ground. Just as we wish to create new political and economic relations, so we shall preserve as sacred all of the past that is dear to our people's hearts.'

He even reached the stage of the new State's flag:

> 'I would suggest a white flag, with seven golden stars. The white field symbolizes our pure new life; the stars are the seven golden hours of our working-day. For we shall march into the Promised Land carrying the badge of honour.'

Herzl was passionately moving the Jewish people along on their journey to return to their homeland. He himself would never see it as he died on 3 July 1904, but his significance in this journey was seen when Herzl Day was created as a national holiday in Israel to honour him. Despite Herzl's thrust for a Jewish State being framed in terms of a political and social necessity, in his heart he held that religious conviction of a Jew in his God being with him in his work, writing in his diary, 'For God would not have preserved our people for so long if we did not have another role to play in the history of mankind'.

The trouble for the Jews continued just as Herzl had predicted and in England the Jews fleeing persecution were not entirely welcomed. An 'Aliens Bill' was brought before Parliament and typical of the hysterical opposition to the Jews was voiced by some MPs:

> 'It was all very well to talk about its being the traditional policy of this country to give to political refugees a domicile, but if that policy was

The Ziggurat of Ur, located in the present-day Dhi Qar Province, Iraq, is a Neo-Sumerian ziggurat in what was the city of Ur, near Nasiriyah.

Nanna, the Mesopotamian god of the moon.

The Merneptah Stele is a stone slab engraved with a description of Merneptah's military victories in Africa and the Near East. It is significant for biblical archeology as it is the earliest extra-biblical reference to the nation of Israel.

The silver shekel was struck during the Bar Kokhba War 132-135 C.E, as a symbol of independence from Rome

The Titus victory arch showing the great menorah from the Temple in Jerusalem.

The infamous Judensau, which was seen as an insult to Jews, depicting them in obscene activities with a pig, sometimes including the Devil. It is often combined with depictions of blood libel.

Charles Netter, a Zionist leader and a founding member of the Alliance Israélite Universelle, 1870.

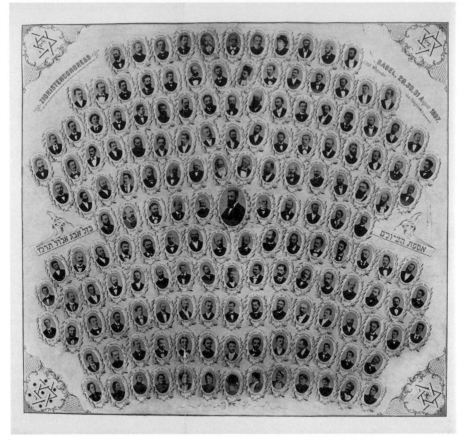

The official portraiture of the delegates of the First Zionist Congress, 1897.

Alfred Dreyfus contemplates his future whilst falsely imprisoned in 1898.

Deuxième Année. — Numéro 87   **Cinq Centimes**   JEUDI 13 JANVIER 1898

Directeur
ERNEST VAUGHAN
ABONNEMENTS

Directeur
ERNEST VAUGHAN

L'AURORE
Littéraire, Artistique, Sociale

J'Accuse...!
LETTRE AU PRÉSIDENT DE LA RÉPUBLIQUE
Par ÉMILE ZOLA

French writer Emile Zola's inflammatory newspaper editorial, entitled "J'accuse," exposed a military cover-up regarding Captain Alfred Dreyfus. Its publication caused a major storm in France.

The Jews of Russia were the victims of three large-scale waves of pogroms that took place between 1881 and 1921, with each one growing in the degree of savagery and brutality inflicted on the helpless victims.

Jewish Legion at the Wailing Wall, 1917.

Russian anti-Jewish propaganda
was used to inflame antisemitism
in 1906 and led to many attacks
on Jews throughout Russia.

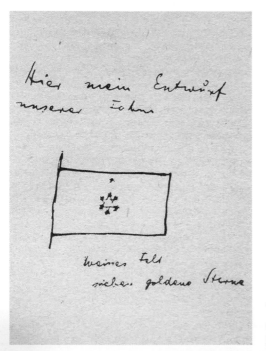

Theodor Herzl's diary drawing
of his proposed flag for the
independent state of Israel.

Foreign Office,
November 2nd, 1917.

The Balfour Declaration brought the reality of an independent state into prominence, thus bringing hope to Jews and dismay to their enemies.

Dear Lord Rothschild,

I have much pleasure in conveying to you, on behalf of His Majesty's Government, the following declaration of sympathy with Jewish Zionist aspirations which has been submitted to, and approved by, the Cabinet

"His Majesty's Government view with favour the establishment in Palestine of a national home for the Jewish people, and will use their best endeavours to facilitate the achievement of this object, it being clearly understood that nothing shall be done which may prejudice the civil and religious rights of existing non-Jewish communities in Palestine, or the rights and political status enjoyed by Jews in any other country"

I should be grateful if you would bring this declaration to the knowledge of the Zionist Federation.

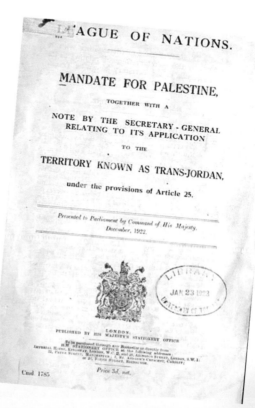

The British Mandate for Palestine was a legal document adopted by the League of Nations on 24 July 1922. It established the United Kingdom as a Mandatory in control of Palestine, which had been held under military government when the British occupied it, displacing the Ottoman Empire during the First World War.

Area Allocated for Jewish National Home
San Remo Conference, 1920

In 1920 the International San Remo Conference gave Britain the Mandate to govern Palestine, but it was not until 1923, after the League of Nations approved and ratified its terms, that the Mandate officially came into full force. Britain excluded the area east of the Jordan (Trans-Jordan) from the area they had proposed for a Jewish homeland.

Menachem Begin (front row, left) was an Israeli politician, founder of Likud and the sixth Prime Minister of Israel. Before the creation of the state of Israel, he was the leader of the Zionist militant group, Irgun.

Hitler was a great manipulator of the German people and stage managed huge rallies, such as this one in 1939. The large organised crowds included many foreigners, and even British aristocratic figures were invited.

British Cartoon on the Evian Conference showing the dilemma of displaced Jews.

Chaim Weizmann was a leading figure in establishing the State of Israel. In 1918 Weizmann was appointed head of the Zionist Commission, and was sent to Palestine by the British government to advise on the future development of the country.

The world was warned of the crisis for Jews in Germany and stands condemned as very little was done to deal with the rising crisis in Germany.

German newspapers carried propaganda against Jews, helping to create the antisemitic atmosphere that contributed to Hitler being seen as the saviour of Germany.

The British Home Secretary, Winston Churchill is escorted by High Commissioner Herbert Samuel, in Jerusalem.

The massacre of Jews in the Ukraine pogroms are a shocking testimony to the terrible record of antisemitism in the country. This image shows the aftermath of one act of mass murder of Jews in 1941.

Auschwitz remains a symbol of depravity, terror, genocide, and the Holocaust, reminding the world how mankind can descend to the greatest depths of evil. It was established by the Germans in 1940 in the suburbs of Oświęcim, a Polish city that was annexed to the Third Reich by the Nazis.

Impassioned with a determination to establish a Jewish State for the protection of their people, many young men joined the Jewish resistance and often laid down their lives for the cause.

Concentration camps were established throughout many of the countries conquered by the Nazis. Some of those who survived the horrors were able to tell the world the truths of the Nazi terrors.

The Nuremberg Trials of leading Nazis brought home to the world the extent of the Nazi evil that had inflicted the horror of the Holocaust on the Jewish people.

The British headlines on the Sergeants Affair when Irgun hanged British soldiers after the execution of their members, 1947.

In 1948, the UN announced the establishment of Israel.

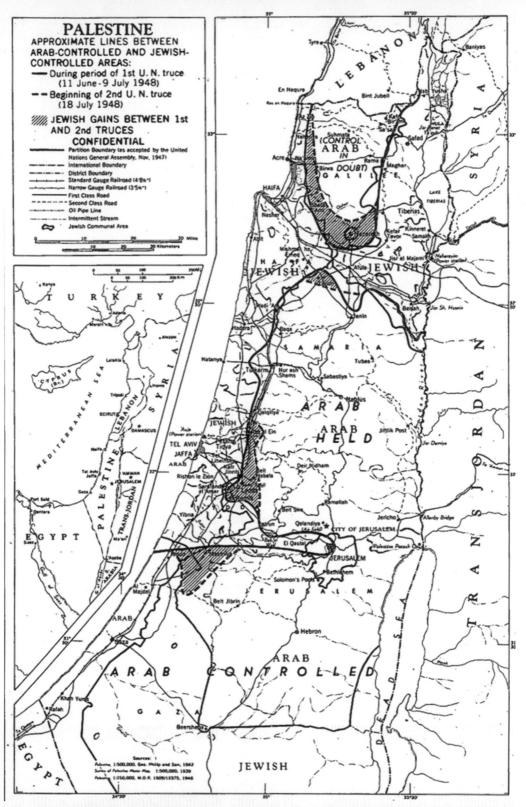

The UN Peace Truce Map in 1948 demonstrates the chaos of the birth of Israel.

This celebration of Jewish independence demonstrates the joy of a persecuted people who have at last returned to their historical homeland.

Jerusalem remains a divided city, even today, yet every year it welcomes millions of visitors who flock to the historic Jewish sites and Yad Vashem, the World Holocaust Center. *© Carol Trow 2017*

to be carried to its logical conclusion nowadays, it meant that we were inviting 5,000,000 oppressed Russian Jews to come to this country, and it was idle to say that because a wrong had been inflicted upon these people in their own country, we were entitled to inflict a further wrong upon our own people by allowing them to come here.'[10]

Thanks largely to Winston Churchill, the restrictions were not imposed, and he was clear in his support of the Jewish people:

'Some people like Jews and some do not: but no thoughtful man can doubt the fact that they are beyond all question, the most formidable and the most remarkable race which has ever appeared in the world'

The Jewish people were mainly coming from Russia where another series of pogroms was being conducted and the 1905 Russian revolution further exacerbated the problem. Churchill again was prominent in their cause, understanding:

'..the supreme attraction to a scattered and persecuted people of a safe and settled home under the flag of tolerance and freedom ... Jerusalem must be the only ultimate goal. When it will be achieved it is vain to prophesy: but that it will someday be achieved is one of the few certainties of the future.'[11]

In Germany, anti-Semitism was once more displaying its ugly face as it was in Ukraine. The cause of the Jewish people was growing more urgent but a darker cloud was gathering over the world. On 28 July 1914, Austria-Hungary declared war on Serbia and the world erupted in the Great War. The Jewish journey would have to come to a halt until the carnage of the war was over.

Chapter Nine

War And The Ending Of Empires

T he tottering Ottoman Empire decided that it would break its neutrality and attacked Russia, aligning itself with Germany. In Palestine, the Arab population was agitating against the Empire's rule and Britain was doing all it could to support the Arabs in their endeavours to wrest Syria/Palestine from the Turks. Hussein ibn Ali al-Hashimi, who was a Hashemite Arab leader, declared himself King of Arabia. Expediently, Britain recognised his kingship as she needed the Arabs as an ally. The war was a dilemma for Jews throughout the world, who, despite the persecutions, in the main remained loyal to their respective countries. Actual numbers are often disputed as to how many were involved on each side. It is thought that 350,000 Jews fought with the Russian army, 100,000 with Austrian army and 30,000 with the German army. The latter were humiliated as they had to take an oath of allegiance in public. About 35,000 Jews fought for the French, 40,000 for the British Empire and 250,000 in the USA forces. Once more, looking at Jewish deaths in the First World War is difficult, with many sources giving vastly different figures but a realistic estimate of the eleven million military deaths in total, 180,000 were Jewish from all sides in the conflict.

Behind the scenes, a secret deal was being carved out by Britain and France in terms of the future of the Middle East, as both parties considered the ending of the war and the defeat of the Ottomans. In January 1915, the British government was presented with a paper marked 'secret' and titled '*The Future of Palestine*'.[1] It recognised that there were twelve million Jews scattered across the world who, with the outbreak of war, believed that there could be a fulfilment of hope and desire that they had 'held with unshakable tenacity for eighteen hundred years, for the restoration of the Jews to the land to which they are attached by ties almost as ancient as history itself'. However, the time was felt not to be right for the fulfilment of such aspirations because of the population mix in Palestine. The British government cautioned that to rush the matter at this time could set back a Jewish State for centuries and that the way forward was a country where Jews could live under the British Empire and after a time be allowed self-government, with the 'sacred sites' given to the control of an international commission. The plan was not altruistic and the benefits to Britain were spelt out in terms of the prestige but more importantly, the belief that the British would do a better job in developing a country that was desolate – after all they had the experience of the British Empire. They also considered the feelings of Protestants throughout the world who would have sympathy for restoring Jews to their homeland in line with the 'fulfilment of prophesies' regarding the 'Hebrew'. There would also be strategic military benefits to Britain along with the 'lasting gratitude' from Jews in America and other lands to see their people freed from 'many centuries of suffering'. The ideas of annexation to France, Egypt, Turkey or an international body were discussed and dismissed and under British suzerainty a Jewish centre could develop in Palestine. It ended with a flourish of praise for the Jews;

> 'For fifteen centuries the race produced in Palestine a constant succession of great men – statesmen and prophets, judges and soldiers. If a body be again given in which its soul can lodge. It may again enrich the world. Till full scope is granted, as Macaulay said in the House of Commons, "Let us not presume to say that there is no genius among the countrymen of Isaiah, no heroism among the descendants of the Maccabees"

Such lofty thoughts interlaced with self-interest were one thing, but the continuing journey of the Jewish people would meet with opposition and *realpolitik*. One such matter was Arabs and their desire for their own territory and Sir Maurice Bunsen in July 1915 gave assurances to them that they would be supported by Britain to gain territory, but Palestine was excluded [2] It was therefore on 19 May 1916, that the Sykes–Picot Agreement (officially the Asia Minor Agreement) was signed, which Russia acknowledged. This would effectively give control to Britain over most of the area that the Jewish People hoped to have as their own. This was moving the responsibility for the realisation of a Jewish State into the hands of the British government. The question of the Jewish homeland was a conundrum for the British and they sought ideas as to a solution. Lord George Curzon, 1st Marquess Curzon of Kedleston, wrote a paper for the Cabinet, which outlined his thoughts. Two questions had been raised; what was the meaning of the phrase 'a National Home for the Jewish Race in Palestine' and the British obligation therein and if the policy was adopted what were 'the chances of a successful realisation'?[3] He did not give a very hopeful answer to the questions as he felt the idea was 'incapacitated' by the conditions of the country. He gave the figures for the Jews throughout the world as twelve million with 3,250,000 in Europe, six million in Russia, two million in the USA and 250,000 in Britain, with 125,000 in Palestine. However, Curzon goes on to say that 'there is no such place as Palestine' because of the way the Ottomans had cut the country up. The population of the area Palestine before the war was between 600,000 and 700,000 with the bulk of Jews living in Jerusalem and they were living in a place of 'abject debasement'. He described it as a poor land with no natural resources living on agriculture and livestock farming. Curzon saw the dream of a Jewish homeland as impossible because of these conditions. He questioned the government's proposals for the idea and outlined his own proposals:

'In reality is not the maximum policy that we can possibly hope to realise one which, if the Turks are defeated and turned out of Palestine, will –

Set up some form of European administration (it cannot be Jewish administration) in that country.

Devise a machinery for safeguarding and securing order both in Christian and in Jewish Holy Places.

Similarly guarantee the integrity of the Mosque of Omar and vest it in some Moslem body.

Secure to the Jews (but not to Jews alone) equal civil and religious rights and the other elements in the population.

Arrange as far as possible for the land purchase and settlement of returning Jews.'[4]

'If this [his proposals] is Zionism' then there was no reason for everyone not to be a Zionist but his ideas fell far short of the object of true Zionists, who still saw a full Jewish State the only way to guarantee the secure protection of the Jewish people. One such was Lucien Wolf, a Jewish English journalist, who wrote to Sir Edward Grey, Secretary of State for Foreign Affairs, promoting the support of the British government for Jews going to Palestine after the war.[5] It was realised within government that the French might not cooperate with any British policy towards the Jews but Lloyd George maintained that after the war, Britain would have conquered Palestine and France would live with it.[6]

In Britain, the hopes of such a Jewish homeland coming out of the horror of the conflict stilled burned in many Jewish hearts. One man, Chaim Weizmann – a bio-chemist and a leader of the Zionist movement – developed an important chemical additive for gunpowder for the British government. He was a good friend of the former Prime Minister and Foreign Secretary in 1917, Arthur Balfour. On 2 November 1917, Balfour wrote a letter to Lord Rothschild, which gave great hope to the Jewish people on their journey home:

'His Majesty's Government view with favour the establishment in Palestine of a national home for the Jewish people, and will use their best endeavours to facilitate the achievement of this object. It being clearly understood that nothing shall be done which may prejudice the civil and religious rights of existing non-Jewish communities in Palestine, or the rights and political status enjoyed by Jews in any other country.'

This became known as the Balfour Declaration, which Lloyd George admitted was in response to Weizmann's help to the government. The declaration was not accepted by all Jews, as some felt that any allegiance to a Jewish State would call into question their commitment to their national country and thus increase anti-Semitism. However, a Foreign Office document confirmed that the vast majority of Jews across the world held a hope of a State in Palestine.[7] Indeed, the USA and France had confirmed their agreement with Balfour, the French calling it '*Un Foyer Nationale* [A National Home]".[8]

Making such a statement was one thing but bringing it about was another with the volatile situation in the Middle East and the Arab populations across the area. Under General Allenby, head of the British Egyptian Expeditionary Force, who had entered Jerusalem on foot to honour the city after the Turks fled in December 1917, T E Lawrence (Lawrence of Arabia) had been sent to work on intelligence with the Arabs and became involved in the actual military actions against the Ottomans. He was concerned that the outcome of the war would result in an Arab national State, and was extremely unhappy that the Sykes-Picot Agreement was not going to facilitate that ambition. Sir Mark Sykes, in a separate report to the government, indicated the issues that working with the Arabs would bring about, including possible violent responses, internal and external.[9] In a report, the government adviser, Professor Oman from Oxford, concluded that the ambition of the Arabs for their State and the fact that the French would have their own plans, would not allow a Jewish State. Oman also noted that 'Tribal disintegration has always been the curse of the Arabs'.[10] Sykes similarly pointed out these issues and therefore the conflict between Jewish and Arab ambitions was clearly known to the British government. On 4 April 1918, the British confirmed to the Sherif of Mecca (who became King Hussain of Jordan) that Balfour was going to be implemented.[11] Even William Ormbsby-Gore (Lord Harlech), an extremely strong supporter of the Zionist aims, indicated, 'Our pledge to assist the formation of the Jewish National Home does not involve the creation – at any rate in the immediate future – of an autonomous Jewish State'.[12] Balfour himself had clearly stated at a dinner on 7 February 1918 of a desire, 'to give the Jews their rightful place in the world; a great nation without a home is not right'. He was further asked to clarify if that meant 'ultimate Jewish sovereignty in Palestine'. His response was carefully made to distinguish his own views from government, 'My personal hope is that the Jews will make good in Palestine and eventually found a Jewish State'.[13]

Others were still pressing for the Jewish State to be created. On 26 February 1918, Balfour received a letter with 'Extremely Urgent and Important' written across the top in pen. It was from Baron Gustave de Coriolis, who declared that a group of Jewish bankers, including the Rothschilds in Paris, were prepared to act as an intermediary to end the war by approaching Prussia to set up an Empire of Middle Europe under the Emperor of Austria.[14] The letter makes clear that Britain now had the Middle East in her hands and could control events there and could now assist the Jews to 'recover their national existence they have been deprived of for so many centuries'. Coriolis argues that there were 2.8 million Jews in Europe who would be on the side of Britain and the idea appears to be that a national Jewish State would be governed by the Empire. Notes on the file indicate that Gustave had offered his services before as intermediary and had been refused. Nothing seems to have been done by Balfour in response to the letter and there were no indications that the Rothschilds knew anything of the contents.

On 2 March 1918, Balfour wrote to General Allenby informing him that a 'Zionist Mission' to the area to explore the establishment of 'National Home for the Jewish people' would be taking place. The letter is very clear that the Mission has his and the government's full support and he is to help in every way possible to give 'concrete form to this Declaration' and bears the hand-written note 'Palestine for the Jews'. The Mission was led by Chaim Weizmann and Lord Harlech, 'the Political Officer' and Balfour gave his high endorsement of Weizmann stating clearly their long term relationship and there is no doubting Balfour's enthusiasm for the project. Despite this encouragement to assist the Zionist Mission, British officials were working against the Balfour Declaration and some generals were even asking for it to be cancelled. The war was now reaching the end game but whilst the war 'ended' on 11 November 1919, the legal end to the war came at the end of the various treaties on 23 August 1923. The war had come to an end and four empires had disappeared, the German, Austro-Hungarian, Ottoman, and Russian and the seeds of the ending of the British Empire were sown in the new world that was emerging after the terrible carnage. Captain Leo Amery, writing to Balfour in October 1918, suggested the Empire should be renamed, 'United Nations of the British Commonwealth' because nations like 'Zionist Palestine, if it happens' would be more comfortable with such an entity rather than the United States.[15]

When the Ottoman Empire capitulated on 30 October 1918 and General Allenby, had based himself in Jerusalem, the way was being made open for British control of Palestine. The post-war Paris conference in 1919 had its problems in respect to the Middle East. The agreed delegations from the different countries did not include the Arab group, the Hedjaz, whose king Feisal fought against the Ottomans with T.E. Lawrence. Eric Drummond, 7th Earl of Perth, the British politician and diplomat, who would become Secretary-General of the League of Nations, writing to Balfour from Paris in January 1919, informed him that 'Lawrence, who has just been to see me, says that Feisal is furious'. This was the first pointer to problems that would arise over the question of a Jewish State. Lord Curzon also wrote to Balfour in January after a visit from Major-General Sir Arthur Wigram Money, the Chief Administrator of Palestine, who had concerns about the promised Jewish State and that 'A Jewish Government in any form would mean an Arab rising'.[16] Curzon indicated that he shared the views expressed and added he had long 'felt that the pretensions of Weizmann & Company are extravagant and ought to be checked'.[17] In a puzzling reply to Curzon Balfour wrote:

> 'As far as I know Weizmann has never put forward a claim for the Government [Balfour had underlined this in pen] of Palestine. Such a claim is in my opinion certainly inadmissible and personally I do not think we should go further than the original declaration which I made Lord Rothschild'.[18]

The statement was puzzling because he had written to Allenby in Jerusalem about the Zionist Mission regarding a 'National Home for the Jewish people'. How could there be a National Home without a government? Harlech wrote to Eric Drummond[19] from the Conference that Weizmann had applied to place before it his request that Britain be given mandatory power over Palestine and that there was concern that Balfour should advise. Drummond made a note that Britain should stand apart from the matter and let Weizmann take his own course to which Balfour had add in pen 'yes'. The eventual proposals turned out to be a clear declaration:

> 'The Zionist Organization respectfully submits the following draft resolutions for the consideration of the Peace Conference:
>
> 1. The High Contracting Parties recognize the historic title of the Jewish people to Palestine and the right of Jews to reconstitute in Palestine their National Home.
> 2. The boundaries of Palestine shall be as declared in the Schedule annexed hereto.
> 3. The sovereign possession of Palestine shall be vested in the League of Nations and the Government entrusted to Great Britain as Mandatory of the League.

4. (Provision to be inserted relating to the application in Palestine of such of the general conditions attached to mandates as are suitable to the case.)'

There were additional provisions securing the rights of government of the new State and defining its boundaries, also included were the justifications for the claims. The submission ended:

'In every part of the world on the Day of Atonement the Jews pray that "all nations may be united by a common bond, so that the will of God may reign supreme throughout the world." In the fulfilment of this prayer, the Jews hope that they will be able to take an honourable place in the new community of nations. It is their purpose to establish in Palestine a government dedicated to social and national justice; a government that shall be guided, like the community of old, by that justice and equality which is expressed in the great precept of our Lawgiver: "There shall be but one law for you and the stranger in the land".'

The document was signed by Rothschild, to whom Balfour had written his declaration, on 'behalf of the Zionist Organization, Nahum Sokolow [a Polish-born Jew and a multilinguistic journalist, prominent in Zionism], and Chaim Weizmann'. The letter from Drummond was passed to Balfour who appeared to be annoyed with it, noting in pen at the top of the letter, 'When did I talk about a Jewish government?' Drummond also noted, 'This hardly requires an answer.' However, an answer was sent to Harlech, indicating he should tell Weizmann to do whatever he wished as the British government wanted no responsibility in the matter. He also had received a letter from Paris to the effect that Lawrence was conducting behind the scene lobbying for the Arabs at the Conference and that there were difficulties with the French as to what territory thy would have influence over and there was concern that British action be taken to deal with it. The atmosphere for the Jewish people's journey to their State was proving very difficult and Balfour seemed to be playing a strange game. In February 1919, he met a Jewish delegation in his hotel in Paris[20] which included Sokolow who had signed the Zionist document laid before the Conference. They thanked Balfour for his statement and for his efforts on their behalf and in his reply, he expressed his 'personal sympathies' and advised them that 'no movement such as theirs could achieve fulfilment without encountering many difficulties' and confirmed that they had many supporters in England and America, even among non-Jews. He went on to say that he 'felt convinced that their movement would succeed. He made no mention of any misunderstanding between his and their understanding of 'government' of the new State which Balfour was confident they would achieve.

The evidence would suggest that whilst Balfour was sympathetic to the Zionist cause, he was in difficulty with what he could actually do. Philip Henry Kerr, 11th Marquess of Lothian, secretary to Lloyd George made Balfour aware in February 1919 of the rising conflicts between ambitions from Arabs, Catholics and Jews in Palestine. Lloyd George had sent a letter to Kerr[21] regarding a letter received by Lord Edmund Talbot, a prominent British politician and Catholic, from Cardinal Bourne in Jerusalem. The letter echoed some of the Catholic anti-Semitism of earlier years headed boldly, 'Zionism'. He wrote that the Balfour statement was 'very vague' and could be 'interpreted in different ways', which indeed confirmed the actions and statements of Balfour which were indeed confusing. The Cardinal demanded an immediate declaration from the British government that the Jewish minority in Palestine would not govern the majority. He criticised the Zionist organisation 'asserting themselves' and beginning to nominate nominees for political posts, claiming he had been approached by both Christians and Moslems. He was also critical of Sir Mark Sykes for supporting them and denied they had the support of the Pope and that the whole movement was contrary to Christian sentiment and tradition. He was happy to have Jews come and dwell there and inadvertently gives the Jews acknowledgement that the land was formerly theirs by writing, 'they should never again dominate and rule the country' as that would be 'an outrage to Christianity and its Divine Founder'. Lloyd George expressed his own concerns, 'If the Zionists claim that the Jews are to have domination of the Holy Land under a British Protectorate, then they are certainly putting their claims too high'. It was suggested that Balfour should clarify the position in a public statement. Lloyd George also expressed the Arab concerns that they were to be removed to make way for Jews and he felt it all would be a bad start for the British as they assumed government of the area and the letter from the Cardinal 'is a revelation to me of the reason why the Catholics hate the Jews so badly'. Harlech was involved in deciding a response and wrote that, 'Cardinal Bourne's letter "reveals a complete misunderstanding of our commitments in regard to Zionism'. He felt a declaration would cause greater difficulties and in that probably reflected Balfour, in that it was better to leave matters vague and therefore no one could then hold the government down to any specific agreement. He wanted to wait for the end of the conference and a mandate given to the British over Palestine. He understood that Weizmann and Feisal had reached an understanding about Syria and Palestine and there was the possibility of disturbance throughout the Arab world. He wanted assurances to be given to the Catholics over the 'Holy Places' and political equality. He then gave his view that many Catholics 'have deep seated anti-Semitic prejudices' and that the 'Jews now living are equally responsible with the Jews 1900 years ago for the crucifixion'. He confirmed he had spoken to Weizmann and pointed out the difficulties before their movement and again reiterated his belief that a public statement should not be made.

He enclosed a memorandum which rejected the Cardinal's core points and stated that Sokolov and Sykes had spoken with Cardinal Gasperi and had made clear the position two years previously. Contrary to Bourne's claims that German Jewish finance was involved, he stated that the money was coming from America and Britain. He also made clear that the British government would assist 'those Jews who wished to return to the land of their ancestors' and that all rights would be safeguarded. The British government, he declared, never contemplated any inequality between groups in Palestine but 'is anxious to facilitate the creation of a National Home for a race, that has been persecuted in so many lands, where they can live in security and can develop freely their own culture and civilisation'. He makes clear that there would be no discrimination and that the land was under-developed and many areas sparsely populated and that the future situation regarding the Jews would depend on how many took up the opportunity to live there. Once more, there is the acknowledgement that 'anti-Semitism still exists among many elements of Palestine as well as of other countries as a discredit to Christian civilisation'. The memorandum ends with the hope that the future will once more see the unity of people revived and that there would be redemption of the land 'regarded as Holy by Jew and Christian alike'.

Such sentiments gave hope that the Jewish people would see a successful end to their journey and an end to their suffering over the centuries.

Balfour himself also took up his pen to write to Lloyd George and urge that no statement should be made. His view was that the government 'rightly decline to accept the principle of self-determination' because any consultation of the present population of Palestine would give an 'anti-Jewish verdict'. The justification for this was that Palestine was 'absolutely exceptional' and that 'we consider the question of the Jews outside Palestine as one of world importance'. He confirmed to the Prime Minister that 'we conceive the Jews to have a historic claim to a home in their ancient land'. The opposition to the Jews from Roman Catholics to the Jewish Zionists was 'very little to their credit' and that the opposition was not so much about the Holy Places – these could be safeguarded by the League of Nations – but more about the 'hatred of the Jews'. He acknowledged that the attitude of the Jews in the matter was not always attractive but 'the balance of wrongdoing seems to me on the whole to be greatly on the Christian side'; he himself was an evangelical Christian.

There was obvious confusion even within government and Edward Montagu of the India office contacted Balfour expressing considerable alarm at the reports he was hearing about the Zionists and Balfour's apparent support for 'reconstituting Palestine as the Jewish national home'. He referred to an announcement Balfour made that contained the words, 'establishing in Palestine a national home for the Jewish people'. He argued that there was a difference between the two phrases 'reconstituting the country as' and 'establishing in the country'. He expressed his 'hatred' of the Balfour Declaration and that Balfour had gone beyond it. He had heard from Sir Louis Mallet that the scheme for the future government of Palestine being proposed by London was the same as his and not Balfour's. He demanded to know where Balfour stood on the matter. Balfour's response was a polite rebuke to Montagu and he accused him of semantics in the whole matter and he saw no difference in the phrases quoted. He also believed that most English Jews were Zionists and that they had support from Britain and America. Montagu did not get the clarification he wanted. His response came back obviously annoyed with Balfour and declaring that, if the reports he was hearing were accurate, that Balfour did support a Jewish homeland, then Moslems would be upset. He asked Balfour to 'refrain from voting me an incorrigible nuisance' and looked to the future official government declaration. Balfour was also under fire from the League of British Jews in London. They objected to a term he used in a book on Zionism which said that, 'Jews are homeless' and declared that Jews had homes in many countries. The Jewish people so often caused themselves problems and frustrated the movement to a national home.

Curzon once more wrote to Balfour[22] expressing concern that Weizmann had gone beyond what was agreed and that the 'ambitions of the Zionists were exceeding all bounds'. He had obtained a copy of a secret meeting which listed a number of intentions of a Zionist government which were very extreme in his view and made him 'shudder'. They included control of all immigration, observed Jewish holidays, control of land and water rights, nationalisation of public land and any surplus private land exceeding a certain size, control of public works, supervision of education and the use of Hebrew as the language in all schools. He foresaw trouble with the Vatican and had reached the view that if the report was the way forward, he wished the mandate would fall on someone other than the British. On 19 March 1919, James de Rothschild had also written to Lloyd George indicating that about £2m would be need to reconstruct Haifa and other places in Palestine and asking for a declaration on the Zionist ambitions in the country. The situation was beginning to cause great pressures within the government. Balfour wrote to Herbert Samuel, who was Jewish but atheist in outlook, to inform him of his concerns that the Zionist cause was being damaged and that their activity was alienating elements of the population in Palestine because of their interference. Writing to Samuel was surprising as he was even more extreme than men like Weizmann, who he 'believed had made demands that were too modest', and even suggested that perhaps the Temple may be rebuilt, as a symbol of Jewish unity. On 27 March 1919, Samuel's reply was polite but firm, pointing out that he would speak with Zionists leaders but also making the case that British administration in Palestine was discriminating against Jews, especially in Jaffa. He repeatedly stressed that the administration did not seem to have heard of Balfour's declaration and the removal of the Jaffa government would help ease the situation. Chaim Weizmann also responded to Balfour in a friendlier but still firm tone. He pointed out that the journey to a Jewish Home had been a long one and now it was in sight it was no surprise Jews talked with enthusiasm, but he acknowledged the needs of 'non-Jewish elements' and he would always seek to protect them. He pointed to the French attempts at both anti-British and anti-Jewish comments in the press to undermine the events in Palestine. He told Balfour that he and Feisal had reached an understanding over the proposals put before the Peace Conference and quotes his response from a letter he had received:

> 'We Arabs, especially the educated among us, look with the deepest sympathy on the Zionist movement. Our deputation is fully acquainted with the proposals submitted yesterday by the Zionist Organization to the Peace Conference, and we regard them as moderate and proper. We will do our best in so far as we are concerned, to help them through, we will wish the Jews a most hearty welcome home.'[23]

This was an important endorsement coming from the chief Arab leader, who himself was expecting a great deal from the British for Arab land in Syria. Weizmann reminded Balfour that Lawrence and Sykes all were in support of the aims of the Jewish people for a homeland and that there was agitation from Damascus and Egypt that were not only anti-Jew but anti-British. The politics of the Jewish homeland were one thing, but the British government had a number of issues on their plate and the persecution and killing of Jews continued especially in Russia and Ukraine. The journey home for the Jews was still a bloody and frustrating one.

Chapter Ten

The British Mandate

On 8 February 1920, Winston Churchill penned an article in the *Illustrated Sunday Herald* in which he wrote:

'If, as may well happen, there should be created in our own lifetime by the banks of the Jordan a Jewish State under the protection of the British Crown which might comprise three or four millions of Jews, an event will have occurred in the history of the world which would from every point of view be beneficial.'

This encouraging belief in the realisation of the hopes and dreams of Jewish people was welcomed but even the road to the British Mandate would not be easy. In June of that year, the proposed draft was placed before the British Cabinet and in its opening paragraph there was the confirmation of the commitment to the Balfour Declaration and a 'national home for the Jewish people'. There was also to be a Jewish Agency with power to advise and cooperate with the Administration and 'the Zionist organisation' was to be recognised as that Agency. There were the usual statements on protection of liberty in political and religious views and importantly for the future 'no person shall be excluded from Palestine on the sole ground of his religious belief'.[1] That would be strongly tested when Jews would want to enter in great numbers at a later date. The appointment of Sir Herbert Samuel was a popular choice as was seen in past correspondence with Balfour, with his strong stance on a Jewish State. In his public statements after his appointment he was clear:

'In accordance with the decision of the Allied and Associated Powers, measures will be adopted to reconstruct the Jewish national home in Palestine. The yearnings of the Jewish people for 2,000 years, of which the modern Zionist movement is the latest expression, will at last be realised.'[2]

There can have been no doubt in anyone's mind what that meant, as the Zionist organisation had made plain to government and others that this would be a self-governing Jewish State and indeed no direct public contradiction from government was ever made. In November, Lord Curzon, the Foreign Secretary informed the government that the French and Italians were unhappy with the 'Zionist complexion' in the mandate's preamble;

> 'Recognising the historical connection of the Jewish people with Palestine and the claim which this gives them to reconstitute Palestine as their National Home.'

Some wished it removed but Balfour insisted that it was appropriate to have some statement regarding the Jewish historical connection to Palestine and a new clause was agreed:

> '… and whereas recognition has thereby (i.e., by the Treaty of Sevres) been given to the historical connection of the Jewish people with Palestine, and to the grounds for reconstituting their National Home in that country.'

This political expediency was accepted by the Cabinet but other Zionists' demands about preferential treatment in other areas were rejected.[3]

The situation in Palestine was very delicate, with tensions simmering under the surface that would break through as they did on 4 April 1920, when Arab mobs attacked Jewish property and looted their premises. The mob was roaring 'independence, independence!' and 'Palestine is our land, the Jews are our dogs'. An enquiry by the British could not find the real causes of the riot as there were claims and counter claims as to who started it. Indeed the Jewish population were becoming concerned because of their minority population and the larger Arab group and self-defence groups were organised, some armed. Yet by 8 December, the Cabinet were informed that the situation between Jews and Arabs in Palestine was good, but by 18 December, Churchill, as the Secretary of State for War, said in a memorandum to the Cabinet that the situation in Palestine was dangerous with 'riots likely to break out' in many of the towns including Jerusalem because of strong feelings within the Arab community that their land was to be given to the

Jews under the proposed mandate.[4] Churchill seemed to have a better grasp of the reality of the situation and on 30 December 1920, a new Middle East department was established under him, with T.E. Lawrence and Lieutenant Colonel Richard Meinertzhagen, who was working with Allenby, as advisers. A number of issues were related to religious differences in celebration of the different festivals and the crowds that gathered at these times. The matter was one that had always been considered and as part of the mandate, a Commission was to be set up behind the scenes, the form of which was being considered. The situation was also bringing financial pressures on Britain and there were continual discussions about troops in both Palestine and Transjordan and the related costs. Whilst the British may have given their support to a Jewish homeland, the financial burden was one that they were finding onerous and there were continuous public assurances to encourage Jewish finance to assist the development of Palestine. In the Cabinet report:

'The Secretary of State for the Colonies, Churchill, paid a high tribute to the success of the Zionist colonies of long standing, which had created a standard of living far superior to that of the indigenous Arabs. His observations had not confirmed current accounts of the inferior quality of recent Jewish immigrants, and by strict control (proportionally to the development of the country by water power, etc.) of the quality and number of the Zionists he hoped to be able to fulfil our undertaking.'[5]

A great deal of the finance for this success was from Jewish sources which were keen to see the realisation of the Jewish homeland, so longed hoped for. Churchill was proving a good ally for this hope and at the Cabinet meeting gave answers to any criticisms that were raised as to the positivity of the Jewish contribution to an improving Palestine. However, the Jewish population were under severe threat and Captain Brunton, General Staff (Intelligence), Palestine, gave a blunt appraisal to the Cabinet in July 1921:[6]

'The High Commissioner, with the assistance of the General Officer Commanding, is taking steps to form a species of "Town Guards" in the Jewish villages and colonies by issuing arms to selected men. It is, however, problematical how far such organizations will be capable of the defence of their localities.'

He offered three possible solutions:

'(a)   An alteration of policy as regards Jewish immigration;
(b)   An increase in the British garrison; or
(c)   The acceptance of serious danger to the Jewish population'

If the journey to a Jewish Homeland was to be fulfilled, the first option could not be accepted as Jewish finance would be at issue. The second was unpopular in Britain due to the cost and the latter, which would deliberately put Jewish lives at risk, was not a palatable choice for the Government. There was an incident in Jaffa in May when an Arab mob attacked a Jewish immigrants' hostel and severe rioting broke out with some deaths. The British officer, when questioned as to why he did not interfere, said, 'When we found it was a question between the Jews and the Arabs we did not think it was for us to interfere ... Which were we to stop?' This reflects a poster that appeared in Jerusalem, 'The Government is with us, Allenby is with us, kill the Jews; there is no punishment for killing Jews'. Furthermore, Meinertzhagen alleged that Colonel Bertie Harry Waters-Taylor had incited the riots and had spoken with the Arab Mayor, Moussa Kasim Pasha to the effect that he had given him a clear opportunity to deal with the Jews.[7] Meinertzhagen was sent back to London. It would appear the third option was being implemented on the ground. The High Commissioner, Samuel, was under great pressure to protect the Jews and the demand was made to revoke the suspension of immigration that had been applied. He told the Zionist leaders that this was 'a war between the Arab nation and the Hebrew nation', when it was suggested the matter was just a local affair. However, he was told that the events echoed the pogroms that many immigrants had fled.

By 13 January 1922, the inter-religious conflict was a concern and the British were seeking to get the mandate and the related Commission to oversee the matter established. The difficulty was that the French and Italians were once more causing delays and the USA was slow in responding to the requests for their views. The government in Britain was still under internal pressure regarding finances in the whole Palestinian project and the matter of the mandate was now growing urgent. In May 1922, the Cabinet agreed a memorandum to be sent to the Council of the League of Nations to bring the matter to a conclusion and outlined once again the agreed mandate and

Commission and confirmed a small Commission of two members each from
the Christian, Moslem and Jewish groups. The memorandum indicated that
the USA had given assurances of their support and these would eventually
be confirmed to the Council. Once more, the journey to a Jewish Homeland
was being frustrated by the countries who had demonstrated their anti-
Semitism over centuries.

However, Churchill was still very clear in the White Paper in June 1922:

'When it is asked what is meant by the development of the Jewish National
Home in Palestine, it may be answered that it is not the imposition of a
Jewish nationality upon the inhabitants of Palestine as a whole, but the
further development of the existing Jewish community, with the assistance
of Jews in other parts of the world, in order that it may become a centre
in which the Jewish people as a whole may take, on grounds of religion
and race, an interest and a pride. But in order that this community should
have the best prospect of free development and provide a full opportunity
for the Jewish people to display its capacities, it is essential that it should
know that it is in Palestine as of right and not on sufferance.'

Furthermore, the true force to oppose the mandate and the Jewish progress
was the one that had demonstrated its anti-Semitism since the first century
was the Vatican. There had been a procedural delay and a frustrated Balfour
wrote to the Cabinet from Paris: [8]

'The second obstacle which has been encountered—unexpectedly so
far as I was concerned—has been the intervention of the Vatican, lhe
result of which has become more and more evident as the deliberations
of the Council proceed. ... the Vatican would seem to have redoubled
its efforts to stir up opposition to the draft mandate for Palestine as it
stands at present. At all events the extent of the campaign undertaken
by the Vatican can scarcely have been realised in London. It is no
exaggeration to say that the reluctance of the French, Polish, Spanish,
Italian and Brazilian representatives on the Council to discuss now the
Palestine mandate or the question of the chairmanship of the Holy
Places Commission has been due to the representations which have
been made to their Governments by the Papal representatives.'

The opposition was not just abroad. Even in London the anti-Jewish forces were at work and on 4 July 1922, a debate in the House of Lords about a hydro-electric project in Palestine turned into an opportunity for the House to try and throw out the Balfour Declaration. The Lords defeated the plan by 60 votes to 29. It was up to Winston Churchill to rescue it and in the House of Commons he made a passionate speech that succeeded in winning the day. The importance of this speech cannot be overstated and the journey to a Jewish Homeland could have ended that day. He made a point of reminding those opposing just what they had said earlier:

> 'The House again and again on most formal occasions has approved of the great series of negotiations in which these were included, and which is associated with the name of Versailles. There is no doubt whatever that the fulfilment of the Balfour Declaration was an integral part of the whole mandatory system, as inaugurated by agreement between the victorious Powers and by the Treaty of Versailles. ... And speaking as Colonial Secretary, charged with the execution of a particular policy, a policy adopted and confirmed by this country before the whole world, I am bound by the pledges and promises which have been given in the name of Great Britain in the past, and by the decisions which Parliament has taken from time to time. ... Let us keep to the question. When the Zionist policy was announced by Lord Balfour, then Mr. Balfour, almost every public man in this country expressed his opinion upon it.'

He then went on to name the Lords, now opposing, who at the time had assented to the Balfour Declaration, adding.

> 'I consider that one of the greatest outcomes of this terrible War will be the rescue of Palestine from Turkish mis-government, and I will do all in my power to forward the views of the Zionists, order to enable the Jews once more to take possession of their own land. This goes far beyond the Jewish National Home; it is a commonwealth; it is almost a complete expropriation.'

Churchill went on for some time to drive home the hypocrisy of the Lords decision and the need to honour British commitments.

The Italians meanwhile were still trying to find ways to delay with Balfour still frustrated with their tactics Churchill said:

'It had come as a complete surprise to him that now, in the middle of July 1922, there should be an objection on the part of the Italian Government to the discussion of the Syrian mandate. ... at least a feeling of something approaching, despair to those who had to work the machinery.'

On 24 July 1922, the mandate was formally adopted by the League of Nations and a great step forward made but there was still going to be trouble ahead. By September, the matter of the Commission for Holy Sites was still unresolved, with new proposals finally agreed which were no more than the extension of the former proposals, obviously showing compromise in its final mixture of numbers, sub-divisions and faiths represented.[9] On 14 September, the British government began to clarify their implementation of the mandate, which, although one mandate, covered Palestine *and* the areas east of the Jordan. They made clear the territory east of the Jordan – Transjordan – was to be separately administered and did not include any plans for Jewish involvement. This decision, to take three-quarters of the Palestine mandate away from the Zionists, was made in the hope that the Arab community would be happy with the territory being allocated to them and thus ease the transition of Western Palestine to a Jewish Homeland. Weizmann was not happy that so much area of land was taken away, arguing that it was much for the Jewish people and little to the Arab people and would not satisfy them anyway. He was right. Yet Britain felt it had to satisfy Arab hopes for their own country. Abdullah I bin al-Hussein, who would become king of Jordan, was made an Emir in 1921 and would eventually become king in 1946. He wanted a Palestine that included Transjordan and Eastern Palestine as an Arab State, but was plainly told, 'The mandate embodied the terms of the Balfour Declaration in which two distinct promises were made – one to the Jews and the other to the Arabs' thus both parties had their promises met. It was a vain hope that this move would satisfy Arabs in the Palestine area. Meinertzhagen, who had not been present at the talks, was furious with the step that was taken, believing it to be a betrayal of the Jewish people and Britain's promise in order to appease Abdullah.[10] In a report to government from the High Commissioner in Palestine on 30 December 1922, he reported that the tensions had eased and that there was little trouble. He noted that:

'The large majority of the population of Palestine are Moslem Arabs, and among them a majority, possibly equally large, favour the general views of what may be termed the opposition to the present Administration. Three currents of thought combine to create and to maintain this opposition. First, there is the Arab national movement, which desires to see the establishment of a great Arab Empire, of which Palestine should form a part; a movement which was always hostile to Turkish rule, and which welcomed the British as the agents of liberation. Second, there is the anti-Zionist movement, which came into existence after the occupation, which is inspired by a dread of submergence under a flood of Jewish immigration and of political subordination, sooner or later, to a Jewish Government. Third, there is the Pan-Islamic movement, which commands the support of numbers of religious Moslems, which sympathises with Mahommedanism wherever it may be found, and feels it be its duty to adopt whatever course in Palestine may best contribute to the advancement of the common cause, paying only secondary attention to the facts of the local situation. These three motives intermingle. The minds of some men may be more influenced by one, of some by another. The majority of the Moslems of Palestine are probably moved, in greater or less degree, by all three.'[11]

Despite the fact that in Syria and Transjordan there were now Arab administrations, that were heading to give substantial territories to the Arab people, there was still this desire for an Arab Empire that wanted to include Palestine and wanted to exclude the Jewish people from any home for themselves. He reported that many Moslems were advocating that no land be given to Jews but at the same time they were in fact selling their land to immigrants to cultivate. Furthermore, the Jews were now greater in number than the Christians, who yet held great power because of their wealth, and were joining with Moslems to oppose Zionism. This cooperation was under strain because of the ideas being promoted of an Arab Empire. It was also noted that the areas under Jewish development were excellent and that money was flowing into the area to assist the development, with the added bonus that it was easing the pressure on British finance. The Commissioner was wary of elements in Britain that may wish to make trouble for the region and makes a footnote in his report:

'Perhaps I may be permitted to deprecate any reference in Parliament to the more peaceful state of the country as a reason why no change of policy is necessary. Such reference may be regarded as a direct invitation to make trouble in order to furnish arguments to the contrary.'

There were still those who wanted to frustrate the Jewish people in making their home in Palestine. In November 1922, a new British government had come to power under Andrew Bonar Law – he had succeeded Balfour in 1911 as Conservative leader – and in February 1923, the Cabinet was asked by Lord Devonshire, the Colonial Secretary, to revisit the previous administrations on Palestine.[12] It addressed three questions that needed answering; did pledges to the Arabs conflict with the Balfour Declaration in favour of setting up a National Home for the Jews of Palestine? If the answer was 'no' should the policy of the 1922 White Paper continue to be implemented and if not, what alternative policy should be adopted? These questions had serious implications for the journey of the Jewish people to their home. The Balfour agreement was summarised as being brought about to 'enlist the sympathies on the Allied side of influential Jews and Jewish organisations all over the world', to oppose the Germans and influence public opinion in the USA, the latter having the effect of bringing the USA into the war sooner. The idea that was abroad, that it was 'one of the many legacies of evil which the [then] Coalition has bequeathed', could not be sustained. The fact was that 'The Jews would naturally regard it as an act of baseness if, having appealed to them in our hour of peril, we were to throw them over when the danger was past.' The Declaration had been accepted by the Allied Powers and included officially in the mandate for Palestine.

The British government were committed to the Zionist policy in the eyes of the whole world. It was under the mandate's Article 2, that the British government were, 'responsible for placing the country under such political, administrative and economic conditions as will secure the establishment of the Jewish national home', which Balfour re-asserted and defended in the Lords. In that provision the Zionist organisation (known in Palestine as the Zionist Executive) had been given a special place to advise and cooperate with the administration. In terms of pledges to the Arabs, there had been none given in respect of Palestine. Sir H. McMahon, then High Commissioner in Egypt, gave an undertaking on 25 October 1915, to the Sherif of Mecca (now King Hussein of the Hejaz) that His Majesty's Government would 'recognise and support' the independence of the Arabs 'within certain territorial limits', McMahon had been subsequently asked if that commitment have anything to do with Palestine, to which he replied in writing that 'it did not'. The White Paper of 1922 also confirmed this was the case and Churchill had made a statement in Parliament on 11 July, when he reinforced that principle. An Arab delegation from Palestine had tried to insist that McMahon's pledge did refer to Palestine, but they were informed that this never was the fact and this evidence, along with statements by Allenby, was presented to them. Balfour himself was angry with Arab claims and on 11 June had made a statement:

'Of all the charges made against this country, I must say that the charge that we have been unjust to the Arab race seems to me the strangest. It is through the expenditure largely of British blood, by the exercise of British skill and valour, by the conduct of British generals, by troops brought from' all parts of the British Empire—it is by them in the main that the freeing of the Arab race from Turkish rule has been effected. And that we, after all the events of the war, should be held up as those who have done an injustice; that we, who have just established a King in Mesopotamia, who had before that established an Arab King in the Hejaz, and who have done more than has been done for centuries past to put the Arab race in the position to which they have attained; that we should be charged with being their enemies, with having taken a mean advantage of the course of international negotiations, seems to me not only most unjust to the policy of this country, but almost fantastic in its extravagance.'[13]

The issue of Palestine was not a problem within the larger Arab world at that time and it was only a group within the Arab population in Palestine that was attempting to frustrate the government's ambitions towards the Jews. There was a problem with the Declaration in that it was not certain what was meant by a 'Jewish Homeland' and the Zionist 'Jewish State'. Were the two the same? Indeed, the records show that Harlech had stated:[14]

'Upon the origins of the Declaration little exists in the way of official records; indeed, little is known of how the policy represented by the Declaration was first given form. Four, or perhaps five, men were chiefly concerned in the labour – the Earl of Balfour, the late Sir Mark Sykes, and Messrs. Weizmann and Sokolov, with perhaps Lord Rothschild as a figure in the background. Negotiations seem to have been mainly oral and by means of private notes and memoranda, of which only the scantiest records are available, even if more, exist'.

The actual text of the Declaration was finalised by Leo Amery, not Balfour.

However, the Cabinet were informed that the High Commissioner and Churchill had agreed on an explanation of the declaration:

'They [i.e., the words of the Declaration] mean that the Jews, a people that are scattered throughout the world, but whose hearts are always turned to Palestine, should be enabled to found here their home, and that some among them, within the limits that are fixed by the numbers and interests of the present population, should come to Palestine in order to help by their resources and efforts to develop the country to the advantage of all its inhabitants.'[15]

This explanation had not satisfied an Arab delegation to London and they called for the declaration to be rescinded and a representative government be established in Palestine. In effect, they wanted an end to a Jewish Homeland. Weizmann of the Zionist organisation had agreed that a special Legislative Council with a majority of Arabs to advise the Administration could be set up and the government were free to refute the Zionist terms being used in relation to Palestine and that the Zionists were not included in government of any form. This was a major statesman-like step by Weizmann and the Zionists but the Arabs rejected it. The further Arab delegation complaint that Palestine had seen a 'flood of alien immigration' was not correct, as the restrictions on immigration had been enforced since May 1922; the figures spoke for themselves with 'Moslems 589,600, the Jews 83,800 and the Christians 73,000'. The Cabinet acknowledged that the Arab delegation was in London to agitate among politicians, and that many of these were also unhappy with the situation. On 13 March, Devonshire again reinforced the facts that no pledges were given to Arabs on Palestine and gave numbers that showed in the highest administration posts there were only three Jews out of thirty-six. On 27 July, Devonshire presented the outcome of a Committee[16] established to advise on the issues raised in the review by government and it concluded that to change course now would be detrimental to Britain's prestige and the handing back of the mandate to another power, which also would harm Britain. It criticised the Zionist organisation for some of its language and advocated that the Arabs be given a role in advising the Administration and so the situation continued with an attempt to involve Arabs more. On 27 October Devonshire had to report back[17] with disappointment that he had offered:

'1.Establishment of Legislative Council on which Arabs would have been represented by ten elected members;
2. Reconstruction of Advisory Council so as to secure effective Arab representation; and
3. Recognition of Arab Agency with functions similar to those assigned to Jewish Agency under terms of Mandate.
Towards all these proposals Arabs have adopted same attitude, viz., and refusal to co-operate.'

The Legislative Council elections were a disaster and boycotted by the Moslem leaders. A record of the meeting between the High Commissioner and the Moslem leaders to encourage them to participate demonstrates clearly their attitude:

'HAFTZ BEY TOUKAN said: Your Excellency, the Fifth Arab Congress, representing all sections of the Arab population of Palestine, has decided to reject the Constitution that was issued in London, about which the Arab population of Palestine was not asked for an expression, of an opinion, and the Arab nation has found it injurious to its interests, and has unanimously decided to reject and boycott the elections. We therefore do not think it necessary to enter into any detailed discussion on the subjects mentioned by your Excellency.

SIR HERBERT SAMUEL: I should like to add to what has been said, that if you, and those you represent, abstain from the elections now you must not complain afterwards if legislation is passed without consulting you and those whom you represent. An opportunity for consultation is offered to you now; if it is not taken, the responsibility for the facts of non-consultation in the future will rest with yourselves and not with the Government.'[18]

The government, Devonshire advised, had no choice. It had to continue to implement the policy of a Jewish Homeland in terms that it had defined and on 7 November, the go-ahead was given for the administration to proceed as it had been doing. On 25 January 1924, the High Commissioner in Palestine sent a report to the Cabinet[19] which was almost a complete copy, with a few alterations, of his report in December 1922, which in essence confirmed that a section of the Arab people still wanted to see an Arab Empire which would include Palestine. He again cautioned against the forces in Britain that wanted to cause agitation and in Palestine there was concern of further violence towards the Jewish population, such that the Commissioner needed more powers to deal with it.[20] The journey to a Jewish Homeland was still facing great opposition.

This journey, and everyone was aware of it, had one central element; immigration. The country needed the people and the finance that would come with it. This of course raised problems with the Arab community, the British and the Vatican. The Arab community feared that a large influx of immigrants would rob them of home and land, the British were concerned about public order and costs of related military involvement whilst the Vatican was concerned about the Holy Sites behind which was the traditional antipathy towards Jews. Chaim Weizmann and the Zionist organisation had their own concerns around the issue of uncontrolled and unplanned immigration and thus were astute enough to offer a solution. Weizmann wrote to the High Commissioner and suggested that the immigration needs were not in the millions but that 100,000 productive workers would be the number that would lead to the hoped for Jewish commonwealth. The journey to a Jewish Homeland was not an easy one and this was typified in the immigrants arriving in Palestine. Many had been the victims of Russian pogroms and had been driven of their property and stripped of most of their valuables. They had, like many refugees today, become the prey of traffickers with their journey to Palestine often in ill-equipped boats with little or no sanitation. This meant the health and cleanliness of the immigrants was poor and pathetic. Their arrival meant they were taken off the boats with reports that their smell caused many British soldiers to vomit, as they were unloaded. They were taken to bathhouses past Arab dock workers, who jeered at them. Stripped naked, searched for weapons, they were put through showers, disinfected and inoculated. Having endured a horrendous journey across continents and the sea, they found the great hope in their hearts for paradise was not immediately to be. Many had to spend nights in tents and make-shift accommodation until they received help from Zionist organisations. However, they were still overjoyed to be away from the persecution, torture and death of the countries from which they had fled. The Jewish National Fund needed land to house the new immigrants and despite many Arabs calling for land not to be sold to Jews, many of the same people were selling their land, including Musa Kazim al-Husseini, the Arab Mayor of Jerusalem; most of the land was agricultural.

On 25 August 1925, Field Marshall Lord Plummer became the new High Commissioner, a non-Jew. This gave encouragement to many Arabs, easing their resentment and with a reduction in Jewish immigration some extreme Arabs wanted to begin a violent resistant, but saner heads ruled, as any violence would alienate public opinion in Britain. They decided to try and influence the British government against a Jewish Homeland with delegations being sent to London to oppose the Zionist delegations that had already had great success there. Their efforts were not very successful with a conference they called being poorly attended and no leading figures in politics giving their support. In Palestine, there was an uneasy quiet with the continual vying for British support behind the scenes. An earthquake hit the region and although there were not many deaths, there was damage, which the international Zionist community responded to, sending aid. The lack of Arab success in London frustrated the more extreme elements within that community and Palestine was on course for bloody conflict – conflict that would eventually bring a withdrawal of the British.

Chapter Eleven

A Journey Through Terror

1 928 was a turning point in Palestine. The place was always a tinder-box with the least excuse a cause for exploding tempers. One such incident involved a simple bedroom modesty screen. On 23 September 1928, as Yom Kippur was approaching, a very sacred festival to the Jews, a screen was spotted against the Western Wall (other names used in Hebrew, *HaKotel HaMa'aravi* and commonly the Wailing Wall). The screen was part of the ceremony of the Jews to segregate the men and women worshippers. This was blown into a charge that it represented Zionism and the implementation of Balfour and that a synagogue would eventually be built there. Despite the assurances of the elderly Jewish beadle that it would be removed at the end of Yom Kippur, the British Constable, Duff, organised a violent heavy-handed attack and removed it. The following months saw hundreds of deaths. This was not the only issue that was fomenting violence as there was also the issue of names. Many local neighbourhoods had been given Arabic names; the Jews wanted them to be bi-lingual and the name Palestine itself became a controversy. This name, given by Romans, was offensive to many Jews and they wanted the name *Eretz Israel* (Land of Israel) to be restored and in classic British fudge, stamps were produced with Palestine E.I. This in turn provoked Arab anger. When a nation is established it has its own national anthem and flag and both these became an issue, with British representatives never knowing how to behave at public functions when they were played or raised. Even Encyclopaedia Britannia became involved, producing the Israel flag as the flag of Palestine.

Weizmann also had issues within the Zionist faction, with David Ben-Gurion on one side and Ze'ev Jabotinsky on the other. Ben-Gurion was born in Płońsk, then part of Russia, and was one of the major figures in the establishment of a Jewish State; he would go on to declare its independence and be its first Prime Minister. He was an astute politician and saw working with Britain as a means to achieve the aims of the Zionists. Jabotinsky was born in Odessa and established the *Betar*, a Jewish young radical group in Latvia. He had separated from the main Zionist movement and formed Union of Zionists Revisionists (*Hatzohar*). He was in a hurry and demanded a Jewish State immediately. The *Irgun Tzvai Leumi* (I.Z.L), a military arm, would emerge under his leadership. Once more, the British Commissioner was replaced and Sir John Chancellor took the hot seat in November 1928. He was totally inexperienced in Palestinian affairs and even suggested that the Zionists should purchase the Wailing Wall, not appreciating the sensitivity of the place. The inevitable happened with the Arab population objecting and calling conferences to protest. The Wall became a place of constant conflict with Jews being pelted with stones as they prayed. The incident was pushing both Jews and Arabs to the extremes. A procession of Jews to change the Ark and scrolls at the wall was considered as a possible flashpoint and the British wanted it cancelled. The Jewish authorities agreed, with many seeing it as weakness and others as sensible in the difficult environment. On 14 August 1929, the Jews called for a fast to recognise the destruction of the Temple and thousands gathered at the wall, with flags and speeches without any trouble. The Arab community then responded a few days later with a counter-demonstration to commemorate Muhammed's birthday. After Friday prayers that day, a number of Arab worshippers left the Mosque and entered the wall area to attack Jews and beat them, defacing sacred Torahs in the process. Young Jews gathered into groups to protect the people as many were stabbed in the attacks. Once more a small incident would create a bloodbath.

A young Jewish boy, Avraham Mizrahi, was playing with a football that rolled into an Arab family's vegetable patch. The attempt to retrieve it led to a young girl from the family refusing to hand it over and a fracas led to Mizrahi being hit by an iron bar and dying. That evening an Arab pedestrian was attacked and injured. An aide to the high commissioner had said the best result was if both died and troubled flared as a result, causing casualties and deaths. The journey was going to get rougher. Hebron on 23 August 1929 saw Arab villagers streaming into Jerusalem to pray at the Temple Mount, but many were armed with sticks and knives and the City was under huge tension. Gunshots were heard on the Temple Mount which sent fear through the Jewish community. An Arab preacher gave a nationalistic sermon calling on 'the Islamic faithful to fight against the Jews to the last drop of their blood'.

Worshippers then ran through the streets attacking Jews and property. The police force, mainly Arabs, and the very small British police were helpless and refused to fire on the mob as long as only Jews were being attacked – it was feared any attempt to deal with the Arab rioters would result in worse trouble. The aide to the High Commissioner considered this a wise decision. Some Jews with weapons in one area defended the population and a request to the British for help was initially ignored. As well as multiple casualties there were eight Jews and five Arabs killed. This would not be the end of the violence.

In Hebron the next day, another brutal event occurred when an Arab mob attacked homes. Raymond Cafferata a British police officer who was in Hebron gave testimony to the horror as he reported:

'an Arab in the act of cutting off a child's head with a sword. He had already hit him and was having another cut but on seeing me he tried to aim the stroke at me but missed: he was practically on the muzzle of my rifle. I shot him on the groin. Behind him was a Jewish woman smothered in blood and a man I recognised as a police constable, named Issa Sherrif from Jaffa ... He was standing over the woman with a dagger in his hand. He saw me and bolted into another room, shouting in Arabic, "your honour I am a policeman". I got into the room and shot him.'

In this incidence sixty-seven Jews and nine Arabs were killed and many other massacres were carried out in other places. The whole series of killings all stemmed from the fear and hatred the Arabs had about the Jewish religion, politics and in some cases envy over Jewish possessions. The good, in the midst of bloody hatred, was that many Arab families protected Jews, hiding them in their homes; otherwise the carnage would have been even greater. Before this current event of disturbances ended, 133 Jews and 116 Arabs had been killed.

The High Commissioner, now Sir John Chancellor, expressed his opinion that the Balfour Declaration was a blunder and by 1930 the Jewish Homeland was no closer as the British became more perplexed as to a solution. Ben-Gurion continued his progress towards a State enthusiastically, founding *Mapai* on 5 January 1930, a merger of the *Hapoel Hatzair* and *Ahdut HaAvoda* which came from the moderate, wing of the Marxist Zionist socialist *Poale Zion* he led. This party would play a major role in Israel's future. Hajj Amin al-Husseini, a Palestinian Arab nationalist and Muslim leader and Grand Mufti of Jerusalem, declared 16 May 1930 as 'Palestine Day' and called for a General Strike which lasted until October. This led to British intervention and the British issued yet another White Paper[1] on Palestine which in its opening stated the obvious:

'In a country such as Palestine, where the interests and aims of two sections of the community are at present diverse and in some respects conflicting, it is too much to expect that any declaration of policy will fully satisfy the aspirations of either party.'

Following the disturbances, the Paper gave a glimpse at frustration in government that, 'they have received little assistance from either side in healing the breach'. Ramsay MacDonald is quoted as confirming the mandate was 'an international obligation from which there can be no question of receding'. It has to be borne in mind that this included the Balfour Declaration. The government were under pressure from Zionists on one hand for a move to a Jewish State and the Arabs wanted a constitution that would give them control of Palestine. The Paper declares:

'It becomes, therefore, essential that at the outset His Majesty's Government should make it clear that they will not be moved, by any pressure or threats, from the path laid down in the Mandate, and from the pursuit of a policy which aims at promoting the interests of the inhabitants of Palestine, both Arabs and Jews, in a manner which shall be consistent with the obligations which the Mandate imposes.'

The White Paper pointed to 1922, when a full statement had been made on the situation and the Arabs would not cooperate with the government, but the Zionist organisation had written to confirm their acceptance of the British position and the paper confirmed the 1922 definition of a 'Jewish Homeland'. The thorny issue of immigration was addressed, confirming the right of Jews to immigrate but reminding everyone that immigration had to be at levels which the country could accomodate. The document criticises the Arab leaders who had rejected all the initiatives to involve them in positions to advise government and effect decisions in Palestine. The Jewish organisations were also criticised for only offering employment to Jews. The document did not appear to offer any real hope for advancement. Weizmann put pressure on the government and the Paper quietly disappeared and immigration was unaffected. One concession that he had gained was a written memo from Ramsay MacDonald that the way must be found to give the Zionists preference. Despite all Weizmann's work, he resigned from the presidency of the Zionist organisation and was replaced by Sokolow but the more aggressive Jabotinsky was determined to force change in policy. At the Zionist Congress in July 1931, he would seek to redirect the thrust of Zionism in Palestine. During the Congress, there were a great number of delegates who protested at Weizmann's policy towards the British, objecting to his full cooperation with them. Jabotinsky and the Revisionists were most strident and called on the organization to adopt a resolution with goals for the establishment of a Jewish majority and Jewish State in Palestine to include Transjordan. The Congress rejected this which led to Jabotinsky destroying his delegate's card and crying, 'This is not a Zionist congress!'

The High Commissioner was again changed in November 1931 with Arthur Wauchope taking the role. From a military background, he was very favourable to the Zionist cause and in his time immigration trebled and it would be said of him that 'the first four years of his term were the heyday of Zionist history in Palestine'. By 1933, the situation was on the surface peaceful with few incidents, but this belied an undercurrent that was growing towards violence on a great scale. In April, Allenby was in Jerusalem at a YMCA ceremony where a stone was engraved with words from his speech with his hope for the future:

'Here is a place whose atmosphere is peace, where political and religious jealousies can be forgotten and international unity can be fostered and developed'

Laudable as these thoughts were, the reality was different as Meinertzhagen wrote in his diary in March of that year, that he, 'would not live to see the actual establishment of the Jewish State'.[2] As a military man, he knew the reality that was Palestine and indeed he was right. The General Strike of 1930 sowed seeds that would grow into violence over the years and in October 1933, a demonstration by Arabs across the country brought clashes with police which flared up and by the end of the protests official figures gave 30 people dead and 200 injured, with one Arab account reading:

> 'Today Palestine became a battlefield ... Demonstrations everywhere, attacks on police and railway stations, hundreds of dead and wounded. The hospitals are overflowing and tempers are hot with anger'.

In 1935, the situation deteriorated when Muhammed Iz-al-Qassam arrived from Syria. He was an Imam and Islamic teacher who had called for a *jihad* against the Catholic Italians when they invaded Libya in 1911 and had joined the Turkish army in the First World War. He returned to Syria and fought as a guerrilla against the French and when he came to Palestine he was appointed as an Imam in Haifa and came into service under the Grand Mufti in Jerusalem travelling around the villages. There, he encouraged the Arab villagers to form terrorist groups to attack the British and the Jews which led to eruptions of violence with deaths and destruction of Jewish farms, and his sermons gave vent to the simmering hatred of both the British and Jews that had had been developing over the years. Al-Qassam took to the hills and conducted a guerrilla war from there.

He was eventually hunted down and killed in a gun battle with British forces, but the fire was lit and the Arab revolt spread. The guerrillas attacked the British forces and attempted assassinations of British officials and Jews and their leaders became the target as the drive for Arab national recognition took hold. Initially, it was mainly the British who were the object of the revolt. It spread and more and more, involving Jews, bringing pressure for Jews to retaliate with their own armed force. Ben-Gurion himself was pressed by the *Haganah* to allow them to act against the revolt. The *Haganah* had grown out of groups who had the role of protecting Jewish settlements since 1911. They were a defence force and had unofficially been helping the British in their dealing with the revolt; now they wanted to be allowed to take a more aggressive stance. Ben-Gurion demanded they refrain and told them he would resign if they refused as he was pursuing talks with Arab leaders and was looking for solutions, even the partition of Palestine into a Jewish and Arab area, believing that half a loaf was better than none. His restraint was not welcomed by another Jewish para-military group, the *Irgun Tsva'i-Leumi* (National Military Organization), also known as 'Irgun' by the British and its Hebrew acronym, '*Etzel*'. They had split from *Haganah* in 1931, seeking to give a more military response to Arab aggression. They saw no need for restraint and began a campaign of terrorism against Arabs with killings and bombings of Arab coffee-houses and market-places. The situation had become a bloody reign of terror from elements within both sides of the Palestinian divide. The British responded and on capturing *Etzel* terrorists, they too were subjected to the same brutal treatment as Arab terrorists. Tensions grew within the Jewish community and violent encounters took place between *Etzel* and *Haganah* members. Eventually, Ben-Gurion could no longer resist the pressure to restrain the *Haganah* and Special Operations Units were formed to find Arabs who had killed Jews and eliminate them but they also would target British soldiers and anyone collaborating with them. Blood was now on the hands of British, Arabs and Jews and many in all three communities were disgusted at the descent into this bloody morass.

In June 1936, a commission came to Palestine to carry out an inquiry under the chairmanship of William Robert Wellesley Peel, 1st Earl Peel, a former Secretary of State to India. Its terms of reference were:

'To ascertain the underlying causes of the disturbances along with enquiring into the manner in which the Mandate for Palestine is being implemented in relation to the obligations of the Mandatory towards the Arabs and the Jews respectively ... and to ascertain whether, upon a proper construction of the terms of the Mandate, either the Arabs or the Jews have any legitimate grievances on account of the way in which the Mandate has been or is being implemented.'[3]

It unremarkably stated that the reasons for the disturbances were, 'the desire of the Arabs for national independence and their hatred and fear of the establishment of the Jewish National Home'. This was not news to anyone familiar with Palestine. With a nod to the developments in Europe and Germany, Peel noted, 'The National Home is bent on forcing the pace of its development, not only because of the desire of the Jews to escape from Europe, but because of anxiety as to the future in Palestine'. The

Commission gave a hint of the government's real intention for it. 'The gulf between the races is thus already wide and will continue to widen if the present Mandate is maintained'. The British now wanted a way out of the mandate. Peel knew the problem was not resolvable under present policies, only palliatives: 'They cannot cure the trouble. The disease is so deep-rooted that in the Commissioners' firm conviction the only hope of a cure lies in a surgical operation'. Once more the partition of Palestine was the solution for Peel. The Arab community rejected the findings and the Zionists were in a quandary. The Arabs would not cede any land to Jews and the Jews in turn thought the idea of a Jewish State of some sort was a foothold into the Jewish Homeland that had been promised whilst others rejected the idea. Indeed, the whole project would have involved what today would be called 'ethnic cleansing' and would have repeated the despicable scenes of India's partitioning. Ultimately the Supreme Muslim Council rejected the plan as did the Zionists, over the area of land they would have been given. A new development was now being added to the Palestinian brew – one that would be terrifying in its consequences.

Chapter Twelve

The Rise of Hitler, War and A Journey to Death

'We want Hitler to be destroyed, but as long as he exists, we are interested in exploiting that for the good of Palestine.'

David Ben-Gurion, 1937

In 1896 in Berlin, Theodor Herzl noted, 'Everything tends, in fact, to one and the same conclusion, which is clearly enunciated in that classic Berlin phrase, '*Juden Raus!*' (Jews Out!)' He was also adamant, 'Oppression and persecution cannot exterminate us. No nation on earth has survived such struggles and sufferings as we have gone through'. These two statements would come together in the greatest ever onslaught against the Jewish people in Germany. Hitler would seek to remove the Jews, not only from Berlin, but from every continent on earth. He became the leader of a political movement that emerged; the National Socialist German Workers' Party, (*Nationalsozialistische Deutsche Arbeiterpartei* or NSDAP). In general, the Arab community tended to side with Hitler and men like al-Husseini sought him out to assist their cause in Palestine. Khalil al-Sakakini was an Orthodox Christian, born in Jerusalem, a teacher, poet and Arab pan-Nationalist. On the appointment of Samuel as High Commissioner, he had resigned because Samuel was a Jew. He hated Zionism because, in his opinion, 'it endeavours to build its independent existence on the ruins of others' and he had supported the Arab attacks on Jews even calling those involved 'heroes'. His hope was that Hitler would succeed and that a weakened post-war Britain would allow Palestine to be liberated from them. His son had carried out a poll in Palestine for the Americans (in 1941) and the results were very clear; 88% of Palestinian Arabs were pro-Germany and 9% pro-British. This reflected the views that were spreading throughout Palestine through men like al-Sakakini.

Arabs seeking out Hitler's help to prevent a Jewish State would be disappointed. As al-Sakakini wrote, 'Up until now we have received no help

from either Italy or Germany. All we have heard from them is fine words.'
They did not fully grasp Hitler's understanding of the Jewish State. He
believed:

> 'The Jewish State has never been delimited in space. It has been spread
> all over the world, without any frontiers whatsoever, and has always
> been constituted from the membership of one race exclusively. That
> is why the Jews have always formed a State within the State. ... That
> is why the Jewish State, which ought to be a vital organization to serve
> the purpose of preserving or increasing the race, has absolutely no
> territorial boundaries.'

He did not offer much help because his whole premise was that the Jews
should not exist anywhere. However, this did not prevent him from giving
his views of a Jewish State, if it ever existed:

> 'When the Zionists try to make the rest of the world believe that
> the new national consciousness of the Jews will be satisfied by the
> establishment of a Jewish State in Palestine, the Jews thereby adopt
> another means to dupe the simple-minded Gentile. They have not the
> slightest intention of building up a Jewish State in Palestine so as to live
> in it. What they really are aiming at is to establish a central organization
> for their international swindling and cheating. As a sovereign State, this
> cannot be controlled by any of the other States. Therefore it can serve
> as a refuge for swindlers who have been found out and at the same time
> a high-school for the training of other swindlers.'

He would go on to write that he would 'rather wipe out the Jewish State
which is now in existence', meaning Jews wherever they existed. With
Hitler there was no place on earth that he would allow Jews to be beyond
his reach; his megalomaniacal drive for world domination had built within
it this principle, such was his hatred for the Jews. There was a paradox in
the Nazi position as was seen in the negotiations between Nazis and Zionists
in Germany in the very early days. The Haavara Agreement of 25 August
1933 was agreed between the Nazis and Jewish groups, including the Jewish
Agency to help facilitate the immigration of Jews to Palestine. It allowed the

Jewish immigrants to gain control of some of their assets and get them to Palestine, using *Hanotea*, a citrus fruit company in Haifa, and allowed them to overcome British bans on immigration under a special visa arrangement. This allowed the Nazis 'to get rid of their Jews' and the Zionist groups in Palestine to get people and finance into the country. The arrangement was not popular with all Zionists such as the Revisionists and Jabotinsky who wanted a boycott of the fascist regime. Chaim Arlosoroff, a key figure in Ben-Gurion's Mapai Party and involved in the negotiations, was assassinated in June 1933, with good evidence that Jabotinsky's party was behind it, one of his men being identified by the victim's wife. Although arrested he was released and the crime remained 'unsolved'. Many, who wish to attack this action by the Jews in Germany, would claim it was 'collaboration' with the Nazis which is to distort the truth. The issue was one of rescue of those who would perish if not taken out of Nazi hands. The Nazis would have eventually taken all the finances of the Jews anyway and here it was expedient to use it for the good of the Jewish people.

Hitler's actions to deal with Jews continued with legislation on 7 April 1933, when laws were enacted to prevent anyone of 'non-Aryan descent' allowed into public service. This at a stroke removed thousands of Jews from any source of livelihood and alongside this the Nazi agitation provoking the boycott of Jewish business had a major effect on the Jews of Germany. The legal implications of the Nazi laws were taken up by a considerable number of non-government businesses, who also applied the rules in their own spheres of influence, again adding to the problems for Jews. The measures created 60,000 Jews who now sought to escape the persecution and move elsewhere. In Britain more than 3,000 Jews had arrived, many 'destitute' and seeking help and the government responded in a typical bureaucratic way and set up a committee to deal with it.[1] The ambassador from Berlin sent the Cabinet a telegram informing them of the plight of the German Jews, in which he painted a picture of successful Jews as the reason it was 'natural' for the persecution of the Jews by the Nazis.[2] This was shared with the High Commissioner in Palestine, but the Cabinet decided not to make it public, 'for the sake of the Jews in Berlin'.[3] At this stage, the full impact of how the Nazis would progress and their plan for wider Europe were not yet understood and for many refugees Palestine was not yet their first thought. This movement of Jews away from Germany suited Hitler as he had written in *Mein Kampf* that 'No Jew, therefore, may be a member of the nation'. The actions against Jews were not just in words and between January 1929 and September 1932, fifty synagogues had been vandalised with 128 Jewish cemeteries desecrated and many attacks on Jews in the streets, especially when entering or leaving synagogues.

Many ordinary Germans, at first neutral, were now being caught up in the constant slogan chanting, bill posting, leafleting and flag waving against the Jews. The *Protocols of The Elders of Zion*, was widely distributed to fan the flames of hate. This book had its origins in the French Revolution, being composed by Hermann Goedsche, a German anti-Semite who worked for the Prussian secret police. *The Times* over 16-18 August 1921 had run a full article detailing the history of the book showing it to be a forgery and discrediting it. The Nazi election's 'on 12 November 1933, in which opposition parties were banned, (98% in their favour – in a contested election in March that year they received less than 50%) was proclaimed as a great victory. The election however, increased the pressure on Jews as it now gave 'legitimacy' to the Nazis and their approval of anti-Jewish actions brought even greater acts of intimidation and murder against the Jewish people. Goering, the Minister of the Interior, said, 'I refuse to turn police into a guard for Jewish stores ... The nation is aroused. For years past we told the people: 'You can settle accounts with the traitors'. We stand by our word'. The slogan '*Kauft nicht beim Juden*' (Don't buy from the Jew) became the cry throughout main German cities and Nazi Storm Troopers were placed outside Jewish premises with placards, '*Deutsche kaufen nicht aus Jüdischen Geschäften*' (Germans don't buy from Jewish Shops). The presence of these troops with their placards terrified the Jewish population. The boycotts were eventually framed in official Nazi policy, when Julian Streicher, the editor of *Der Sturmer* and an extreme anti-Semite, who had always argued for it, became chair of the party's Boycott Committee. Hitler himself would declare that the boycott was necessary and Goebbels, Propaganda Minister, concerned about reports from abroad, issued a formal statement to the foreign press stating that 'the boycott will be carried out, by the organisations concerned, with a most rigid discipline and without violation of any law. Nobody will be physically endangered by this boycott'. This was a lie. 15 September 1935 saw one of the greatest anti-Semitic laws of Nazi Germany brought to the Statute Book – the Nuremberg Laws for the

Protection of German Blood and German Honour. In November the British Cabinet agonised over whether there should be a boycott of the Olympic games over the Jewish persecutions but decided it was better to 'keep out of it', again 'for the sake of the Jews'.[4] There was no question of the direction that was being taken; the Jewish people were beginning to see the writing on the wall; not only was there a need to escape Germany but more and more a Jewish Homeland was becoming a necessity.

By March 7 1936 Hitler had moved into the Rhineland defying the Treaty of Versailles. In Palestine, although initially reluctant, the Grand Mufti decided to back the Arab revolt and a General Strike was called in April 1936. The situation was extremely dangerous and the British were searching for military and political solutions. The military response was brutal with arrests, torture and deaths of many Arabs. The Nazis' activities in Germany resulted in many joining refugees from Russia, Poland and Europe that saw 60,000 Jews immigrating into Palestine that year. They were coming into a very difficult situation. The bloody consequences of the Arab revolt were evident, a British soldier describing the aftermath of an attack on Jews in Tiberius, wrote, 'They had left behind one of the worst sights I have ever saw in my life. The place is strewn with the bodies of men, women and children. The naked bodies of the women exposed the evidence that the knives had been used in the most ghastly way'. By 9 May of that year Italians had taken control of Ethiopia and the clouds of war hung heavily over the whole of Europe. The British focus was beginning to shift accordingly. In 1937 Britain poured more troops into Palestine and instituted military courts to deal with the violence. In September Wauchope had been worn out without much success and William Battershill took charge on a temporary basis. Meanwhile Hitler was considering his options for war at the Hossbach Conference, where the military reviewed the world and various scenarios that might develop. The Zionists also looked at Hitler and tried to understand his plans so that they themselves might develop a strategy to support Britain and at the same time gain advantages towards the Jewish Homeland. Indeed, the British government also realised that they were essential to them in the fight against the Arab revolt and accepted that they and Zionists were standing together against a common enemy. So began joint enterprises between the British and para-military Jewish forces not only against Arabs but the Agency's leaders also promised they would attempt to prevent attacks by Etzel against Arab civilians. The Jewish Agency was heavily involved in controlling events and their leaders recognised that this was good preparations for a future army in the Jewish State.

In 1938 Hitler once more flaunted his power and marched into Austria breaking the Versailles Treaty without any interference from the allies. The Jews of Germany and Austria were becoming more alarmed. There was a need to provide a strong support for the Jewish plight which was becoming obvious to anyone who wanted to see. Yet the British government was still in a state of paralysis towards Hitler. Britain also wanted to close the doors to Jewish immigration into Palestine and another Commission led by Sir John Woodhead was still offering partition as a solution as he laid out in great detail the plans.[5] A new permanent High Commissioner arrived, Harold MacMichael, a civil servant who had come from his post as Governor of Tanganyika. The concerns of the officials in Jerusalem and Amman about the German situation were now being expressed to London.[6] They believed that if there was conflict in Europe the Arabs would do all they could to embarrass the British in Palestine. There was even the suggestion that the Arabs should be given an independent State 'to keep them friendly' in the hope that they would not go against Britain in the next war. With the dark storms gathering over Europe and the reign of terror in Palestine, the British did what they always did, when they did not know what else to do in Palestine: they called a conference in London - one that they knew would achieve nothing. Even agreeing who was to be invited was fraught with difficulty, with Britain objecting that five Arab 'extremists' should be reconsidered and called on king Ibn Saud of Saudi Arabia to intervene to get a better balance of Arab views.[7] Ben-Gurion noted that, 'The Arabs see themselves as victors, and they really have won – first they practice terror and then they are invited to negotiate with the government', a lesson that would have a bitter outcome in later days. For the Zionists, they asked the government to allow 20,00 adults and 10,000 child refugees to enter Palestine, otherwise they would withdraw, but the government refused to do anything until after the conference discussed immigration, rightly noting that the Zionists would not carry out their threat.[8]

Whilst the manoeuvring around the conference was raging Prime Minister Chamberlain had much larger concerns and went off to meet Hitler in September 1938. This resulted in the Munich Agreement, in which

Chamberlain was completely deceived by Hitler and returned to England to assure the world that there would be 'peace for our time', convinced that there would be no war and that Hitler would not make any further moves into other territory. He would be disappointed – on 15 October, German troops occupied the Sudetenland and the Czech government resigned. Germany also began to demonstrate that its anti-Jewish policy was continuing. On 27 October 1938, Reinhard Heydrich, second-in-command of the SS, expelled about 17,000 Jews of Polish origin, including over 2,000 children. The appeasement of Hitler allowed continued assaults on the Jews of Germany and between November 9 and 10 1938, Kristallnacht saw Jewish homes, hospitals, synagogues and schools attacked and destroyed and over 100 Jews killed. Many disappeared and were tortured and murdered in subsequent days. 25,000 Jewish men were taken and sent to Dachau, Buchenwald and Sachsenhausen concentration camps; many of them were tortured and killed by the SS. On January 30, 1939, Hitler made clear threats to the Jews during a Reichstag speech – the world now knew, if it cared, that the Jews were in grave danger and needed a place of safety.

With this horror as a background, the London Conference started on 7 February 1939 and the Cabinet minutes clearly show that they were ready to set proposals and adjust them to any Arab objections, the matter was clearly an attempt to get the Arabs on the side of the British.[9] However, the next day the Cabinet was told that there were difficulties with the Arab delegation as they could not agree a unity within their group and no progress had been made with them.[10] By 22 February, the reports to the Cabinet[1] said that the Jewish delegation 'had shown themselves ready to make quite considerable concessions' whilst on the Arab side 'discussions had been very difficult'. They had made three demands: 'recognition of an independent Arab Palestine State, complete stoppage of all immigration, complete stoppage of land sales to Jews', the first being the most important. Neighbouring Arab states present at the talks did not want Britain to leave Palestine for at least twenty years. There was confusion as to whether the demand was for an Arab or Palestinian State; the consensus was the latter. It was remarkable that the discussion on stopping immigration took no regard of the events in Europe and German actions and the mass displacement of Jews. The question of the State was clarified[12] and it was agreed that what was being asked was an Arab State with an Arab majority.

This was the Cabinet meeting when the British government killed the Balfour agreement and betrayed the Jewish people. The decisions led to a plan on an independent State that would have an Arab majority. Despite caution that the State should only come into being with an agreed British presence remaining to safeguard the minority Jews, the Cabinet ploughed on with its intentions. Furthermore it was argued that if an independent State was declared with British oversight, experienced had showed that at some point the State would divide from Britain, with or without its agreement. The sentiment was agreed that a, 'great difference to the Moslem world if we were able to make a public declaration that our ultimate goal was an Independent Palestine State' and the need to keep the Arabs happy. The feeling was that the Jews were in a weak position and they could be encouraged to believe that they would start as a minority but immigration would make them the majority. This was cynical as at the same time they agreed to restrict immigration to very small numbers. Once more the effect of Nazi aggression was ignored. On 2 March 1939, another Cabinet meeting[13] heard that there was a dispute over promises given in 1915 that the Arabs could have an Independent State. The government had to review past statements to argue that this was not so. Sir Maurice Bunsen in July 1915 had confirmed no such commitment was given and McMahon, who had written the original letter, later confirmed explicitly that no such promise was made:

'12th March, 1922

With reference to our conversation on Friday (10th) I write you these few lines to place on record the fact that in my letter of the 25th October, 1915, to the Sherif of Mecca, it was my intention to exclude Palestine from independent Arabia, and I hoped that I had so worded the letter as to make this sufficiently clear for all practical purposes. My reasons for restricting myself to specific mention of Damascus, Hama, Horns and Aleppo in that connection in my letter were (1) that these were places to which the Arabs attached vital importance, and (2) that there was no place I could think of at the time of sufficient importance for purposes of definition further south of the above. It was as fully my intention to exclude Palestine as it was to exclude the more northern coastal tracts of Syria. I did not make use of the Jordan to define the limits of the southern area because I thought it might possibly be considered desirable at some later stage of negotiations to endeavour to find some more suitable frontier line east of the Jordan and between that river and the Hejaz Railway. At that moment, moreover, any detailed definitions did not seem called for. I may mention that I have no recollection of ever hearing anything from the Sherif of Mecca, by letter or message, to make me suppose that he did not also understand Palestine to be excluded from independent Arabia. I trust that I have made my intention clear.

Sir H. McMahon'[14]

There had also been a leak from the Conference in Egypt, which had threatened to derail the talks and had caused bombings in Palestine. However, the belief was that the talks would continue and the proposed policy on an independent State should be pursued. By March 8 the Cabinet[15] now understood the talks were moving to deadlock and that whilst constitutional items might reach agreement there was still no agreement on immigration. For the first time, explicit mention was made of the plight of Jews in Germany and limits of around 20,000 immigrants per year might be made acceptable to the Arabs for five years but after that they wanted a veto on any further immigration which the Zionists rejected. They themselves were in dispute with one another over the proposals and one member of the Cabinet rightly predicted negative reactions from the Jewish population in the USA as well as violence in Palestine. It was agreed that a White Paper be produced which apparently did not seem to matter what the Conference finally did or did not agree – the British wanted out of Palestine.

On March 15 the final feedback to the Cabinet[16] was not positive, whilst the Jewish delegation had moved on, accepting a Palestine State, they had insisted it must be Federal and that they should be allowed to control immigration into those areas. There were also extreme divisions on land transfers which would restrict the places for immigrants to settle. The Arabs of course did not agree. Furthermore because of the lack of progress the Jewish delegation had become 'embittered' because the Arabs appeared to be given dominance in the proposals that would mean the realisation of a Jewish Home would be betrayed. Weizmann had given an ominous warning that the British proposals were 'a betrayal of the Jews, and they would result in worse bloodshed in Palestine than ever before', the responsibility for this he said rested on British shoulders. For the Arabs it was reported that there had been a lot of agreement but on a few points, despite all the concessions made, they were unhappy and would probably reject the proposals. The intention was therefore to proceed unilaterally with a White Paper if the parties would not agree. Both delegations would eventually reject the proposals of the British.

On the same day the reality of Chamberlain's appeasement policy became home to roost – Germany took control of Czechoslovakia and this despite concessions the Czech government made to appease Hitler, by banning the Communist Party and suspending all Jewish teachers in ethnic-German majority schools. The invasion had always been Hitler's plan even whilst talking to Chamberlain who had stated in considering Palestine's future, 'If we must offend one side, let us offend the Jews rather than the Arabs'.[17] This was in effect done and on 26 April, when the Cabinet was informed[18] that the consideration of sending Jewish immigrants to British Guiana rather than Palestine had been discussed but had ran into difficulties with the colony's government. It was also told that because of Egyptian pressure the word 'Federal' was being dropped from the White Paper, which would be shown to the Egyptians, Saudis and Iraqis first for their approval and then it would be shown to the two sides in Palestine. It was recognised that violence was likely in Palestine and therefore great concern was expressed that the White Paper should be delayed or postponed indefinitely. A decision on the matter was postponed until May and then the Cabinet agreed[19] in principle all that had already been discussed with a few more concessions to the Arab lobby in order to keep the surrounding Arab states on board. The Jews were hardly referred to – the matter appeared to be a *fait accompli*.

The Nazis signed a 'Pact of Steel' with Italy on May 22, which had the potential of expanding Hitler's wish to pursue Jews wherever he could find them. German appointed Reich Protector, Konstantin von Neurath, a German diplomat, issued a long list of anti-Jewish orders in Czechoslovakia on 21 June 1939. They were the same as those in Germany, designed to destroy the economic viability of the Jewish population and confiscate all Jewish property. The continued drumbeats of war were echoing throughout Europe and Polish and Romanian Jews were becoming concerned and making plans to leave their countries. On 19 July, the Cabinet were informed[20] that the United Nations Permanent Mandates Committee was unhappy with the proposed White Paper as it broke the mandate the British had been given. This, if followed through, would have been a severe blow to Britain after all its efforts to placate the Arab peoples and it was to be challenged by a reply and also by diplomatic lobbying of the dissenting countries.

The issue of immigration in Palestine was also a problem, with British patrols stopping illegals from Germany, Romania, Hungary and Poland, along with others who had destroyed their papers. These could not be returned to their own countries and a solution was needed urgently as the situation was inflaming Arab opinion that Britain was reneging on its commitments. The idea of concentrating them in 'camps' and preventing them entering Palestine was floated and was referred to the government's Palestine Committee. The full impact of events that were pressing the Jews into such desperation was not considered. The potential for further Nazi aggression against the Jews was seen on 23 August, when the Nazis signed a pact with the Soviets. This sent waves of anxiety across British minds and on 25 August, Britain signed a Mutual Assistance Treaty that guaranteed Poland's borders. This was a foolish pact as Britain was never fully ready for a full-scale war with Germany. The realisation was that Hitler would invade Poland and so on 31 August, the British fleet was mobilised and civilians were evacuated from London. On 1 September, the Nazis invaded Poland and by 3 September, Britain, France, Australia and New Zealand declared war on Germany. This was one of the most serious situations for the Jewish people as Poland would become the major country where Jews would be shipped to from Nazi conquered countries; the Lublin Plan. Indeed, in October, the first Czech Jews were deported to concentration camps in Poland and by 1942, seventy-five percent of Czechoslovakian Jews had been deported. The majority of them would perish.

Despite the events that were happening Britain still proceeded to issue its White Paper on Palestine which appeared on 9 November.[21] It was basically all that had been previously discussed and stated on Palestine, 'It should be a State in which the two peoples in Palestine, Arabs and Jews, share authority in government in such a way that the essential interests of each are shared'. The Zionist 'Federal' did not appear and the British intention to rid itself of the mandate and withdraw was made clear:

'The objective of His Majesty's Government is the establishment within 10 years of an independent Palestine State in such treaty relations with the United Kingdom as will provide satisfactorily for the commercial and strategic requirements of both countries in the future. The proposal for the establishment of the independent State would involve consultation with the Council of the League of Nations with a view to the termination of the Mandate.'

It ended with a, no doubt sincerely meant, pious plea:

'Each community has much to contribute to the welfare of their common land, and each must earnestly desire peace in which to assist in increasing the well-being of the whole people of the country. The responsibility which falls on them, no less than upon His Majesty's Government, to cooperate together to ensure peace is all the more solemn because their country is revered by many millions of Moslems, Jews and Christians throughout the world who pray for peace in Palestine and for the happiness of her people.'

By December the cabinet was told that there was no way any constitutional change could proceed at that time and that land sales and immigration was being dealt with despite criticism from America. The naïve statement that there would be no problem with immigration was unbelievable in the maelstrom that was the Second World War which was displacing masses of people including a great number of Jews fleeing the Nazi tide.

In Palestine the White paper did not go down well with the Jewish community. Etzel was carrying out bombings and attacks against Arab civilians, there were demonstration and protests, often violently put down. A lengthy discussion by the Cabinet on a memorandum from the High Commissioner,[22] showed Britain's difficulties in dealing with Jewish armed groups. They had to consider upsetting the Arabs, inflaming Jewish resistance and hampering the war effort, with a military who wanted heavy handed action and a government who wanted a middle road – it was the latter who won out. The war against Hitler took priority and the military proceeded with caution but still did uncover caches of arms and munitions, often hidden in homes and stations of Jewish police officers.[23] Discussions in London, far away from the reality of Palestine, did not deter Ben-Gurion who did not abide with the immigration rules and conducted an 'immigration rebellion'. Both the needs of the Jewish hopes for Palestine and the European madness, necessitated allowing fleeing Jews into the country. He was adamant in his actions, 'We will bring thousands of young people from Germany, Austria and other countries and confront the English with the necessity of either shooting the refugees or sending them back'. Indeed the High Commissioner told the Cabinet[24] that an agreement to let in 25,000 in the year could not be certain to be adhered to as illegal immigration was adding to the numbers entering. The British also had the issue of land sales to deal with as they wanted them tightly controlled but land was necessary for incoming immigrants and the reality on the ground was that Arabs were still willing to sell land to Jews. When they decided to try and implement a policy on the matter, Weizmann sent an urgent telegram to Churchill, who was then First Lord of the Admiralty, and advised him to stop the policy as it would cause difficulties with both Arabs and Jews.[25] The Arab revolt was also coming to an end in late 1939 as the contentment with British plans was understood. There was the usual dispute about figures as if that was the most important point of the tragedy that should have been avoided. According to official British figures the army and police killed more than 2,000 Arabs in actions, 108 were hanged, and 961 died in gang and terrorist related activity. Arab sources insisted that 5,032 deaths had occurred, 3,832 who had been killed by the British with 1,200 killed in other acts of terrorism. The figures were horrific, but they would be dwarfed by events under the jackboots of Hitler's troops. In 1940, the notorious Auschwitz concentration camp was opened – this was the German's most industrialised killing centre and in Poland the Warsaw ghetto was walled in with 400,000 Jews now contained, the Nazis were now set on a course of extermination of Jews.

The outbreak of war had seen Britain turn Palestine into a giant manufacturing plant for war materials and thus helping the very high unemployment figures reduce. Chamberlain had given the nod to Ben-Gurion that the White Paper would never last and he believed that that was true and therefore he decided to support the British in their war. The Zionists believed that the ending of the war and the realisation of its effect on the Jewish people would result in a Jewish State. Winston Churchill remained a great friend to the Zionist cause and he was on the verge of becoming Prime

Minister. The *Haganah* continued their military training and when arrested were tried and received punitive sentences but these were revoked by Field Marshall Ironside, Chief of the Imperial General Staff, who thought them ridiculous. Indeed, they were allowed to build up a special elite force, the Palmach, in full cooperation with the British. 134,000 Jews wanted to join the British army with 30,000 finally enlisting. Etzel stopped its campaign of terror and some went to support the British operations overseas. Palestine was bombed from the air in June 1940 and the advance of Hitler seemed to threaten Egypt, which in turn could mean the occupation of Palestine by the Nazis. The action at El Alamein by the British stopped that advance. An Etzel leader, Avraham Stern, refused to accept the decision of the military groups to support the British and in September 1940 formed *Lehi* (Hebrew acronym for 'Fighters for the Freedom of Israel'), which was given the nickname the Stern Gang. This group would carry out attacks and conduct a propaganda campaign against the British. Despite this fly in the ointment, in general things were such that Britain was reasonably content with the situation. The Arab revolt had ended, and many thousands of Jews were in the army, cooperating in the fight against the Nazis. However, the gathering of black clouds was beginning over the country and once more terror would stalk its streets and even spread to England itself.

Chapter Thirteen

Home At Last

" Israel was not created in order to disappear – Israel will endure and flourish. It is the child of hope and the home of the brave. It can neither be broken by adversity nor demoralized by success. It carries the shield of democracy and it honors the sword of freedom."[1]

Despite all this collaboration with the British, things were still deteriorating. Etzel had decided to renew its campaign under Menachem Begin, who was born in Poland and had served in the Free Polish Army as well as being an interpreter in the British army. He was much later to become both a Prime Minister of the new Jewish State and a co-recipient of the Nobel Peace Prize. He could not trust the British as he had seen the betrayal of the British too often, had watched their handling of India and Ireland and had seen the Arab terrorism squeeze concessions out of them. The only way to achieve a Jewish State, he believed, was to drive the British out and take it from them. Thousands of Jews were escaping from Europe and on 25 November 1940 the Cabinet were informed that a ship named the *Patria* was to be diverted to a camp in Mauritius (in line with British policy on illegal immigration) but it had sunk after an explosion. Of 1835 illegal immigrants and 37 crew, 1,450 survivors[2] had been accounted for and an enquiry was being carried out. The facts were that three ships of immigrants sailing from Romania after being released by the Nazis were met at the docks by the British who were determined they would not enter Palestine. The British High Commissioner for Palestine, Sir Harold MacMichael, issued a deportation order on 20 November and the immigrants were put on the *Patria*.

The *Haganah* were also determined that the ship should not leave Haifa and placed a bomb to disable it. Their calculations as to the strength of the bomb and its placement were a disaster and the ship sank with the loss of life. The British knew what had happened, but the true picture did not emerge until many years later – the incident help to solidify anti-British feeling. The British Cabinet agreed that as a humanitarian gesture the survivors should be allowed to remain in Palestine but that would be the only exception; everyone else who were caught would be sent to the internment camp in Mauritius.[3] Cabinet after Cabinet meeting continued to agonise in London and there is no doubt that Churchill and his ministers had concerns for the plight of the Jews and were wrestling with this alongside the wider problem of Hitler and his aggression. Churchill had said on 19 May 1941, in a secret memorandum, he wrote of his hope for the establishment after the war of a 'Jewish State of Western Palestine' with not only the fullest rights for immigration and development, but also with provision 'for expansion in the desert regions to the southwards' which they would gradually reclaim. However, the urgency of safety for Jewish people was reinforced when Germany invaded Russia in 1941 and formed the death squads know as *Einsatzgruppen*. These squads followed advancing German troops and hunted down Jewish people and executed them (they had also worked in Poland earlier). Their savagery was staggering, with 33,771 Jews killed in two days (*Babi Yar*) and about 25,000 killed in another two days (*Rumbula*), by the end of the war these squads shot and killed more than 2 million people, 1.3 million of them Jews. At Chelmno in Poland, a death camp was set up to systematically kill Jews and reinforced once and for all their intentions. The Jews were literally marked for humiliation and killing, being made to wear a yellow star by the Nazis. The result of these actions was the continued illegal immigration of many Jews fleeing the murderous flames of Europe who went to sea in unworthy boats; many drowned as these vessels sank on the high seas.

On 20 January 1942, the Nazis called a conference at Wannsee. Here, the senior government officials of Nazi Germany and Schutzstaffel leaders, coldly sat around a table and agreed the industrialisation of the slaughter of the Jews. The effects of the decision had already begun to be implemented even before the conference; it was the Nazi bureaucratic mind that needed to have a formal process to follow and to make their deadly task more efficient. It is no wonder that those Jews, still able to, were desperate to get to safety. That is why on 24 February 1942, 800 Jews set sail from Romania and headed for Palestine in the *Struma*, a boat that was un-seaworthy' desperate people do desperate things. The vessel broke down many times and eventually was towed into Istanbul where the authorities would not allow her passengers to disembark. The British and the Turks disputed over what should happen with the British insisting she should not be allowed to continue to Palestine in line with the 1939 White Paper immigration policy. The result was that the ship was towed out to sea despite her condition and was eventually destroyed by a torpedo, initially thought to be from a German submarine; many years later it was suggested the submarine was Russian.

The detail of the submarine was irrelevant, and the fact was that nearly 800 Jews, men, women and children perished because of British policy in Palestine. This indeed was the conclusion of many politicians back in Britain and it is important to look at the matter closely as it was a point that deepened the determination for armed resistance in Palestine and the determination for a Jewish State, that even British officials were voicing. Of course, the government in Britain could not be seen as callous and Harold McMillan gave their view,[4] 'His Majesty's Government greatly deplore the tragic loss of life which occurred in this disaster', but they could not 'give any guarantee, nor can they be party to any measures which would undermine the existing policy regarding illegal immigration into Palestine'. Lord Wedgewood was blunt in the House of Lords:[5]

'My Lords, may I ask one supplementary question? When all hope was lost, the Jewish garrison at Masaba, rather than hand their wives and children over to the Romans, slew them all and fell on their swords. About a year ago, a ship similar to the "*Struma*" was refused permission to land those on board in Palestine, and blew up in Haifa harbour, when over a hundred were drowned. May I ask the noble Lord whether he is not as sure as I am that the bomb which destroyed the "*Struma*" was the last hope of the unfortunate refugees to save them from being handed back to Hitler? And may I ask him whether he does not think that the blood of these people is on our hands?'

Asked in a later written question,[6] 'whether he has instructed the Palestine Administration in any further case of Jewish refugees similar to that of the *Struma*, that entry into Palestine to Jewish victims of Nazi persecution will not be refused?', MacMillan answered he had 'nothing to add'. The tirade against the government continued when Sir Geoffrey Mander pointedly asked him[7] on another occasion, 'Does not my Hon. Friend think it was a very cruel thing that these persons should be sent to almost certain torture and death without any alternative arrangements being made, and could not anything have been done for the children in the six weeks that were available?' Again, he had 'nothing to add'. Samuel Silverman highlighted the issue of fairness in treating Arabs and Jews,[8] 'Will the hon. Gentleman include in the inquiry the question of how the Palestinian Administration reconciles its refusal to admit these refugees with the ease with which it has admitted into Palestine the friends and relatives of the Mufti, who have acted in opposition to this country?' No answer was given at this time, but the matter was later dealt with in a House of Lords debate when it was explained that criminal elements connected with the Mufti had been admitted but had been kept under scrutiny by the security forces. Lord Wedgewood later that year in a debate on Palestine was passionate,[9] 'I hope yet to live to see those who sent the *Struma* cargo back to the Nazis hung as high as Haman cheek by jowl with their prototype and Führer, Adolf Hitler'.

On 10 March, Lord Davies tabled a motion in the House of Lords[10] which raised important questions about Britain in Palestine:

'We all know the facts with regard to the loss of the *Struma*. Here were a lot of refugees fleeing from the Nazi tyranny in Rumania and in other Balkan countries, men, women and children who otherwise would have found themselves in concentration camps subject to all the tortures and sufferings which they would have had to undergo in those camps'.

He placed the responsibility for the refusal to admit the refugees on:

'the Palestinian authorities, who, I suppose, had received their instructions from Whitehall, to allow these unfortunate refugees, flying from the Nazi terrors, to enter into Palestine and join their co-nationals in that country ... It is difficult to imagine where they could have found any refuge or asylum other than in Palestine ... we have never recognized, so far as I am aware, the services which Jews have already rendered on all fronts in the Middle East. If you go to their [the government's] Commanders you will hear lots of praise of the Jews, but when it comes to reporting it in the Press or to extending any official recognition, not a word has been said or published ... The whole thing has a Nazi smell about it'.

He reminded the Lords:

'This pledge (Balfour) of a home of refuge, of an asylum, was not made to the Jews in Palestine but to the Jews outside Palestine, to that vast, unhappy mass of scattered, persecuted, wandering Jews whose intense, unchanging, unconquerable desire has been for a National Home ... another declaration, which was made in November of last year, when General Smuts said: The case for the Balfour Declaration has become overwhelmingly stronger. Instead of the horror of new ghettos in the twentieth century, let us carry out the promise and open up the National Home. The case has become one not merely of promises and International Law, but for the conscience of mankind. We dare not fold our hands without insulting the human spirit itself. That, I think, goes to the root of the matter. This is not merely a question of expediency; this is really a moral question. Since Hitler has for years past made the Jews the target of his persecution and of his outbursts of hate, I feel that anyone who refuses to accept the challenge is playing a double-faced game and is injuring the cause for which we are fighting. I do not believe that there can be any neutrality in this matter, and I believe that the whole attitude of the administration in Palestine has been in complete contradiction of our declared war aims, the rescue from oppression of all the oppressed peoples of the world'.

Lord Wedgewood added another sobering fact:

'I should like to say a ward on which all of us will agree. Dr. Weizmann has long been the leader of the Zionist Movement, and I have known him for twenty-five years. He has done a great work for the Jewish people. The other day one of our bombers did not return, and Dr. Weizmann's son is dead. I think that we ought to say a word of tribute and sympathy to Dr. Weizmann now that we are discussing a question which relates to Palestine. I think that the whole gist of the speech of

my noble friend Lord Davies points to one self-evident truth, which is
that the Administration in Palestine is Anti-Semitic.'

The truth was that there were those who held anti-Semitic views in the
administration in Palestine, but there were also a number who did support
the Jewish aspirations and could never be classed as anti-Semitic. The
problem was that the government policy was in a mess trying to reconcile two
irreconcilable ambitions; an Arab Independent State and an Independent
Jewish State. They had granted their support and assistance to establish a
number of Arab independent States in the Middle East and had intentions
for another one in Transjordan. If they had taken decisive action and
grasped the nettle when Balfour made his Declaration, the whole Middle
East situation may have been different, whereas now the crisis of Hitler's
aggression made a Jewish Independent State inevitable. The British would
now have to endure a rough passage until it was achieved.

The onslaught from the Nazis against the Jews continued with more
death camps being established at Belzec, Sobibor, and Treblinka, with mass
deportations happening all across Nazi-occupied Europe, and the whole
world knew it was happening. On 18 October 1942, Oscar Chapman, the
Assistant Secretary of the USA Department of the Interior, called a meeting
in Washington, to look at ways help could be given to the Jews from all
countries including the UN.[11] On 11 June 1943, Himmler ordered the
liquidation of all Jewish ghettos in Poland, realising the end was drawing
close for the Nazis. In Warsaw, a Jewish revolt had demonstrated that the
Jewish people were no longer prepared to passively accept their treatment
at the hands of the Nazis and that violent spirit was seeping into Palestine.
Avraham Stern was caught and killed by British police officers in suspicious
circumstances as the Stern Gang continued its actions against British targets
through smaller groups that splintered from the main group. Menachem
Begin officially declared war against Britain and published his vision of an
even greater Jewish State that would also take in Transjordan. Attempts
by Lehi to assassinate the High Commissioner failed, whilst Lord Moyne
was murdered by them in Egypt which caused Winston Churchill great
problems in supporting the Zionist cause. The assassination also led to
Haganah cooperating with the British to track down the killers and resulted
in the arrest of many Irgun members. Attempts by Ben-Gurion to get the

immigration issue sorted out and thus reduce Jewish antipathy to the British fell on deaf ears. Jewish detainees were receiving harsh treatment and ships were still sinking at sea killing hundreds of refugees or being intercepted by the British who refused landings in Palestine, which was beginning to deteriorate into one violent act being met with another between British and Jews and internecine conflict with the Jewish groups. Ben-Gurion was concerned that the extreme actions of armed Jewish groups would destroy the dream of the Jewish Homeland.

By 1944, the British government was sitting down and trying to create the final policy for Palestine with Anthony Eden, the Foreign Secretary, setting before the Cabinet his plan.[12] He re-affirmed the policy of partition along the Peel Commission's line tied to 'a Greater Syria plan' that included Transjordan. He advised that the 1939 White Paper should be abandoned because it had proved ineffective and un-workable especially immigration which was likely to see the House of Commons insisting the current plans were dropped. He stated clearly, 'if there is to be a Jewish State, it could hardly be elsewhere than Palestine'. This made clear at last those ideas of Madagascar, Uganda, and British Guiana were now dead. He recognised that the Jews would be unhappy with the size of the State proposed and that Arabs would be unhappy with Israel having a State at all. Also, the inclusion of Transjordan in the deal would mean that Emir Abdullah, currently in charge of it, would have to 'be retired on a pension' if he was not chosen for the Greater Syria concept. The Ambassador in Cairo had written to Eden making clear that this plan would render dead the Balfour Declaration and the provision for non-Jews, 'it being clearly understood that nothing shall be done which may prejudice the civil and religious rights of non-Jewish communities in Palestine'. He believed that there would be violent reactions from Arabs because the British action would be seen as a betrayal and they would also reject the Greater Syria plan, believing that 'the best bit of their land was being taken away'. He was for leaving the matter alone until after the war, when more direct steps could be taken to protect the strategic interest of Britain, particularly oil. He concluded that 'the Balfour Declaration has been from the start a millstone around our necks'.

The Ambassador in Baghdad gave a similar view with the addition that eventually the two-state solution would result in the larger Arab forces in the area taking action to reclaim the territory, a far sighted and true view of what would actually happen in the future. Despite the talk, the situation in Palestine was still unstable with kidnappings and violence which was still taking lives and destroying property. The American CIA report on Irgun noted that they were responsible for the majority of attacks and that, 'Irgun activities are condemned by the rest of the Palestine Jewish community as irresponsible, misguided and harmful to the Zionist cause'.[13] The report also credited Irgun with the responsibility of bringing the bulk of 50,000 illegal immigrants into Palestine between 1937 and 1944 and that in their activities they tried to avoid the 'shedding of blood'. This is belied by the ambushes they carried out resulting in wounding and death.

On 7 May 1945, the unconditional surrender of all German forces to the Allies brought an end to the war in Europe. The discoveries by the Russian, American and British troops began to reveal the true extent of the Nazis' persecution of the Jewish people. Now there was no doubt about the reality of what refugees were fleeing from when they tried to get to Palestine; it was no longer theory or intellectual debate, but before the eyes of the world, the grotesque images on still and moving film of piled up bodies waiting to be incinerated spoke in the loudest volume ever for a Jewish Homeland. The starved haggard skeletal faces of the survivors looked out with vacant eyes at the world, not victims but human beings who had been to hell. Corrie Ten Boom belonged to a family of Christians who were active in social work in their home town of Haarlem, in the Netherlands. During the Nazi occupation, they chose to act out their faith through peaceful resistance to the Nazis by active participation in the Dutch underground. They were hiding, feeding and transporting Jews and underground members hunted by the Gestapo out of the country. It is estimated they were able to save the lives of 800 Jews, in addition to protecting underground workers. She wrote, 'Surely there is no more wretched sight that the human body unloved and uncared for'. These people had been betrayed by the world great powers including Britain, who had turned Jewish refugees away and ignored what the Nazis were doing to the Jews. In Cabinet meetings throughout 1941 and 1942, discussing whether the Jewish leaders in Palestine could relax the immigration rules for those fleeing persecution, the mantra was the same; not to offend the Arabs and maintain the immigration policy of the failed 1939 White Paper. One of the many survivors, Elie Wiesel wrote, 'I have more faith in Hitler than in anyone else. He alone has kept his promises, all his promises, to the Jewish people'. Those promises of Hitler to wipe out the Jewish people, gave 6 million reasons to the world why the Jewish People should be free to establish a National Home. Theodor Herzl had written in 1896:

'But the distinctive nationality of Jews neither can, will, nor must be destroyed. It cannot be destroyed, because external enemies consolidate it. It will not be destroyed; this is shown during two thousand years of appalling suffering. It must not be destroyed, and that, as a descendant of numberless Jews who refused to despair, I am trying once more to prove in this pamphlet [The Jewish State]. Whole branches of Judaism may wither and fall, but the trunk will remain.'

The war with Hitler was over, but another bloody period of history was to continue in Palestine with the establishment of the Jewish Resistance Movement, with the *Haganah*, Irgun, and Lehi under the Jewish Agency cooperating in a united campaign against the British. The truth is that the campaign did not bring honour to anyone, British, Jew or Arab, in its ferocity. The buildings of British administration were attacked as were people connected with it. In June 1946, mass action was taken by the British against Jewish areas, searching for men and weapons – a gentle touch was not applied. The actions were retaliated against and on 22 July, the King David Hotel in Jerusalem was bombed by Irgun. This was where the British had their central offices for the British Mandatory authorities and was the headquarters of British forces in Palestine and Transjordan. The action resulted in 91 people killed, including 28 British soldiers, policemen and civilians; 46 people were injured. The Irgun insisted they had telephoned warnings of the bomb which were not acted on. The terrorist act was condemned by the majority of Jews and the Jewish newspapers carried their own condemnations It was also a step too far for the other armed Jewish groups and the *Haganah* condemned it and broke off its links with them, although there was suspicion from the British that *Haganah* had tacitly approved the attack.[14] Irgun continued to attack police and army targets which brought down the wrath of the British who introduced draconian measures which included arrests, torture, hangings, and house searches throughout the country. The Jewish Bar Association described the measures as worse than those perpetuated in Nazi Germany, whilst others criticised the British for not treating the Jews as harshly as they did the Arabs during their revolt. The situation was the usual mixture of truths, half-truths and lies that occur in such circumstances. The pressure was coming from America that the British should allow an immediate 100,000 immigrants to enter Palestine and permit the purchase of more land to accommodate them, but Britain was maintaining their opposition to any immigration above the 1939 limits. Following the execution of Irgun members, they retaliated in a barbarous way in the execution of two British soldiers, leaving their bodies booby-trapped. The images that flashed around the world brought discredit to the Zionist cause and took the focus away from what was being done for immigrants. Ben-Gurion called the Irgun action a 'Nazi act', he and the Irgun leader, Begin, were enemies and stood in opposition to one another as to tactics to achieve the same aim. A CIA report[15] noted that the Jewish Agency had informed the UN that they could not be responsible for the 'dissident' elements in Jerusalem as they were unable to control Stern Group and Irgun elements and handed lists of Irgun members to the British administration.

The British Security files[16] show that the *Haganah* were opposing Irgun and had conducted operations against them and there was the thought that should Britain withdraw, there could be a civil war between the two groups. Irgun made a further strategic decision, that they would take their war with Britain to the streets of England, which also infuriated the Jewish Agency leaders. Irgun hatched a plan to assassinate Ernest Bevin, the Foreign Secretary, a plan which came to the attention of the British Security Services:

'... Several agents have reported that Jewish terrorists have had the assassination of Mr. Bevin under consideration for some time, and that they are prepared a plan for carrying out the outrage, if necessary, in the United Kingdom.'[17]

Bevin had been particularly strong in opposing immigration and resented the interference of America, making remarks that were considered anti-Semitic. The Security Service files show through phone tapping and letter interception that the plot was well advanced for an attack in Egypt or England, with the attempts to purchase explosives in Glasgow and the discovery of explosives in England. Dover House, a colonial administration building, was a target but the device was discovered before it exploded. The plotters were under secret observation in England and Paris as they organised their activities. There was also pressure brought against Britain with letter bombs being sent to Bevin and other politicians and colonial administrators. Another directed campaign was against Roy Farran, who had been involved in the kidnapping and murder of a teenage Jewish boy, Alexander Rubowitz. Farran was a loose cannon and conducted many unauthorised and brutal actions against Jews, and this particular incident resulted in a letter bomb being sent to his home in England which ended up killing his brother. Farran and a number of others were unceremoniously sent back home as it became clear what he had done.

On 15 January 1947, the Cabinet discussed[18] the possibility that the USA might take on the mandate and if not them then the matter would have to go to the UN. The records show that the USA would not take on such a task as they knew it could never have a happy outcome. Once more the options were rehearsed, but the conclusion was that any Jewish State would be rejected and would create a hostile Moslem Arab world. An Arab Independent State would also be rejected as they would not allow Jewish immigration and a half-way house of an Arab State with Jewish immigration and special areas within that State would never work either. To any observer, it would appear to be creating ghettoes for Jews. On 16 January, the Palestinian High Commissioner, wrote[19] that any unified State was impossible and partition was the only answer. At a further meeting on January 22, the government were still perplexed as to a solution and once more the discussion[20] turned to some way to get the problem off their hands. A question which is still asked is, how could he [Bevin] not find a way to balance the British interest in the Arab world with a more forthcoming attitude to the historic return of the Jews to Zion? Was the only solution partition? Hugh Gaitskell gave his approval to it, stating that, 'if Britain had to choose between friendship with Arabs or Jews, they should choose Jews', but did point out that the experiences of Egypt and India suggested this would never be an easy choice. There was also concern expressed that if there were a discussion at the UN, it could be embarrassing for Britain as it had failed to solve the issues. 6 February reports[21] to the government from the Secretaries of State for Foreign Affairs and the Colonial Office show that they had had held meetings with Arabs and Jews and 'there was no prospect of a settlement', even when they were threatened with the matter being handed over to the UN. The Cabinet meeting the next day was depressing for the government, as the Prime Minister told them that it was, 'doubtful whether any scheme on partition which would be acceptable to the Jews would be regarded by His Majesty's government as defensible'.[22] Grasping at straws, they considered a plan of 'Trusteeship' of an Arab majority state, with restrictions on immigration of Jews, but the military implications to enforce it were costly in money and lives. By the middle of February,[23] the British had reached the end of their tether and the possibility of an immediate withdrawal, letting the UN sort it out was discussed, but this was unacceptable because of the humiliation and bloodshed that would ensue. However, it was now definite; the matter would be handed over to the UN for a motion to be tabled in September of that year. The British feeling was that the Jewish terrorists would not bomb them into a decision but there was no doubt it contributed to their decision. By this time no convictions had come in Britain for the terrorist activity. The British Government announced publicly that responsibility for Palestine would be handed back to the UN and troops would be withdrawn from Palestine by June 1948. Ya'akov Cohen from *Haganah*, with reflection on the Jewish journey to a homeland, had earlier written:

'The Egyptians, Babylonians, Assyrians, Greeks, Romans, Persians, and others have all been here, they've all been here and now they are gone. You will also be thrown out. England, know you what your end will be if you persist in your mistreatment and your provocations.'

He advocated disobedience to the British administration as their end drew near but the Jewish Agency called on people to 'turn in' their family members involved in terrorism. The Cabinet had been informed[24] that Ben-Gurion wanted a delay in the British decision and offered to try and bring terrorism to an end, if there was a granting of 100,000 immigrant visas, which was refused. Surprisingly, a former devotee of the anti-Semitic Oswald Mosley, John Strachey, now the Minister for Food, thought support should still be given to a Jewish State as it would be the most likely to be an ally in the future, but this was a minority view. The journey to a Jewish Homeland was now in international hands.

It was agreed[25] that there would be no concessions on Jewish immigration whilst waiting for the UN's plans, with Bevin suggesting[26] that Attlee's decision to give the Arabs a veto had made the situation worse, while Attlee's view was that the 'military action has been ineffective in checking terrorism'.[27] By March, the situation was deteriorating, with violence in Palestine. Martial law had to be imposed a number of times in different areas, and it was now seen as 'a means of government' for the British. Immigration was still a major issue and four Royal Navy ships had to be sent to deal with it, with tented camps being set up in Cyprus. The matter of withdrawal and how it would be done was also a problem for the British, with Sir Alexander Cadogan, the country's ambassador to the UN, favouring the acceptance of whatever the UN decided and cooperating with it whereas the Cabinet felt there should be no advanced commitments to anything and abstaining on any votes on the matter.[28]

In May 1947, the cost in prestige, casualties and money was mounting and the latter became a subject of concern with £82m a year for Palestine coming from the Imperial budget along with £8m from local funds for security plus £2.5m in compensation for relatives of British officials killed in Palestine. The response exposed the attitude of the government to the Jewish people, especially when the situation was one of Britain preparing to leave. The Cabinet proposed to impose a new tax of £344,000 on Jews in Palestine and £133,000 on Arabs, with the Arab funds being returned through 'social funds' to offset any anger from them. On top of this, the government would sequestrate £5m from 'certain Jewish communal funds' which belonged to groups such as the Jewish Agency, Jewish institutions and the Revisionist organisation.[29] This was fair according to the government, because Jews were responsible for the terrorism, despite the fact that the Jewish agency was active against Irgun and cooperating with the British. Against the background of continued violence, immigration remained a difficult issue for Britain with the incident of SS *President Warfield*, renamed *Exodus* by the Jewish organisations, which brought tension between her and France. The project of *Aliyah Bet* which was the programme of illegal immigration into Palestine had a planned a total of 100,000 immigrants from camps throughout Europe, where Jewish Holocaust survivors, displaced by the war, had been gathered, sent 4,500 immigrants to Palestine via France. The incident brought shame to Britain from the UN and from media reports throughout the world, as a large naval force had been used to stop the ship docking in Palestine and the immigrants were returned to Germany by force, which was anathema to many of the Holocaust survivors who wanted to return to a Jewish Homeland. The British tried to discharge them in France, but the French refused cooperation and the government had to see what, 'alternative arrangements might be made for the disposal of the illegal immigrants'.[30] Despite being put into camps in Germany, many would escape and make it to Palestine, until eventually all of them would reach their heart's desire and settle in a free Israel.

The incident demonstrated that the British government had not yet grasped the burning passion of the Jewish people to return to their roots. A burning passion that Primo Levi, a survivor of the Holocaust, experienced:

'In Szob, an extra wagon had been added to the sixty in the convoy. It had been brought, and coupled to the train, by a group of very young Jewish men and women, still in their teens, refugees from Eastern Europe, who had decided to go to British-run Palestine and build the Jewish state. Levi was staggered by their nerve, independence, and strength of mind: it amazed him that they could have hitched their wagon without asking anyone's permission. When he expressed this to their leader, "with his intense hawk-like glance," his answer was: "Hitler's dead, isn't he?" Levi was fascinated by these young Jews who, having fought as partisans against the Nazis, were making their escape from Eastern Europe, the graveyard of European Jewry, to create a new country where they intended to become the masters of their fate.'

The result of British actions against the refugees was an increase in Irgun activity with barrel bombs being used to destroy police and military property. By September, the government were expressing a desire for the mandate to end 'as early as practically possible' and in September 1947, the UN advised them of their decision, which Britain decided they did not like. They were on the horns of a dilemma as to how to handle the UN decision which had a majority view and a minority view. The majority view would hold, which was to partition Palestine into a Jewish State and an Arab State with Jerusalem as an international city. At last, the Jews had a Jewish Homeland but to arrive at it would involve more death and suffering.

Cadogan was instructed to make a speech to the UN and the draft produced by the Cabinet ended in a clear statement that no matter what happened at the UN, Britain was getting out. They had had enough of Palestine and knew that the Arab population would never agree to a Jewish State in any form:

'In conclusion, and in order that there may be no misunderstanding of our attitude and policy, I have been instructed by His Majesty's Government to state-with all solemnity that, if it proves impossible as a result of the deliberations of the General Assembly to reach a settlement His Majesty's Government will be forced to base their policy on the assumption that they will have to surrender the mandate under which they have sought for twenty five years to discharge their obligations to facilitate the growth of a Jewish National Home and to protect the interests of the Arab population. This task has now become impossible, and in the absence of a settlement His Majesty's Government must plan for an early withdrawal of British forces and of the British Administration from Palestine.'[31]

The British had decided that they would not oppose the plan, but they would abstain in the vote on it, and they would not agree to allow the UN Commission overseeing the implementation to enter even one day before they evacuated. Bevin made clear his priorities in the handover:

'On the other hand our withdrawal from Palestine, even if it had to be effected at the cost of a period of bloodshed and chaos in the country, would have two major advantages. British lives would not be lost, nor British resources expended, in suppressing one Palestinian community for the advantage of the other. And (at least as compared with enforcing the majority plan or a variant of it) we should not be pursuing a policy destructive of our own interests, in the Middle East.'[32]

Creech Jones, Secretary of State for Colonies, was equally pessimistic about the withdrawal, 'His Majesty's Government would have to face the prospect of leaving Palestine in a state of chaos which would make it difficult to safeguard British interests, such as airfields and oil installations'.

In November 1947 the UN made its announcement as to the decision to partition Palestine.

By February the British government had told the UN of the date of its withdrawal, 15 May 1948, and the British Cabinet were given a report[33] of the situation in Palestine. The withdrawal of British police from certain areas had started and control was being handed over to the Jewish Guard Forces in Jewish areas and the Palestine Police Force in Arab districts. British administration families had begun to leave Palestine on specially chartered vessels which all had the effect of difficulties beginning to appear in commercial activities and in the collection of revenues. All Transjordanian, Egyptian and Syrian police and military had to be gone before withdrawal and they were sent back to their own territory. Large groups of armed Arabs were coming across the border from Syria, dispersing themselves throughout Arab villages, with the various Arab governments surrounding Palestine doing nothing to stop them. The Foreign Secretary was sent to the UN, 'to defend Britain's handling of Palestine and the withdrawal' and confirm there would be no admission of the UN Commission until the British had completely left.[34] Britain would also not contribute personnel to any military force that would implement the UN plan on the population.

In Jerusalem, a large explosion killed 50 Jews and injured 70; the government were keen that statements should be made to clarify that they were not involved. There were also problems for the UN, with the USA withdrawing backing for partition and initially backing a 'Trusteeship' arrangement, which again everyone knew was never going to work. The British government (who still supported the idea despite their doubts it would work) made plans for an earlier withdrawal if the plan was implemented and advised their administration:

'The British civil and military authorities in Palestine should make no effort to oppose the setting up of a Jewish State or a move into Palestine from Transjordan, but should now concentrate on the task of withdrawing the civil administration and the British forces from Palestine.'[35]

This order to not oppose the Jewish State was necessary because 'there was an abundance of experts in the Foreign Office who would argue the Arab case and few who would defend Israel's security imperatives'. They knew[36] that the

Jews would 'probably establish a State in some area' and then commence more immigration and the Arabs would retaliate from Transjordan. Bevin advised that Britain should not interfere and that 'nature may partition'. Some Cabinet members wanted troops out immediately, but that was thought unwise by the majority. Indeed, the situation was spiralling into conflict and the refusal of Arabs to accept partition alongside a Jewish determination to have a homeland was the backdrop to behind the scene attempts to bring a truce and peace that would facilitate the withdrawal of Britain and establishment of the two states. The Jewish leaders had received a promise from King Abdullah of Transjordan that he would not attack the Jews if they established their State, as he would include the UN areas designated for Arabs into Transjordan. Before they declared their new State, Golda Meir went secretly to Abdullah to confirm whether he would keep his promise. He did not reply, but asked 'Why are you in such a hurry to proclaim your State?' to which she replied, 'I don't think that people who have waited 2000 years should be described as being in a hurry'. He was told the Jews would honour the UN plans for the Arab area and sought his support but all he offered was to incorporate the whole of Palestine into Jordan and allow the Jews representation in his Parliament which of course was not an acceptable solution. He was warned of what was to come and the horror of war. He said he was under pressure from the other Arab States and he was not going to keep his promise.

The clock ticked relentlessly onward and it became clear that Britain would withdraw and that the Arabs would not accept any Jewish State, it was therefore decided by the Jewish Agency that they must take the initiative for the 650,000 Jewish people living in Palestine, even if it meant all-out war. On 14 May 1948, on the day in which the British Mandate over a Palestine expired, the Jewish People's Council gathered at the Tel Aviv Museum, because Jerusalem was under siege by Arab forces, and a declaration of the establishment of the State of Israel was read by David Ben-Gurion and remains one of the most powerful and important Jewish documents (See Appendix 2). In it Ben-Gurion declared:

'On the 29th November, 1947, the United Nations General Assembly passed a resolution calling for the establishment of a Jewish State in Eretz-Israel; the General Assembly required the inhabitants of Eretz-Israel to take such steps as were necessary on their part for the implementation of that resolution. This recognition by the United Nations of the right of the Jewish people to establish their State is irrevocable. This right is the natural right of the Jewish people to be masters of their own fate, like all other nations, in their own sovereign State.

ACCORDINGLY WE, MEMBERS OF THE PEOPLE'S COUNCIL, REPRESENTATIVES OF THE JEWISH COMMUNITY OF ERETZ-ISRAEL AND OF THE ZIONIST MOVEMENT, ARE HERE ASSEMBLED ON THE DAY OF THE TERMINATION OF THE BRITISH MANDATE OVER ERETZ-ISRAEL AND, BY VIRTUE OF OUR NATURAL AND HISTORIC RIGHT AND ON THE STRENGTH OF THE RESOLUTION OF THE UNITED NATIONS GENERAL ASSEMBLY, HEREBY DECLARE THE ESTABLISHMENT OF A JEWISH STATE IN ERETZ-ISRAEL, TO BE KNOWN AS THE STATE OF ISRAEL.'

The USA gave immediate recognition to the new state which annoyed Bevin:

'"Just as I was getting it all right, Truman [US President] stepped in and recognised Israel."[37] he continued, Arabs will never recognise Israel.'

Russia followed three days later. Britain would not do so until 13 May 1949 in practice (De Facto) and April 28 1950 by law (De Jure).[38] The journey of the Jewish people to a homeland was now at and end but the birth of this state would not be an easy delivery.

On that very day the Arab states rejected Ben-Gurion's call for peace and cooperation and launched an all-out attack on the fledgling State. Egypt, Syria, Jordan, Lebanon and Syria unleashed their forces to kill the new nation at its birth. Not one country lifted a finger to assist the Jews in their struggle. For nearly a year the battles would rage, interspersed with truces until in July 1949 the final peace agreement had been signed with Israel and all the States that had attacked her. After nearly two millennia of expulsions, dispersals, pogroms and ultimately the horror of the *Shoah* (Jewish term for the Holocaust) and 6500 (1% of the Jewish population) dead in the independence war, the Jewish people's journey to a National Homeland was over, now it would be built with sweat and more blood.

Chapter Fourteen

Reflections - 70 Years On

'Finally, it cannot be too often repeated that somehow and at some time the Jews and Arabs in Palestine will have to learn to live together in peace.'

Neville Chamberlain, 1940[1]

During the first Arab/Israeli war, about 750,000 Palestinian Arabs left their homes in the newly created state. Some of this was at the urging of Arab leaders, who expected they could send them back after a certain Arab victory over the new Jewish State and included some who did not wish to live under Israeli rule, whilst others were victims of individual or extreme Jewish groups. It is regrettable that the latter action was from a people who themselves had experienced similar treatment and did no credit to the new Israel. This action was out of fear and indeed may have contained an element of revenge, but it was also part of a strategy of the new army concerned with the infiltration of fighters from other Arab areas. General Yigael Yadin, Chief of Staff in 1948, said:

'The aim of the plan is the control of the area of the Jewish State and the defence of its borders [according to the UN partition plan] and the clusters of [Jewish] settlements outside the boundaries, against regular and irregular enemy forces operating from bases outside and inside the Jewish State.'

About a third of those who left went to the West Bank under Jordanian control, a third went to the Gaza Strip, under Egypt's control, and the rest went to Jordan, Lebanon and Syria. The Arab nations refused to allow any of these Palestinians to become citizens of their country and settled them into refugee camps. Only King Abdullah of Jordan conferred citizenship on the 200,000 Palestinian living in Jordan and the Jordanian-controlled West Bank and East Jerusalem. On the establishment of the State of Israel, from 1948-1951, almost 800,000 Jews were expelled from their native Arab and Moslem countries or forced to flee as a result of state-sponsored anti-Zionist violence from the nations attacking Israel. They were stripped of their property and the lives they had built in these lands over hundreds of years were destroyed. As many as 500,000 of these refugees fled from Iraq, Tunisia, Syria, Egypt, Yemen, Algeria, Libya and Morocco and were welcomed with open arms by the new State of Israel. Others fled to Europe and North and South America.

In 1951, Israel declared Jerusalem as its capital, but this was seen as unacceptable by many and today it remains a divided city.[2] Israel moved to a parliamentary democracy comprised of legislative, executive and judicial branches. The population as of 2015, were 74.8 per cent Jewish, of which 75.6 per cent were Israel-born, 16.6 per cent Europe/America/Oceania-born, 4.9 per cent Africa-born, and 2.9 per cent Asia-born. 25.2 per cent were non-Jewish (mostly Arab).[3] Many make the mistake, similar to those made about Ireland, of making the issue simply a religious one, which ignores the wider dimensions of cultural, social and political factors and how they relate to religious attitudes. The issue is one of a people who for millennia have been persecuted and slaughtered in millions and who wanted to return to the land from where they were driven, so that they can live in peace and security in religious, cultural, social and political freedom. The danger, again like Ireland, is that the concept of memory can often dominate and blur solutions. Do people want to recall the terror incidents and the dates that this or that happened and continue to add more dates to the bloody calendar? Or do they sit down and reason that enough have died and it is time for peace so that no more die from violence?

In Judaism, every fifty years is considered a year of Jubilee, a year of freedom and release and for many the last Jubilee was in 1967, the year that Israel went to war and reclaimed a great deal of territory. Therefore, 2017 would be a jubilee year but yet there is still no peace or release for Israel and her people and she finds herself continually attacked by rockets, suicide bombers and random assaults were death and injury result. There have also been Israeli attacks against the source of these incidents, resulting in many deaths on either side. It has to be said that Israel has not always responded evenly or appropriately and there indeed have been occasions where the boundaries of justice have been transgressed. The tragedy is that many get caught up in counting of bodies as if that is the important point rather than an examination of the human tragedy and loss and how all violence in that region can be ended.

A fresh acceptance of the reality of the problems and the conflict in the Middle East, free from political correctness, is required. International and national legal restraints need to be imposed to stop incidents occurring that inflame the situation, accompanied with education of all involved with regulations on behaviour that are rigorously enforced against offending parties. Britain's problem in trying to find a solution was trying to ensure neither side was offended or seeking not to offend the side that could give them a national advantage, which disastrously failed. This was combined with unclear promises to both Jews and Arabs. The UN opted for a solution that was designed to fail, with partition already being a deadly choice as seen in Ireland and India. One complicating factor has always been that the majority of Arab nations refuse to accept the right of Israel to exist or to sanction the terrorists who also will not accept her legitimacy. They are the key to a solution. Nelson Mandela wisely said, 'I cannot conceive of Israel withdrawing [From Gaza] if Arab states do not recognize Israel, within secure borders'.[4]

If political barriers were erected that stopped the attacks on Israel and the Arab nations enforced it and Israel agreed to sit down (as they have done many times already) without the threat of rockets and terrorism, then movement to peace could happen. A reformed Menachem Begin was correct in saying:

'My colleagues and I have gone in the footsteps of our predecessors since the very first day we were called by our people to care for their future. We went any place, we looked for any avenue. We made any effort to bring about negotiations between Israel and its neighbours, negotiations without which peace remains an abstract desire.'[5]

There would also be the need for clear declarations from all nations of Israel's right to exist and to remain in her native land. On both sides, from children to adults, a programme of education is needed that begins to explain 'the other' without judgement and in universities, mosques and synagogues, serious reflection on truth, forgiveness and the true evaluation of history, unclouded by bias. Some of these things are already happening and need greater recognition and support. Finally, there need to be both International and National regulations with sanctions that stop extreme behaviour and these must have the support of all nations involved in the Middle East. In asking this from the world it should also be recognised that Israel has been a tremendous blessing to that world and over the past 70 years she has contributed great scientific and medical advances and inventions that have brought benefit to millions (See Appendix 1 for some examples). Israel has not been inward-looking and many countries have been given assistance they needed to develop and grow. Even in places where there are no Israeli embassies, Israeli experts have taught developing nations many skills on improving medical facilities, schools and food growing. Israel, despite its size, has given many foreign assistance programs to the world.

Israel understand the genocide of the Jewish people and in both Rwanda and Sudan she provided humanitarian aid to the refugees. In Rwanda, a field hospital was built and several doctors, nurses, medical supplies and vaccinations were sent. $5 million in aid was sent to relieve the plight of Sudanese refugees. Israel contributed to relief efforts after earthquakes, floods, hurricanes and other natural disasters hit many areas, sending medicine, water, food and other supplies in tragedies such as the tsunami in 2004, the victims of the New Orleans suffering after Hurricane Katrina and the 2010 Haiti earthquake that affected that country. Since 1959, Israel has established medical outreach programmes, including eye clinics in developing countries, such as Nepal, Mauritania, Tonga, Liberia and Micronesia. This demonstrates that Israel had not just demanded a home but from that home has given to the world with great generosity.

As to the future, it is right to acknowledge that the problems of the Middle East are more than just religious divisions, but it has also to be faced that religion does drive much of the hate against the Jewish people and therefore society also needs to address the area of 'freedom of religion' and the issues that arise when one religion or group seeks to impose its ideas on others by force. There has to come a time when an individual is free to choose their belief system or way of life in accordance with their conscience without threat and that liberty must take priority over the freedom to practice a religion or lifestyle that would seek to impose itself on others with violence.

'Religious freedom, as currently understood, is the condition in which individuals or groups are permitted without restriction to assent to and, within limits, to express and act upon religious conviction and identity in civil and political life, free of coercive interference or penalties imposed by outsiders, including the state.'

There must be liberty in how one decides to, or not to, practise a religion. The three major religions of Judaism, Christianity and Islam have their views on this freedom of religion. For Judaism, they have their internal belief that all Jews should follow the precepts of that religion and that all non-Jews should obey the Noachide laws[6] which they believe God gave as universal principles for mankind to follow. However, neither of these should be imposed by the State but freedom to follow a religion should be guarded by the State. Israel itself has a law that gives freedom of religion. Christianity has a chequered past on religious freedom, believing that the tenets of Christianity were necessary for the preservation of society and for the salvation of souls of men and women. The Catholic Church's attitudes in enforcing their belief system resulted in the horror of persecutions of both Jews and Moslems over many centuries, whilst the emergence of Protestantism had its own branches that sought to impose belief by force on others. Today, modern Christianity has evolved into an understanding that seeks to preach their ideas on religion, but no longer seeks to use force to gain acceptance and as with Judaism looks to the State to protect its practices. With Islam, the situation is more complicated in these modern times:

'As it stands today, religious freedom is a contested human right within Islam. While Qur'an 2:256 famously states that there is to be "no coercion in religion," other texts seem to endorse contradictory principles, appearing to enjoin coercion, sometimes even violent coercion, in matters of conscience and religious practice. Modernist Muslim interpreters increasingly advocate an approach toward the Qur'an and Islamic jurisprudence that would place Islam on a path toward broader appreciation of religious freedom, including equality under the law for all religious individuals and groups. On the other hand, some Islamists invoking these same texts urge a return to an earlier, "purer" Islam that forbids conversion from Islam, as well as proselytization on the part of non-Muslims. This interpretation of Islam denies both non-Muslims and disfavoured Muslims equal status in law and society.'

There is also the injunction in the Qur'an, 'The truth is from your Lord, so whoever wills — let him believe; and whoever wills — let him disbelieve'. Furthermore Sheikh Ali Gomaa of Egypt said, 'Unto you your religion, unto me my religion' to pronounce that if a Muslim leaves Islam, no power on earth has the right to punish him or her. This is anathema to many Moslems. Islam is the only religion that has its tenets officially and legally adopted by certain States as the national religion and uses penalties to enforce its observances on their populations. At the time of writing, Afghanistan, Iran, Mauritania, Saudi Arabia, Sudan, Yemen are examples of states where the tolerance of non-Moslems is in varying degrees allowed but have heavy restrictions and penalties, even death, on any show of non-Moslem religious/atheist expression. Many other countries also have Islamic law as their basis, allowing considerable freedom of religious expression but still imposing restrictions on behaviour in public that offends Islamic principles. The Vatican is the only State where Christianity is imposed as the official religion but there is no persecution advocated by the authorities. Solutions to the Middle East problems are tied up with this position of certain Islamic streams, to cultural, social and political life, being intrinsic to the religion and the demanding of others to conform. This requires modern liberal Islamic theologians to be more vocal as to the interpretation of Islam that demonstrates an understanding and respect of the other to differ and for society at large to become more intolerant of those who will not accept the true freedom of religion. It has to be noted that the state and religion can still clash over specific religious practices.[7]

There is also the matter of free speech and the right to express whatever one feels like no matter what the cost to others. This has been the cause of anti-Semitism and indeed offence to other religions and peoples. It is an area that regularly sees both Israel and Jews becoming the object of much offensive material and radically incites many to attack them, verbally and physically. It is of note that in recent times of Islamic terrorism, many are wary of offending Islam and the consequences of some stepping out to do so, rightly or wrongly, have resulted in bloody retaliation. Steven Spielberg commented, 'As a Jew I am aware of how important the existence of Israel is for the survival of us all. And because I am proud of being Jewish, I am worried by the growing anti-Semitism and anti-Zionism in the world.'[8]

There is therefore a need to revisit the concept and to question what exactly 'free speech' means. The term can only be understood better if there is another concept understood which I term 'costly speech'. The latter is any speech that has the direct effect of inciting behaviour that has the potential to result in hatred or violence that 'costs injury or death'. It is this type of activity that has resulted in so much pain, suffering and death on the Jewish journey to their national home and its peaceful existence. In a debate over Salmon Rushdie's *Satanic Verses*, Ronald Dhal controversially wrote, 'In a civilized world we all have a moral obligation to apply a modicum of censorship to our own work in order to reinforce this principle of free speech'. Whilst Dhal may have been wrong to criticise Rushdie's book, which did not incite hared or murder, often the 'moral obligation' is ignored and the question raised as to whether that obligation needs legal strengthening. There have been steps to try and regulate costly speech, but the evidence is that there is a long way to go.

It is important to note that this does not mean the abandonment of fair criticism of religion or even nations, such as Israel, and peoples, but it does set a limit on how far that criticism can go. Nor does it mean suppressing discussion on difficult issues, such as abortion, same-sex relationships, and homosexuality and so on, but again holds those discussions within boundaries which will not incite hatred and violence. It is legitimate to argue about religious doctrine and belief and to disagree with the tenets of any faith or to argue about political matters and dogma, and even national attitudes of any country, but it is illegitimate to provoke behaviour that would result in violence and death because of disagreements with any area of dispute. Society needs to recognise the boundaries between these two approaches and politics and religion particularly, must not be sacred cows that cannot be passionately discussed and debated but the advocating of violence can never be allowed to silence debate.

I was born into the arena of sectarian division and have personally experienced the discrimination, violence, hatred and persecution of a minority that struggles for self-determination. These life experiences, alongside the study of the psychology of child development, suggest that no child is born to hate or to seek the extermination of the other, rather it is the education and example shown, that forms prejudice or the lack of it. The bankruptcy of Hitler's perverted application of Darwinian Theory was shown by the observable altruism of many who resisted him to rescue others. In working among a divided community, I have seen people willing to sacrifice themselves for others and have seen many change from hatred to love, from violence to peace, from suspicion to understanding, from rejection to acceptance of the other; these changes of heart can and do happen. Jonathan Sacks, Chief Rabbi of the United Hebrew Congregations of the Commonwealth from 1991 to 2013, speaking of how things should be, wrote:

> 'Religion creates community, community creates altruism and altruism turns us away from self and towards the common good ... There is something about the tenor of relationships within a religious community that makes it the best tutorial in citizenship and good neighbourliness'.

Martin Luther King Jr, who gave his life for the emancipation of his people, when preaching to his Baptist church in 1957 said, 'Every man must decide whether he will walk in the light of creative altruism or in the darkness of destructive selfishness'. It is only in the light of such wisdom will the Middle East ever see peace.

The final words belong to those who live in Israel today and a research poll carried out in October 2017 suggests that Israel is not an apartheid state where the majority of Arabs are unhappy. Carried out by the Konrad Adenauer Program for Jewish-Arab Cooperation Center at Tel-Aviv University's Dayan Center, and Kivun, a research, strategy and communications company, the survey asked local Arab residents how they viewed the State of Israel. A 60 per cent majority of Arabs overall said they hold a favourable view Israel, 37 per cent described their view as unfavourable. With Arab Muslims, the view was 49 per cent to 48 percent in favour, and among Christian Arabs the view was 61 per cent to 33 per cent in favour. Of the Druze population, 94 per cent said they view the State of Israel favourably whilst 47 per cent of Arab respondents overall said they 'felt unequally treated' compared to the country's Jewish population. However, 63 per cent said Israel is a good place for Arabs to live. Michael Borchard, Israeli director of the Konrad

Adenauer Stiftung, said that the results once again demonstrated that among local Arabs 'there is more identification with Israel than with a possible Palestinian state'.[9] Ibtisam Barakat brought up in the West Bank, has made that journey from hatred to love, from violence to peace, from suspicion to understanding, from rejection to acceptance of the other. In an interview she said:

'It is sad how the world lives on misinformation until great violence is carried out extensively. The Holocaust was played down and the Jews were blamed until 6 million people perished. And with Palestine, as well as with many other places too, the world stands silent, or settles for not knowing, or just blames this or that group, until big, indelible wounds are done. There is really no one to blame since everyone has suffered greatly one way or another. But I think we can find ways to prevent the destruction of human beings. First it's necessary to claim everyone as our people.'[10]

In her book, *Tasting the Sky: A Palestinian Childhood*, she wrote:

'To Alef,

The letter that begins the alphabets of both Arabic and Hebrew - two Semitic languages, sisters for centuries.
    May we find the language that takes us to the only home there is – one another's hearts.
    Alef knows that a thread of a story stitches together a wound'.

Speaking with a Messianic Jew in Jerusalem, he was concerned that there should be an awareness of the very different attitudes and the different streams of thought within both the Arab and Jewish groups and that within each group there were differences. He believed that the issue of religion cannot be avoided and ultimately only an individual's change of heart can determine how the situation in Israel is seen and how the future peace of Israel will be determined. Within the Jewish population there are four groups: *Haredi* (ultra-Orthodox), *Dati* (religious), *Masorti* (traditional) and *Hiloni* (secular). Surveys suggest that the more orthodox and religious

Jews see the Arab population as a problem and would welcome their leaving Israel, whereas the less religious see the need for a solution that allows both communities to exist in peace. This was also true of the Arab population where there were secular, Moslem and Christian Arabs. Christian Arabs held very differing views from Moslem Arabs with Christian Arabs holding more tolerant positions and It is also the case that there is great emotional conflict within the Arab Christian population as to the fact that they wish to identify with their Arab background but recognise that they are free to practice their faith in Israel whereas in Arab lands that becomes quite difficult, if not impossible;

'Today 60% more Christians live in Israel than in the Palestinian territories. A small new Christian party, B'nai Brith, calls on its youth to serve in the Israeli army and hundreds each year do so. Its leader, Reverend Nadaff, declares, "We love this country"'.

After 70 years of existence, it is therefore time for the Jewish people to be allowed to enjoy their homeland, free from the persecution and suffering that has been inflicted on them and a resolution for those in Israel, the West Bank and Gaza must be found. It is not naïve to believe that a solution is possible with the goodwill and determination for peace of all involved. The whole world, especially Arab nations, needs to acknowledge the right of Israel to exist and for the Jews to live in that land from where they were historically driven. It is not only this but also the six million reasons from Hitler's brutal attempt at extermination and the additional huge deaths from the terrible journey down the ages that give justification to a Jewish State.

Appendix 1

Some of Israel's Scientific Achievements Over 70 Years

1. Given Imaging, a world leader in developing and marketing patient-friendly solutions for visualizing and detecting disorders of the GI tract, is best known for its PillCam (aka capsule endoscopy), now the gold standard for intestinal visualization.

2. Netafim is a worldwide pioneer in smart drip and micro-irrigation, starting from the idea of Israeli engineer Simcha Blass for releasing water in controlled, slow drips to provide precise crop irrigation. The kibbutz-owned company operates in 112 countries with 13 factories throughout the world.

3. Ormat Technologies designs, develops, builds, owns, manufactures and operates geothermal power plants worldwide, supplying clean geothermal power in more than 20 countries.

4. Pythagoras Solar makes the world's first solar window, which combines energy efficiency, power generation and transparency. This transparent photovoltaic glass unit can be easily integrated into conventional building design and construction processes.

5. Hazera Genetics, a project of two professors at the Hebrew University Faculty of Agriculture, yielded a cherry tomato that ripens slowly and doesn't rot in shipment.

6. BabySense is a non-touch, no-radiation device designed to prevent crib death. Made by HiSense, the device monitors a baby's breathing and movements through the mattress during sleep. An auditory and visual alarm is activated if breathing ceases for more than 20 seconds or if breath rate slows to

7. 3G Solar pioneered a low-cost alternative to silicon that generates significantly more electricity than leading silicon-based PV solar modules at a lower cost per kilowatt hour.

8. MobileEye combines a tiny digital camera with sophisticated algorithms to help drivers navigate more safely. The steering system-linked device sounds an alert when a driver is about to change lanes inadvertently, warns of an impending forward collision and detects pedestrians. MobileEye has deals with GM, BMW and Volvo, among others.

9. Leviathan Energy innovated the Wind Tulip, a cost-effective, silent, vibration-free wind turbine designed as an aesthetic environmental sculpture, producing clean energy at high efficiency from any direction.

10. Rav Bariach introduced the steel security door that has become Israel's standard. Its geometric lock, whose cylinders extend from different points into the doorframe, is incorporated into doors selling on five continents.

11. BriefCam video-synopsis technology lets viewers rapidly review and index original full-length video footage by concurrently showing multiple objects and activities that actually occurred at different times. This technology drastically cuts the time and manpower involved in event tracking, forensics and evidence discovery.

12. GridON makes the Keeper, a three-phase fault current limiter developed at Bar-Ilan University. The device, which blocks current surges and limits the current for as long as required to clear the fault, won an Innovation Award from General Electric's Ecomagination Challenge and is of interest to major utilities companies around the world.

13. Better Place electric car network, Israeli Shai Agassi's brainchild, is implementing the Israeli pilot that will provide a model for a worldwide electric car grid.

14. Intel Israel changed the face of the computing world with the 8088 processor (the "brain" of the first PC), MMX and Centrino mobile technology. Israeli engineers at Intel in the 1990s had to convince sceptical bosses to take a chance on MMX technology, an innovation designed to improve computer processing. It's now considered a milestone in the company's history.

15. Disk-on-Key, the ubiquitous little portable storage device made by SanDisk, was invented by Dov Moran as an upgraded version of disk and diskette technology through the use of flash memory and USB interface for connection to personal computers.

16. TACount real-time microbiology enables the detection and counting of harmful microorganisms in a matter of minutes, rather than the conventional method of cell culture that takes several hours to a few days. The technology applies to the fields of drinking and wastewater, pharmaceuticals and food and beverage production.

17. Solaris Synergy innovated an environmentally friendly and economically beneficial way to float solar panels on water instead of taking up valuable land, generating energy while protecting and limiting evaporation from reservoir surfaces.

18. HydroSpin is developing a unique internal pipe generator that supplies electricity for water monitoring and control systems in remote areas and sites without accessibility to electricity.

19. The Volcani Research Center of the Ministry of Agriculture and Rural Development aims to improve existing agricultural production systems and to introduce new products, processes and equipment. Basic and applied research is conducted at six institutes and in two regional research centers by more than 200 scientists and 300 engineers and technicians.

20. Rosetta Green, a 2010 spinoff of the agro-biotechnology division of Rosetta Genomics, develops improved plant traits for the agriculture and biofuel industries, using unique genes called microRNAs.

21. Mazor Robotics' Spine Assist and other surgical robots are transforming spine surgery from freehand procedures to highly accurate, state-of-the-art operations with less need for radiation.

22. The optical heartbeat monitor developed by Bar-Ilan University's Prof. Ze'ev Zalevsky is a revolutionary medical technology using a fast camera and small laser light source.

23. Elya Recycling developed and patented an innovative method for recycling plastic based on a specialized formulation of natural ingredients. Making the new raw material for handbags, reusable totes and lumber products requires 50 percent less energy than current recycling methods and 83% less energy than virgin manufacturing.

24. Like-A-Fish unique air supply systems extract air from water, freeing leisure and professional scuba divers, as well as submarines and underwater habitats, from air tanks.

25. Itamar Medical's WatchPAT is an FDA-approved portable diagnostic device for the follow-up treatment of sleep apnoea in the patient's own bedroom, rather than at a sleep disorders clinic. 26. WatchPAT lets patients spend the night at home. Photo courtesy of Bloomfield Science Museum

27. Zenith Solar developed a modular, easily scalable high-concentration photovoltaic system (HCPV). The core technology is based on a unique, proprietary optical design to extract the maximum energy with minimal real estate.

28. AFC (Active Flow Control) was developed at Tel Aviv University as an intelligent gas-air mixing system to replace all existing mixing technologies.

29. The Space Imagery Intelligence (IMINT) unit of Elbit Systems makes a "space camera," a compact, lightweight electro-optic observation system for government, commercial and scientific applications.

30. Decell Technologies is a global leader in providing real-time road traffic information based on monitoring the location and movement of phones and GPS devices. Swift-i Traffic, Decell's premium product, is incorporated in leading navigation systems, fleet management services, mapping operations and media channels in several countries.

31. PrimeSense revolutionizes interaction with digital devices by allowing them to "see" in three dimensions and transfer control from remote controls and joysticks to hands and body. It is the leading business provider of low-cost, high-performance 3D machine vision technologies for the consumer market.

32. Takadu provides monitoring software to leading water utilities worldwide. The product offers real-time detection and control over network events such as leaks, bursts, zone breaches and inefficiencies.

33. Hewlett Packard (HP)'s Indigo digital printing presses for general commercial printing, direct mail, photos and photobooks, publications, labels, business cards, flexible packaging and folding cartons print without films and plates, allowing for personalized short runs and changing text and images without stopping the press.

34. Cubital's solid rapid prototyping machines craft 3D models of engineering parts directly from designs on a computer screen. They're used in the automotive, aerospace, consumer products and medical industries, as well as engineering firms and academic and research institutions.

35. The Zomet Institute in Jerusalem is a non-profit, public research institute where rabbis, researchers and engineers devise practical solutions for modern life without violating Sabbath restrictions on the use of electricity. Zomet technology is behind metal detectors, security jeeps, elevators, electric wheelchairs and coffee machines that can be used on Shabbat, as well as solutions requested by the Israeli ministries of health and defence, Ben-Gurion Airport, Elite Foods, Tnuva Dairies, Israeli Channel 10 Television and others.

36. The EarlySense continuous monitoring solution allows hospital nurses to watch and record patients' heart rate, respiration and movement remotely through a contact-free sensor under the mattress. The system's built-in tools include a wide range of reports on the status of patients, including alerts for falls and bedsore prevention.

37. TourEngine significantly reduces fuel consumption and harmful emissions by common engines through a sophisticated thermal management strategy. It can also be easily integrated with future hybrid engines, further improving their efficiency and environment-friendly attributes.

38. The superconducting fault current limiter (FCL), designed for limiting short currents, comes out of a $2 million project developed over two years by RICOR Cryogenics and Vacuum Systems with the Institute of Superconductivity at Bar-Ilan University.

39. Heliofocus led an industry trend to provide solar-energy boosting for existing coal or gas power plants, reducing carbon emissions and overall costs.

40. Transbiodiesel makes enzyme-based catalysts (biocatalysts) used in the production of biodiesel.

41. SolarEdge makes a module that optimizes every link in the solar PV chain, maximizing energy production while monitoring constantly to detect faults and prevent theft.

42. The 3D tethered particle motion system developed by three professors at Bar-Ilan allows for three-dimensional tracking of critical protein-DNA and protein-RNA cell interactions in the body.

43. Panoramic Power provides a current monitor solution that enables enterprises and organizations to reduce their operational and energy expenses using a breakthrough power flow visibility platform.

44. SniffPhone – Mobile Disease Diagnostics, Prof. Hossam Haick, Technion – Israel Institute of Technology. The system is a pipeline technology that promises a rapid and noninvasive diagnostic tool for cancer and other diseases. Easily deployed and equipped with nanosensors, the system samples exhaled breath and decodes it. Data is then transferred via mobile phone to a data processing system for analysis. From there, results and recommendations are sent to the physician.

Appendix 2

Israeli's Declaration of Independence

'ERETZ-ISRAEL [(Hebrew) - the Land of Israel i.e. Palestine] was the birthplace of the Jewish people. Here their spiritual, religious and political identity was shaped. Here they first attained to statehood, created cultural values of national and universal significance and gave to the world the eternal Book of Books. After being forcibly exiled from their land, the people kept faith with it throughout their Dispersion and never ceased to pray and hope for their return to it and for the restoration in it of their political freedom. Impelled by this historic and traditional attachment, Jews strove in every successive generation to re-establish themselves in their ancient homeland. In recent decades they returned in their masses. Pioneers, ma'pilim [(Hebrew) - immigrants coming to Eretz-Israel in defiance of restrictive legislation] and defenders, they made deserts bloom, revived the Hebrew language, built villages and towns, and created a thriving community controlling its own economy and culture, loving peace but knowing how to defend itself, bringing the blessings of progress to all the country's inhabitants, and aspiring towards independent nationhood. In the year 5657 (1897), at the summons of the spiritual father of the Jewish State, Theodor Herzl, the First Zionist Congress convened and proclaimed the right of the Jewish people to national rebirth in its own country. This right was recognized in the Balfour Declaration of the 2nd November, 1917, and re-affirmed in the Mandate of the League of Nations which, in particular, gave international sanction to the historic connection between the Jewish people and Eretz-Israel and to the right of the Jewish people to rebuild its National Home.

The catastrophe which recently befell the Jewish people - the massacre of millions of Jews in Europe - was another clear demonstration of the urgency of solving the problem of its homelessness by re-establishing in Eretz-Israel the Jewish State, which would open the gates of the homeland wide to every Jew and confer upon the Jewish people the status of a fully privileged member of the community of nations. Survivors of the Nazi holocaust in Europe, as well as Jews from other parts of the world, continued to migrate to Eretz-Israel, undaunted by difficulties, restrictions and dangers, and never ceased to assert their right to a life of dignity, freedom and honest toil in their national homeland. In the Second World War, the Jewish community of this country contributed its full share to the struggle of the freedom- and peace-loving nations against the forces of Nazi wickedness and, by the blood of its soldiers and its war effort, gained the right to be reckoned among the peoples who founded the United Nations.

On the 29th November, 1947, the United Nations General Assembly passed a resolution calling for the establishment of a Jewish State in Eretz-Israel; the General Assembly required the inhabitants of Eretz-Israel to take such steps as were necessary on their part for the implementation of that resolution. This recognition by the United Nations of the right of the Jewish people to establish their State is irrevocable. This right is the natural right of the Jewish people to be masters of their own fate, like all other nations, in their own sovereign State.

ACCORDINGLY WE, MEMBERS OF THE PEOPLE'S COUNCIL, REPRESENTATIVES OF THE JEWISH COMMUNITY OF ERETZ-ISRAEL AND OF THE ZIONIST MOVEMENT, ARE HERE ASSEMBLED ON THE DAY OF THE TERMINATION OF THE BRITISH MANDATE OVER ERETZ-ISRAEL AND, BY VIRTUE OF OUR NATURAL AND HISTORIC RIGHT AND ON THE STRENGTH OF THE RESOLUTION OF THE UNITED NATIONS GENERAL ASSEMBLY, HEREBY DECLARE THE ESTABLISHMENT OF A JEWISH STATE IN ERETZ-ISRAEL, TO BE KNOWN AS THE STATE OF ISRAEL.

WE DECLARE that, with effect from the moment of the termination of the Mandate being tonight, the eve of Sabbath, the 6th Iyar, 5708 (15th May, 1948), until the establishment of the elected, regular authorities of the State in accordance with the Constitution which shall be adopted by the Elected Constituent Assembly not later than the 1st October 1948, the People's Council shall act as a Provisional Council of State, and its executive organ, the People's Administration, shall be the Provisional Government of the Jewish State, to be called "Israel".

THE STATE OF ISRAEL will be open for Jewish immigration and for the Ingathering of the Exiles; it will foster the development of the country for the benefit of all its inhabitants; it will be based on freedom, justice and peace as envisaged by the prophets of Israel; it will ensure complete equality of social and political rights to all its inhabitants irrespective of religion, race or sex; it will guarantee freedom of religion, conscience, language, education and culture; it will safeguard the Holy Places of all religions; and it will be faithful to the principles of the Charter of the United Nations.

THE STATE OF ISRAEL is prepared to cooperate with the agencies and representatives of the United Nations in implementing the resolution of the General Assembly of the 29th November, 1947, and will take steps to bring about the economic union of the whole of Eretz-Israel.

WE APPEAL to the United Nations to assist the Jewish people in the building-up of its State and to receive the State of Israel into the comity of nations.

WE APPEAL - in the very midst of the onslaught launched against us now for months - to the Arab inhabitants of the State of Israel to preserve peace and participate in the upbuilding of the State on the basis of full and equal citizenship and due representation in all its provisional and permanent institutions.

WE EXTEND our hand to all neighbouring states and their peoples in an offer of peace and good neighbourliness, and appeal to them to establish bonds of cooperation and mutual help with the sovereign Jewish people settled in its own land. The State of Israel is prepared to do its share in a common effort for the advancement of the entire Middle East.

WE APPEAL to the Jewish people throughout the Diaspora to rally round the Jews of Eretz-Israel in the tasks of immigration and upbuilding and to stand by them in the great struggle for the realization of the age-old dream – the redemption of Israel.

PLACING OUR TRUST IN THE "ROCK OF ISRAEL", WE AFFIX OUR SIGNATURES TO THIS PROCLAMATION AT THIS SESSION OF THE PROVISIONAL COUNCIL OF STATE, ON THE SOIL OF THE HOMELAND, IN THE CITY OF TEL-AVIV, ON THIS SABBATH EVE, THE 5TH DAY OF IYAR, 5708 (14TH MAY,1948).'

Endnotes

Chapter One

1. The Amarna Letters are a body of fourteenth century BCE correspondence on clay tablets exchanged between the rulers of the Ancient Near East and Egypt.
2. HANDCOCK, Percy, *Selections from the Tell El-Amarna letters*, Society for Promoting Christian Knowledge, The Macmillan Company 1920, p.6.
3. Hendel, Ronald, *Remembering Abraham: Culture, Memory, and History in the Hebrew Bible*, Oxford University Press, 2005, p.7.
4. KING, The Rev, James, *Moab's Patriarchal Stone, Being an account of the Moabite Stone, its story and its teaching*, London, Bickers & Son, 1878, PP.54FF, (Translation adapted to translate 'Jehovah' to 'Yahweh' by the author).
5. LUCKENBILL, Daniel David, Benhadad and Hadadezer, The American Journal of Semitic Languages and Literatures 27, no. 3, 1911 p267.

Chapter Two

1. PETTINATO, Giovanni, *Archives of Ebla: An Empire Inscribed in Clay* (Translation of Ebla: Un Impero Inciso Nell'Argilla), Doubleday,, 1981, p.315.
2. WATSON, James, *A Letter to the Readers: [Discoveries at Ebla]*, The Biblical Archaeologist, 40(1), doi:10.2307/3209565, 1977, pp.2-4.
3. ALTHANN, Robert. *The Impact Of Ebla On Biblical Studies - Religion in Southern Africa*, vol. 2, no. 1, www.jstor.org/stable/24763954, 1981, pp. 39–47.

Chapter Three

1. GLASSNER, Jean-Jacques and Foster, Benjamin R, *Mesopotamian Chronicles* (Writings from the Ancient World), Atlanta, Society of Biblical Literature, 2004, p.235.

Chapter Four

1. A monk Dionysius developed a Christian calendar but when he did his work, it was later found that he had made mistakes and his dates were wrong. Therefore Jesus was not born at the start of year 1 AD but before this. Using Matthew 2:1 and Luke 2:1-4 along with historic dates for King Herod who died in 4 BC and

Cyrenius who ruled twice; once in 7 BC to 1 BC and once in 6 AD to 10 AD we can pinpoint the time of birth to 6 B.C.E.

2. Luke 3:23 gives Jesus starting his ministry at 30 years old and in Luke 13:7 has him ministering for 3 years, therefore dying in 27 C.E. Furthermore John 19:31 gives the death during a 'special Sabbath' which was not the normal Saturday and using three Jewish nights and days (6 p.m. to 6p.m.) in the tomb for the reported resurrection early on a Sunday, the only special Sabbath that fits is Thursday 10th April 27 C.E. therefore the crucifixion was 9th of April in 27 A.D.

3. YONGE, Charles Duke, *The Works of Philo: Complete and Unabridged* – Flaccus VIII (53), Henry G Bohn, 1855, pp.72-73.

4. GORDON, Thomas, *The Works of Tacitus Vol. IV*, London, Rivington, Davies, Hawes & Co, 1770 Chapter V (Updated to modern prose).

5. See the argument in RAWLINSON, George, *A History of Herodotus:* A New English Version, Vol II, Appleton & Co, 1866, p.63.

6. Theodosian Code 16.8.1 (Constantine the Great, 329 CE).

7. Theodosian Code 16.8.7 (Constantine II, 353 CE).

8. Greek: ἄριστοι and was used of noblemen in ancient Greece, particular ancient Athens. The term is 'best' in direct translation, meaning best in terms of birth, rank, or nobility, but also implies being best morally.

9. DUBNOV, Simon, Spiegel, *Moshe, History of the Jews*, Thomas Yoselof, pp181-182.

10. JEROME, *Comm. in Es., III*, 2; PL, XXIV, 58 f.

Chapter Five

1. Canon XI, The Canons of The Council of Truro.

Chapter Seven

1. Toaff, 2004, pp.239ff.

2. LW 45:199-229.

3. An auto-da-fé or auto-de-fé (from Portuguese auto da fé, meaning "act of faith") was the ritual of public penance of condemned heretics and apostates that took place when the Spanish Inquisition, Portuguese Inquisition or the Mexican Inquisition had decided their punishment, followed by the execution by the civil authorities of the sentences imposed.

4. http://www.fact-index.com/t/ti/timeline_of_jewish_history.html   Retrieved 10/12/2016

5. CARLYLE, Thomas, *The Letters and Speeches of Oliver Cromwell, Vol 1*, Methuen & Co, 1904. P.148.

6. It is believed this practice was related to the Messiah arriving at Tabernacles. Avraham Vaakov Finkel, , wrote 'true happiness is found only in the eternal values of Torah and mitzvot, that material possessions offer no security, and that THE SHIELD OF FAITH is the only protection he can rely on'.
7. Aliyah is the immigration of Jews from the diaspora throughout the world to the Land of Israel (Eretz Israel in Hebrew) it is mainly 'the act of going up to Jerusalem' and is echoed in the diaspora Passover celebration in the words, la-shanah haba'ah bi-Yerushalayim (Next year in Jerusalem and has Messianic overtones), in modern times making 'Aliyah' by moving to the Land of Israel is one of the tenets of Zionism.

Chapter Eight

1. *The Times*, London, 24 January 1839.
2. *The Times*, London, 9 March 1840.
3. The Palestine Royal Commission on the Maritime Plain, 1913, Chp. 9 para.43.
4. Innocent III was pope from 1198 to 1216 and showed extreme hatred towards the Jews bring in an edict that they should were a distinguishing badge.
5. This was the kidnapping of the Jewish Mortara child and his Christian baptism that caused a world-wide outcry. Sir Moses Montefiore tried to intervene with Cardinal Antonelli who told him that once a child had been baptised the laws of the Church prevented the child being given back to the parents.
6. Adolf Stoecker, was party to this petition presented to Prince Otto Von Bismarck and it was conceived by Bernard Förster, who claimed he had the idea whilst attending a Richard Wagner Bayreuth Festival.
7. *La Croix*, February 23 1898, page 4
8. The Thule Society website, https://thulesociety.nfshost.com/index.php/ideas-and-suggestions/ retrieved 12/9/2017.
9. Ibid. p.72.
10. Mr. Claude Hay MP for Shoreditch, Hoxton speaking in the House of Commons, HC Deb 03 July 1905 vol 148 cc847-76.
11. Winston Churchill papers, WSC II c 495-6.

Chapter Nine

1. Cabinet Papers, National Archives, Ref: CAB 37_123_43.
2. Cabinet Papers, National Archives, Ref: CAB 24_159_40.
3. Cabinet Papers, National Archives, Ref: CAB 24_30_6.
4. Ibid.
5. Foreign Office Papers, National Archives, FO 800_176.
6. Ibid.

7. Ibid. FO 800_176.

8. Ibid. CAB 24_159_40.

9. Foreign Office Papers, National Archives, FO 800_214 & CAB 24_37_64.

10. Ibid.

11. Ibid.

12. Foreign Office Papers, National Archives, FO 371_3399_35210.

13. MEINERTZHAGEN, Richard, Middle East Diary, Thomas Yoseloff, 1960, February 7 entry.

14. Foreign Office Papers, National Archives, FO 800_212.

15. Foreign Office Papers, National Archives, FO 800_207.

16. Foreign Office Papers, National Archives, FO 800_215

17. Ibid.

18. Ibid.

19. Ibid.

20. Ibid.

21. Ibid.

22. Ibid.

23. Ibid. FO 800_215.

Chapter Ten

1. Cabinet Papers, National Archives, Ref: CAB 24_107_7.

2. Cabinet Papers, National Archives, Ref: CAB 24_107_75.

3. Cabinet Papers, National Archives, Ref: CAB 24_115_98.

4. Cabinet Papers, National Archives, Ref: CAB 24_117_24.

5. Cabinet Papers, National Archives, Ref: CAB 23_25_29.

6. Cabinet Papers, National Archives, Ref: CAB 24_126_30.

7. Ibid. Meinertzhagen, pp.3ff.

8. Cabinet Papers, National Archives, Ref: CAB 24_136_99.

9. Cabinet Papers, National Archives, Ref: CAB 24_138_76.

10. Ibid. Meinertzhagen June 21 1921 entry.

11. Cabinet Papers, National Archives, Ref: CAB 24_140_79.

12. Cabinet Papers, National Archives, Ref: CAB 24_159_6.

13. Speech in House of Lords, June 21 1922.

14. Cabinet Papers, National Archives, Ref: CAB 24_158_61.

15. Cabinet Papers, National Archives, Ref: CAB 24_159_6.

16. Cabinet Papers, National Archives, Ref: CAB 23_46_15.

17. Cabinet Papers, National Archives, Ref: CAB 24_162_33.

18. Cabinet Papers, National Archives, Ref: CAB 24_159_79.

19. Cabinet Papers, National Archives, Ref: CAB 24_165_37.

20. Cabinet Papers, National Archives, Ref: CAB 24_165_54.

Chapter Eleven

1. Palestine - Statement of Policy by His Majesty's Government in the United Kingdom. CMD3692, 1930.
2. Ibid. Meinertzhagen, March 16 1933 entry.
3. Mandates Palestine Report of the Palestine Royal Commission 1937.

Chapter Twelve

1. Cabinet Papers, National Archives, Ref: CAB 23_75_23.
2. Cabinet Papers, National Archives, Ref: CAB 22_240_11.
3. Cabinet Papers, National Archives, Ref: CAB 23_75_27.
4. Foreign Office Papers, National Archives, FO 371_18863_7600.
5. Palestine Partition Commission Report, CMD. 584, 1938.
6. RHL, Chancellor Papers, 22:MF40, ff., 20 Dec. 1937 and FO 371/20035 E3483 and Policy in Palestine on the Outbreak of War, FO 371/21865 E56C/G, 26 Sept. 1938.
7. Cabinet Papers, National Archives, Ref: CAB 23_96_10.
8. Cabinet Papers, National Archives, Ref: CAB 23_96_11.
9. Cabinet Papers, National Archives, Ref: CAB 23_97_3.
10. Cabinet Papers, National Archives, Ref: CAB 23_97_6.
11. Cabinet Papers, National Archives, Ref: CAB 23_97_8.
12. Cabinet Papers, National Archives, Ref: CAB 24_284_3.
13. Cabinet Papers, National Archives, Ref: CAB 23_97_9.
14. Cabinet Papers, National Archives, Ref: Cab 24_158_6.
15. Cabinet Papers, National Archives, Ref: Cab 23_97_10.
16. Cabinet Papers, National Archives, Ref: Cab 23_98_1.
17. Cabinet Papers, National Archives, Ref: 24_285.
18. Cabinet Papers, National Archives, Ref: 23_99_3.
19. Cabinet Papers, National Archives, Ref: 23_99_4.
20. Cabinet Papers, National Archives, Ref: 23_100_6.
21. Statement on Palestine, White Paper - CMD. 1019, 1939.
22. Cabinet Papers, National Archives, Ref: 67_4_17.
23. Cabinet Papers, National Archives, Ref: 67_4_25.
24. Cabinet Papers, National Archives, Ref: 67_4_11.
25. Cabinet Papers, National Archives, Ref: 67_5_11.

Chapter Thirteen

1. Speech by Senator John F. Kennedy, Zionists of America Convention, Statler Hilton Hotel, New York, NY August 26, 1960.
2. Cabinet Papers, National Archives, Ref: 65_10_15.

3. Cabinet Papers, National Archives, Ref: 63_10_17 and 61_10_19.

4. McMillan, Harold, House of Commons, March 11 1942

5. Lord Wedgewood, House of Lords, 26/2/1942.

6. McMillan, House of Commons, 12/3/1942.

7. Mander, Sir Geoffrey, House of Commons, 12/3/1942.

8. Silverman, Samuel, House of Commons,4/3/1942.

9. Lord Wedgewood, House of Lords, 9/6/1942.

10. Lord Davies, House of Lords, 10/3/1942.

11. Letter to Mr & Mrs Rogers, Jr, dated October 18 1943. National Archives USA, Dept. of Interior.

12. Cabinet Papers, National Archives, Ref: 66_50, May 15 1944.

13. CIA Secret Files, R & A No. 2612, The Objectives of the Irgun Tzvai Leumi, 13/10/1944.

14. National Archives, KV 3_438 1947.

15. CIA intelligence report, CIA-RDP78-01617A, 15 Jun 1948.

16. Ibid. National Archives, 1947.

17. National Archives, KV 2_3428-46, Aug 3 1946.

18. Cabinet Papers, National Archives, Ref: 128_16_30.

19. Cabinet Papers, National Archives, Ref: 129_16_3.

20. Cabinet Papers, National Archives, Ref: 128_11_3.

21. Cabinet Papers, National Archives, Ref: 129_16_49.

22. Cabinet Papers, National Archives, Ref: 129_16_18.

23. Cabinet Papers, National Archives, Ref: 129_17_9.

24. Cabinet Papers, National Archives, Ref: 129_16_22.

25. Cabinet Papers, National Archives, Ref: 128_9_23.

26. Cabinet Papers, National Archives, Ref: 195_5_23.

27. Cabinet Papers, National Archives, Ref: 129_5_29.

28. Cabinet Papers, National Archives, Ref: 129_18_40.

29. Cabinet Papers, National Archives, Ref: 129_19_11.

30. Cabinet Papers, National Archives, Ref: 128_10_17.

31. Cabinet Papers, National Archives, Ref: 129_21_9.

32. Ibid.

33. Cabinet Papers, National Archives, Ref: 129_24_10.

34. Cabinet Papers, National Archives, Ref: 129_24_12.

35. Cabinet Papers, National Archives, Ref: 128_12_24.

36. Cabinet Papers, National Archives, Ref: 195_6_23.

37. Cabinet Papers, National Archives, Ref: 195_6_32.

38. Cabinet Papers, National Archives, Ref: 128_17_25.

Chapter Fourteen

1. Cabinet Papers, National Archives, Ref: 67_4_38.
2. President Trump of the USA has controversially signalled his intention to establish America's Embassy in Jerusalem, thus recognising it as Israel's capital.
3. CIA World Fact Book https://www.cia.gov/library/publications/the-world-factbook/geos/is.html retrieved 09/10/2017.
4. Interview with David Levy, Israel Radio's English News, December 6 2013.
5. Menachem Begin in his acceptance speech at the Nobel Lecture, December 10, 1978 when he and Egypt's Mohamed Anwar al-Sadat jointly won the Nobel Peace Prize.
6. The seven Noachide laws, as traditionally understood: Do Not Deny God, Do Not Blaspheme God, Do Not Murder, Do Not Engage in Incestuous, Adulterous or Homosexual Relationships, Do Not Steal, Do Not Eat of a Live Animal, Establish Courts/Legal System to Ensure Law Obedience.
7. There are certain issues where state and religion clash as in 2012, when a court in Cologne, Germany ruled that circumcision involving a four-year-old Muslim boy constituted bodily harm, which would have caused issues for Jews, however, In December 2012, the Bundestag voted 434-100 to allow the practice of male circumcision, overruling the Cologne court, and leaving the question of Jewish practice of circumcision unanswered and still a matter of controversy. Other countries are also reviewing the practice.
8. Steven Spielberg Interview with Der Spiegel, January 26 2006. Quoted in Israeli Today, October 09, 2017, http://www.israeltoday.co.il/NewsItem/tabid/178/nid/32520/Default.aspx, retrieved 12/09/2017.
9. Interview With By Molly Bennet, *The Nation*, June 4, 2007
10. Jonathan Adelman, The Christians of Israel: A Remarkable Group, Huffington Post, https://www.huffingtonpost.com/jonathan-adelman/the-christians-of-israel_b_8055770.html, retrieved 1/9/2017

Bibliography

ACKERMAN, Susan, (Ed.), **Cohen**, Ada and **Kangas** Steven E., (2010), 'Assyria in the Bible', in *Assyrian Reliefs from the Palace of Ashurnasirpal II: A Cultural Biography*, Hanover, N.H, University of New England

ADLER, Joseph, (1997), *Restoring the Jews to their Homeland*, New Jersey, Jason Aronson Inc.

AL MAWAIZ, (1364–1442), Islamic historian, in, **FALK**, Avner, (2010), *Franks and Saracens: Reality and Fantasy in the Crusades*, London, Karnac Books

ANISSIMOV, Myriam, (2006), *Primo Levi – Tragedy of An Optimist*, London, Little Books Ltd.

ARKEL, Dik van, (2014), *The Drawing of the Mark of Cain: A Socio-Historical Analysis of the Growth of Anti-Jewish Stereotypes*, Amsterdam, Amsterdam University Press

AVI-YONAH, Michael, (2003), *A History of Israel and the Holy Land*, London, Continuum International Publishing Group Ltd.

BAASTEN, Martin. (2003), *A Note on the History of 'Semitic'. Hamlet on a Hill: Semitic and Greek Studies Presented to Professor T. Muraoka on the Occasion of His Sixty-fifth Birthday*, Leuven, Peeters Publishers

BAMFORTH, Iain, (2006), *The Good European: Essays and Arguments*, Manchester, Carcanet Press

BARAKAT, Ibtisam, (2007), *Tasting the Sky: A Palestinian Childhood*, New York, Farrar, Straus and Giroux

BAUMGARTEN, Elisheva, **KARRAS**, Ruth Mazo, **MESLER**, Katelyn, (Eds.), (2007), *Entangled Histories: Knowledge, Authority, and Jewish Culture in the Thirteenth Century*, Philadelphia, University of Pennsylvania Press

BELL, Dean Phillip, (2007), *Jews in the Early Modern World*, New York, Rowman & Littlefield Publishers, Inc.

BENBASSA, Esther, (2001), *The Jews of France: A History from Antiquity to the Present*, Princeton, Princeton University Press

BEN-SASSON, H. H., (Ed.), (1976), *A History of the Jewish People*, Massachusetts, Harvard University Press

BERKEY, Jonathan Porter, (2002), *The Formation of Islam: Religion and Society in the Near East, 600-1800*, Cambridge, Cambridge University Press

BIETAK, Manfred, (1996), *Avaris: The Capital of the Hyksos*, London, British Museum Press

BIRAN, A., (Ed.), (1981), 'To the God who is is Dan', in *Temples and High Places in Biblical Times*, Jerusalem, Hebrew Union College

BLOCH, Abraham, P., (1987), *One Day: An Anthology of Jewish Historical Anniversaries for Every Day of The Year*, New York, Weekly Jewish Post & Opinion

BOOM, Corrie Ten, (2006), *The Hiding Place: The Triumphant True Story of Corrie Ten Boom*, Grand Rapids, Chosen

BOSWORTH, C.E., **Donzel**, E. van, **Heinrichs**, W.P., **Pellat**, Ch.,(Eds.), (1998), *Encyclopaedia of Islam, Volume VII*, Leiden, Brill Academic Publishing

BRENER, Milton, E., (2006), *Richard Wagner and the Jews*, Jefferson, McFarland & Company Inc.

BRETT, Michael, (2001), *The Rise of the Fatimids: The World of the Mediterranean and the Middle East in the Fourth Century of the Hijra, Tenth Century CE. The Medieval Mediterranean*, Leiden, Brill Academic Publishing

BREWER, Catherine, (2005), *The Status of the Jews in Roman Legislation: The Reign of Justinian 527-565 CE*, European Judaism

BRYANT, E. E., (1985), *The Reign of Antonius Pius*, Cambridge, Cambridge University Press

CAFFERATA, Raymond, (1930), *Testimony at the Markha Trial, Report of the Commission of Inquiry* (Hebrew), 2nd Ed, Tel Aviv

CALIMANI, Riccardo, **WOLFTHAL**, K. S., (Translator), (2013), *The Venetian Ghetto: The History Of A Persecuted Community*, New York, Open Road Media

CHAZAN, Robert, (1996), *European Jewry and the First Crusade*, Berkley, University of California Press

CHRISTIE, Niall, (2014), *Muslims and Crusaders: Christianity's Wars in the Middle East, 1095-1382, from the Islamic Sources (Seminar Studies)*, Abingdon, Routledge

Cohen, Mark R., (1994), *Under Crescent and Cross: The Jews in the Middle Ages*, Princeton, Princeton University Press

D'AMATO, Raffaele, **Salimbeti**, Andrea, (2015), *Sea Peoples of the Bronze Age Mediterranean c.1400 BC - 1000 BC*, Oxford, Osprey Publishing

DAVIES, William David, **FINKELSTEIN**, Louis, **KATZ**, Steven T, (Eds.), (2006), *The Cambridge History of Judaism: Volume 4, The Late Roman-Rabbinic Period*, Cambridge, Cambridge University Press

DE HASS, Jacob, (2013), *History of Palestine – The Last Two Thousand Years*, Oxford, Nielsen Press

DEVER, W. G., (2006), *Confronting the Past: Archaeological and Historical Essays on Ancient Israel in Honor of William G. Dever*, Indiana, Eisenbrauns

Devries, LaMoine F, (2006), *Cities of the Biblical World*, Eugene, Oregon, Wipf & Stock

DIMONT, Max, (2004), *The Sealed Coffin - Jews, God, and History (2nd ed.)* New York, Signet Classic

DONNER, Fred M., (1981), *The Early Islamic Conquests*, Princeton, Princeton University Press

DUBNOV, Simon, **SPIEGEL**, Moshe, (1980), *History of the Jews*, London, Thomas Yoselof

GLÖCKNER, Olaf, **FIREBERG**, Haim, (Eds.), (2015), *Being Jewish in 21st-Century Germany*, Berlin, De Gruyter Oldenbourg

EDWARDS, I. E. S., **GADD**, C. J., **HAMMOND**, N. G. L., **SOLLBERGER**, E. (Eds.), (1973), *The Cambridge Ancient History Vol 2*, Cambridge, Cambridge University Press

ELAD, Amikam, (1995), *Medieval Jerusalem and Islamic Worship Holy Places, Ceremonies, Pilgrimage*, Leiden, Brill Academic Publishing

FINKEL, Avraham Vaakov, (1993), *The Essence of the Holy Days: Insights from the Jewish Sages, New Jersey*, Jason Aronson Inc.

FINKELSTEIN, Israel, **SILBERMAN**, Neil Asher, (2017), *The Bible Unearthed: Archaeology's New Vision of Ancient Israel and the Origin of Its Sacred Texts*, New York, Simon and Schuster

FINKELSTEIN, Louis, (1960), *Their History, Culture and Religion Vol II*, London, Peter Owens Limited

FIRESTONE, Reuven, (1990), *Journeys in Holy Lands: The Evolution of the Abraham-Ishmael Legends in Islamic Exegesis*, Albany, NY, State University of NY Press

FLEMING, Daniel E., (2012), *The Legacy of Israel in Judah's Bible: History, Politics, and the Reinscribing of Tradition*, Cambridge, Cambridge University Press

FRANK, Heynick, (2002), *Jews and Medicine, An Epic Saga*, New York, KTAV Publishing House

FRANKOPAN, P., (2012), *The First Crusade: The Call from the East*, London, Random House

FREDERIC, William Madden, (1957), *History of Jewish Coinage, and of Money in the Old and New Testament*, Cambridge, Pegasus Pub. Co.

GEARY, Patrick J. (Ed.) (2013), *Readings in Medieval History*, Toronto, Broadview Press

GERSHOM, Gerhard Scholem, (1976), *Sabbatai Sevi: the Mystical Messiah, 1626-1676*, Princeton, Princeton University Press

GIL, M., (1997), *A History of Palestine (634 – 1099)*, Cambridge, Cambridge University Press

GILBERT, Martin, (2010), *In Ishmael's House*, Toronto, Yale University Press (McClelland & Stewart)

GILBERT, Martin, (1998), *Israel, A History*, London, Doubleday

GINSBURY, Philip, **CUTLER**, Raphael, (**Weissman**, Toby Ed.), (2005), *The Phases of Jewish History*, Tel Aviv, Devora Publishing,

GLASSNER, Jean-Jacques and **FOSTER**, Benjamin R., (2004), *Mesopotamian Chronicles (Writings from the Ancient World)*, Atlanta, Society of Biblical Literature

GOLB, Norman, (1998), *The Jews in Medieval Normandy: a social and intellectual history*, Cambridge, Cambridge University Press

GORSKY, Jeffrey, (2015), *Exiles in Sepharad: The Jewish Millennium in Spain*, Philadelphia, The Jewish Publication Society

GOULET, Jean-Guy, **MURPHY**, Liam D., (2015), *Religious Diversity Today: Experiencing Religion in the Contemporary World*, Santa Barbara, Praeger

GRAETZ, Heinrich, (**Lowy**, Bella, Ed.), (2009), *History of the Jews: From the Rise of the Kabbala (1270) to the Permanent Settlement of the Marranos in Holland (1618)*, New York, Cisimo Classics

GROSSER, Paul E., **HALPERIN**, Edwin G., (1978), *The causes and effects of anti-Semitism: the dimensions of a prejudice :an analysis and chronology of 1,900 years of anti-Semitic attitudes and practices*, New York, Philosophical Library

GRUEN, Erich S., (1993), 'Hellenism and Persecution: Antiochus IV and the Jews', in **Green**, Peter, (1993), *Hellenistic History and Culture*, Berkeley, University of California Press

GUNKEL, Hermann, (1964), *The Legends of Genesis*, New York, Schoken Books

HALE, Vincent, (2013), *Mesopotamian Gods & Goddesses*, New York, Britannica Educational

HALLO, W. H., and **YOUNGER**, K. L., (2003), *The Context of Scripture. Vol. II: Monumental Inscriptions from the Biblical World*, Brill Academic Publishing, Leiden

HANDCOCK, Percy, (1920), *Selections from the Tell El-Amarna letters*, New York, Society for Promoting Christian Knowledge, The Macmillan Company

HANFSTAENGL, Ernst, (2005), *The Unknown Hitler: Notes from the Young Nazi Party*, London, Gibson Square

HANSON, K. C., and **OAKMAN**, Douglas E., (1998), *Palestine in the Time of Yeshua: Social Structures and Social Conflicts*, Minneapolis, Fortress

HASAN, Israr, (2006), *Believers and Brothers: A History of Uneasy Relationship*, Bloomington, Indiana, Author House

HAYES-HEALY, Stephanie A., Ed. (2005), *Medieval Paradigms: Essays in Honor of Jeremy DuQuesnay Adams, Volume 2*, New York, Palgrave MacMillian

HEGERMANN, Harald, 'The Diaspora in the Hellenistic Age', in **DAVIES** and **FINKELSTEIN** (Eds.), (2008), *The Cambridge History of Judaism, Vol. 2*, Cambridge, Cambridge University Press

HELLER, Celia Stopnicka, (1993), *On the Edge of Destruction: Jews of Poland Between the Two World Wars*, Detroit, Wayne State University Press

HERZL, Theodor, (Patai, Raphael Ed.), (1960), *The Complete Diaries of Theodor Herzl, Vols 1-5*, New York, Dover Publications

HERZL, Theodor, (1896) (**LIPSKY**, Louis, **BEIN**, Alex, Commentators), (Harry Zohn Trans.), *The Jewish State*, New York, The Herzl Press, Thomas Yoseloff, (This Dover edition, first published in 1988, is an unabridged, unaltered republication of the work originally published in 1946, by the American Zionist Emergency Council, New York, based on a revised translation published by the Scopus Publishing Company, New York, 1943, which was, in turn, based on the first English-language edition, 'A Jewish State', translated by Sylvie d'Avigdor, and published by Nutt, London, England, 1896. The Herzl text was originally published under the title 'Der Judenstaat' in Vienna, 1896)

HILBERG, Raul, (2003), *The Destruction of the European Jews Vol III*, Yale University Press, New Haven

HILLEL, Geva, et al, (1994), *Ancient Jerusalem Revealed*, Washington, Biblical Archaeology Society & Israel Exploration Society

HITLER, Adolf, (1939), *Mein Kampf,* London, Hurst & Blacket

HOLLOWAY, Steven W., (2002), *Aššur is King! Aššur is King! - Religion in the Exercise of Power in the Neo-Assyrian Empire*, Leiden, Brill Academic Publishing

HOSCHANDER, Jacob, (1923), *The Book of Esther in the Light of History*, Oxford, Oxford University Press

HOULDEN, James L., (2003), *Yeshua in History, Thought, and Culture: Entries A - J*, Santa Barbara, ABC-CLIO

HOWARTH, Stephen, (2006), *The Knights Templar,* London, Bloomsbury

HYAMSON, Albert Montefiore, (1942), *Palestine: A Policy*, London, Methuen

INWOOD, Stephen, (1998), *A History of London*, London, Macmillan

IRVING, M. Zeitlin, (2007), *The Historical Muhammad.* Cambridge, Polity

JACOB, Alexander, (1997), *Eugen Dühring on the Jews, A translation of The Jewish Problem as a Problem of Race, Morals and Culture*, Brighton, Nineteen Eighty Four Press

JAMES, Peter, (1993), *Centuries in Darkness*, New Jersey, Rutgers University Press

JOSEPHUS, Flavius, (Paul Meyer, Commentary), (1999), *The New Complete Works of Josephus*, Grand Rapids, Kregel Publications

KAEGI, Walter Emil, (2003), *Heraclius, Emperor of Byzantium*, Cambridge, Cambridge University Press

KANTOR, Máttis, (2007), *Codex Judaica: Chronological Index of Jewish History*, New York, Zichron Press

KANTOR, Máttis, (1993), *The Jewish Time Line Encyclopaedia: A Year-by-Year History From Creation to the Present*, New York, Jason Aronson, Inc.

KENYON Kathleen M., (1985), *Archaeology in the Holy Land 4th ed.* London, Thomas Nelson Inc.

KING, P. D., (1972), *Law And Society In The Visigothic Kingdom*, Cambridge, Cambridge University Press

KESEN, Ramazan, (1993), *History of Harran, Ankara, Turkey*, Ankara, Turkish Religious Foundation Publishing Printing and Trade Office

KIMMERLING, Baruch, (2010), *Clash of Identities: Exploration in Israeli and Palestinian Societies*, New York, Columbia University Press

KLIEMAN, Aaron S., (1970), *Foundations of British Policy in the Arab World: The Cairo Conference of 1921*, Baltimore, John Hopkins Press

LANGMUIR, Gavin I., (1996), *Toward a Definition of Antisemitism*, Berkley, University of California Press

LAZARE, Bernard and **WISTRICH**, Robert, (1995), *Antisemitism: Its History and Causes*, Lincoln, University of Nebraska Press

LEMCHE, Niels Peter, (1998), The Israelites in History and Tradition, London, Westminster John Knox Press

LEVENE, Mark & **ROBERTS**, Penny, (1999), *The Massacre in History*, New York, Berghahn Books

LEVENSON, Alan T., (2012), *The Wiley-Blackwell History of the Jews and Judaism*, Oxford, Wiley Blackwell

LEVENTHAL, Michael, **GOLDSTEIN**, Richard, (2013), *Jews in Britain*, London, Bloomsbury Publishing

LEVY, Richard S., (2005), *Antisemitism: A Historical Encyclopaedia of Prejudice and Persecution, Volume 1 A-K*, Santa Barbara, ABC-CLIO

LEWIS, Bernard, (1984), *The Jews of Islam*, Princeton, Princeton University Press

LINDER, Amon, (1987), *The Jews in Roman Imperial Legislation*, Detroit, Wayne State University Press

LLOYD GEORGE, David, (1934), *War Memoirs, Vol 2*, London, Ivor Nicholson and Watson

LOEWE, L, Dr, (Ed.), (1890), *Diaries of Sir Moses and Lady Montefiore Vol 1,*Chicago, Belford-Clarke Co.

MACAGG, William, (1989), *A History of Hapsburg Jews – 1670-1918*, Bloomington, Indiana University Press

MADDEN, Thomas F., (2002), *The Crusades: The Essential Readings. (Blackwell Essential Readings in History),*Hoboken, Wiley-Blackwell

MANN, Jacob, (1920), *The Jews in Egypt and in Palestine*, Oxford, Oxford University Press

MARCUS, Jacob Rader, (1938), *The Jew in the Medieval World: A Sourcebook, 315-1791*, New York, JPS

MARCUS, Jacob Rader, (2000), *The Jew in the Medieval World: A Source Book, 315-1791 (Revised ed.)*, Pittsburgh, Hebrew Union College Press

MAYER, Hans, (1988), *The Crusades*, Oxford, Oxford University Press

MEINERTZHAGEN, Richard, (1960), *Middle East Diary*, New York, Thomas Yoseloff

MELTON, Gordon J., (2014), *Faiths Across Time, 5000 Years of Religious History Vol 1: 3500 BCE-499CE*, Santa Barbara, ABC-CLIO

MICHALOWSKI, Piotr, (1993), *Letters from Early Mesopotamia, Society of Biblical Literature Translations Series*, Atlanta, Scholars Press

MIKABERIDZE, Alexander, (Ed.,), (2013), *Atrocities, Massacres and War Crimes – An Encyclopaedia, Volume 1:A-L*, Santa Barbara, ABC-CLIO

MITCHELL, Thomas G., (1957), *Likud Leaders: The Lives and Careers of Menachem Begin, Yitzhak Shamir, Benjamin Netanyahu and Ariel Sharon*, Jefferson, McFarland & Company Inc.

MORAN, William L., (1992), *The Amarna Letters*, Baltimore, Johns Hopkins University Press

MORRILL, John, (1990), *Oliver Cromwell and the English Revolution*, Cambridge, Longman

MORRIS, Benny, (Quoted in) (1948), *A History of the First Arab Israeli War*, Connecticut, Yale University Press

MULLER, James W., (2002), Churchill As Peacemaker, Cambridge, Woodrow Wilson Center Press & Cambridge University Press

MUNDILL, Robin R., (2010), *The King's Jews: Money, Massacre and Exodus in Medieval England*, London, Bloomsbury

MUNN-RANKIN, J.M., (1975), 'Assyrian Military Power. 1300-1200 BC', in Edwards, E.S., (1975), Cambridge *Ancient History, Vol. 2*, Cambridge, Cambridge University Press

MYERS, Susan E., **MACMICHAEL**, Steven J., (1999), *The Friars and Jews in the Middle Ages and Renaissance*, Leiden, Brill Academic Publishing

MYLOD, E.J., **PERRY**, Guy, **SMITH**, Thomas W., **VANDEBURIE**, Jan, (2016), *The Fifth Crusade in Context: The Crusading Movement in the Early Thirteenth Century*, Abingdon, Routledge

NEUSNER, Jacob, (2008), *A History of the Jews in Babylonia, Part V: Later Sasanian Times*, Leiden, Brill Academic Publishing

NICOSIA, Francis R., (2008), *Zionism and Anti-Semitism in Nazi Germany*, New York, Cambridge University Press

NIGOSIAN, Solomon A., (1987), *Islam, The way of submission*, Bath, Crucible, The Aquarian Press

OPPENHEIM, A. L., **PRITCHARD**, J. B., (Eds.), (1969), *Babylonian and Assyrian Historical Texts in Ancient Near Eastern Texts Relating to the Old Testament*, Princeton, Princeton University Press

OPPENHEIMER, Stephen, (2007), *The Origins of the British: The New Prehistory of Britain: A Genetic Detective Story*, London, Robinson

PARSONS, Nicholas, (2008), *Vienna: A Cultural History*, New York, Oxford University Press

PETERS, Edward, (1989), *Inquisition*, Berkley, University of California Press

PETERS, F. E., (1994), *Mecca: A Literary History of the Muslim Holy Land*, Princeton, Princeton University Press

PETTINATO, Giovanni, (1981), *Archives of Ebla: An Empire Inscribed in Clay (Translation of Ebla: Un Impero Inciso Nell'Argilla)*, London, Doubleday

PHILLIPS, Jonathan, (2005), *The Forth Crusade: And the sack of Constantinople, (New Edition)*, London, Pimlico, A Penguin Random House Company

PIERSON, Paul Everett, (2009), *The Dynamics of Christian Mission: History Through a Missiological Perspective*, Pasadena, William Carey International University Press

PINKUS, Benjamin, (1989), *The Jews of the Soviet Union: The history of a National Minority*, Melbourne, Cambridge University Press

POLLOCK, John, (1985), *Shaftesbury The Reformer*, Eastbourne, Kingsway Publications

POPKIN, Richard Henry, (1992), *The Third Force in Seventeenth Century Thought*, Leiden, E J Brill

POWELL, Mark Allan, (1998), *Yeshua as a Figure in History: How Modern Historians View the Man from Galilee*. Louisville, Westminster John Knox Press

QUATRIGLIO, Giuseppe, (2005), *A Thousand Years in Sicily: From the Arabs to the Bourbons*, Ontario, Legas Publishing

RAPHAEL, Jospe, **WAGNER**, Stanley M., (Eds.), (1981), *Great Schisms in Jewish History*, New York, Ktav Publishing House

RAST, Walter E., (1922), *Through the ages in Palestinian archaeology: An Introductory Handbook (Illustrated ed.)*, Continuum International Publishing Group

RAVIV, Moshe, (1998), *Israel at Fifty – Five Decades of Struggle For Peace*, London, Weidenfeld & Nicolson

REINHARZ, Jehuda, (Ed.) (1977), *The Letters and Papers of Chaim Weizmann, vol. IX*, New Jersey, Transaction Books

RICHARDSON, Peter, (1999), *Herod: King of the Jews and friend of the Romans*, New York, Continuum International Publishing Group

RILEY, Thomas, (1873), *Chronicles of the Mayors and Sheriffs of London*, London, Trubner & Co.

REILLY, Thomas, **KAUFMAN**, Stephen, **BODINO**, Angela, (2002), *Racism: A Global Reader (Sources & Studies in World History)*, New York, M E Sharpe

RILEY-SMITH, Jonathan, (2005), *The Crusades: A Short History (Second ed.)*, London, Yale University Press

ROCCA, Samuel, (2008), *The Forts of Judaea 168 BC – AD 73*, Oxford, Osprey Publishing

RODGERS, Zuleika, (2006), *Making History: Josephus and Historical Method*, Leiden, Brill Academic Publishing

ROHL, David M., (1995), *Pharaohs and Kings: A Biblical Quest*, New York, Crown

ROSENBERG, Elliot, (1997), *But Where They Good for the Jews*, Secaucus, Carol Publishing Company

ROSENZWEIG, Franz, (2012), *Between East and West, in Ninety-Two Poems and Hymns of Yehuda Halevi*, New York, The State University of New York Press

ROTH, Norman, (2014), *Medieval Jewish Civilisation: An Encyclopaedia*, New York, Routledge

ROUX, Georges, (1964), *Ancient Iraq*, London, Penguin Books

RUSSELL, Ada, (1914), *Alexander the Great*, New York, Frederick A. Stokes Co.

Schwarz, Joseph Rabbi, (Lesser, Isaac, Trans.), (1850), *A Descriptive Geography and Brief Historical Sketch of Palestine*, Philadelphia, A. Hart

SARTRE, Maurice, (2005), *The Middle East under Rome*. Massachusetts, Belknap Press (Harvard University Press)

SCHAFER, Peter, (2003), *The Bar Kokhba War Reconsidered: New Perspectives on the Second Jewish Revolt Against Rome*, Tübingen, Mohr Siebeck

SCHARMA, Simon, (2014), *The Story of the Jews: Finding the Words (1000 BCE – 1492)*, London, Vintage

SCHARMA, Simon, (2017), *Belonging: The Story of the Jews 1492–1900*, London, Vintage

SCHARFSTEIN, Sol, (1997), *Chronicle of Jewish History: From the Patriarchs to the 21st Century*, New York, Ktav Publishing House Inc.

SCHECHTER, S., (1908), *Studies in Judaism*, Philadelphia, The Jewish Publication Society of America

SCHREIBER, Mordecai, (2008), *The Shengold Jewish Encyclopaedia*, New York, Shengold Publishers Inc.

SCHULTZ, Joseph P., (1981), *Judaism and the Gentile Faiths: Comparative Studies in Religion*, New Jersey, Fairleigh Dickinson University Press

SEAVER, James Everett, (1952), *The Persecution of the Jews in the Roman Empire (300-428)*, Kansas, The University of Kansas Press

SEGEV, Tom, (2000), *One Palestine Complete*, New York, Metropolitan Books

SHACHAR, Isaiah, (1974), *The Judensau : a medieval anti-Jewish motif and its history*, London, University of London

SHACHAR, Isaiah, quoted in, **KATZ**, Steven T., & **ROSEN**, Alan, (Eds.) (2013), *Wiesel, Elie, Jewish, Literary, and Moral Perspectives*, Indiana, Indiana University Press

SKINNER, Patricia, (Ed.), (2003), *The Jews in Medieval Britain: Historical, Literary and Archaeological Perspectives*, Woodbridge, The Boydell Press

SKOLNIK, Fred, **Berenbaum**, Michael, (2007), *Encyclopaedia Judaica, Vol. 13*, New York, Macmillan Reference USA

SLACK, Corliss K., (2013), *Historical Dictionary of the Crusades*, Lanham, Scarecrow Press

SMALLWOOD, E. Mary, (2001), *The Jews under Roman Rule from Pompey to Diocletian: Vol 20: A Study in Political Relations*, Leiden, Brill Academic Publishing

SMALLWOOD, E. Mary, in **WILLIAMSON**, G. A., (Trans), (1981), *Josephus, the Jewish War*, rev. ed, London, Penguin

SOMBART, Werner, (2015), (M. Epstein, Trans.), original publication in the German as *Die Juden und das Wirtschaftsleben* (1911),*The Jews and Modern Capitalism*, Eastford, Martino Fine Books

STEIN, Leonard, (1961), *The Balfour Declaration*, New York, Simon and Schuster

STEM, E., (1982), *Material Culture of the Land of the Bible in the Persian Period 538-332 B.C.*, Warminster, Aris & Phillips

TALIAFERRO, Karen, (Ed.), (2014), *Christianity And Religious Freedom Sourcebook Scriptural Theological Legal Texts, The Religious Freedom Project*, Berkley, Berkley Center for Religion, Peace & World Affairs

TALIAFERRO, Karen, **ANDERSON**, Matthew, (Eds.), (2014), *Islam And Religious Freedom: Sourcebook Scriptural Theological Legal Texts, The Religious Freedom Project*, Berkley, Berkley Center for Religion, Peace & World Affairs

TAYLOR, J. E., (2012), *The Essenes, the Scrolls, and the Dead Sea*, Oxford, Oxford University Press

TETA, Magda, (2006), *Jews and Heretics in Catholic Poland: A Beleaguered Church in the Post-Reformation Era*, Cambridge, Cambridge University Press

THOMSON, Professor R. W., **Howard-Johnston**, James (Trans), (1999), *The Armenian History Attributed to Sebeos*, Liverpool, Liverpool University Press

TOAFF, Ariel, **MACMICHAEL**, S. J., **MYERS**, S. E., (2004), (Eds.), *Jews, Franciscans, and the First monti di Pieta in Italy (1462–1500)*, Leiden, Brill Academic Publishing

TYERMAN, Christopher, (2006), *God's War: A New History of the Crusades*, Massachusetts, Belknap Press (Harvard)

URBANI, Rossana, **ZAZZU**, Guido Nathan, (Eds.), (1999), *The Jews of Genoa: 507-1681*, Leiden, Brill Academic Publishing

VAJDA, G. Haman in **Menage**, Lewis, B. V. L., **Pellat**, C., and **Schacht**, J., (Eds.), (1971), *Encyclopaedia of Islam Volume III*, (New Edition), Leiden, Brill Academic Publishing

VAN VOORST, Robert E., (2000), *Yeshua Outside the New Testament: An Introduction to the Ancient Evidence*, Michigan, Wm. B. Eerdmans Publishing

WEATHERFORD, Jack, (2004), *Genghis Khan and the Making of the Modern World*, New York, Three Rivers Press

WEIZMANN, Chaim, (1983), *The Letters and Papers of Chaim Weizmann: August 1898-July 1931*, New Jersey, Transaction Publishers

WIESEL, Elie, (1982), *Night*, Bantam Books, London

WOOD, Leon James, **O'BRIEN**, David, (1986), *A survey of Israel's history*, Zondervan, Grand Rapids

ZACK, Naomi, (1993), *Race and Mixed Race*, Philadelphia, Temple University Press

Journals, Articles & Extracts

A Letter to the Readers: [Discoveries at Ebla]. (1977). The Biblical Archaeologist, 40(1), 2-4. doi:10.2307/3209565

ADLER, Michael, (1893) *The Emperor Julian and the Jews*, The Jewish Quarterly Review, vol. 5, no. 4, 1893

ALBRIGHT, W. F. *Is the Mesha Inscription a Forgery?*, The Jewish Quarterly Review, vol. 35, no. 3, 1945, pp. 247–2502017. JSTOR, www.jstor.org/stable/1452186. Retrieved 17/05/2017

ALTHANN, Robert, *The Impact Of Ebla On Biblical Studies - Religion in Southern Africa*, vol. 2, no. 1, 1981, pp. 39–47., www.jstor.org/stable/24763954

Anti-Semite's' Petition (1880-1881) http://germanhistorydocs.ghi-dc.org/docpage.cfm?docpage_id=2630, retrieved 21/6/2017

BEŠKA, (1934), Emanuel, *Khalil al-Sakakini and Zionism before WWI*, https://www.academia.edu/19348984/Khalil_al-Sakakini_and_Zionism_before_WWI, Retrieved 26/09/2017

Biotechnology and Biological Sciences Research Council, (2007, July 19), *New Research Proves Single Origin Of Humans In Africa*, Science Daily. Retrieved March 22, 2017 from www.sciencedaily.com/releases/2007/07/070718140829.htm

BRESSLAU, M. H. (Ed.), (1860), *The Hebrew Review and Magazine for Jewish Literature*, Vol 1, London

CAMPBELL, Duncan B., (2010), *Capturing a desert fortress: Flavius Silva and the siege of Masada*, Ancient Warfare Vol. IV, no. 2

CANON XI, *The Canons of The Council of Truro*, https://sourcebooks.fordham.edu/basis/trullo.asp, retrieved 12/07/2017

CARPENTER, A., (1904), *Naturalization in England and the American Colonies*, The American Historical Review, 9(2), 288-303. doi:10.2307/1833367, retrieved 20/08/2017

COHEN, Mark R., (1991), *The Neo-Lachrymose Conception of Jewish-Arab History*, Tikkun 6 (May-June):55–60

CHURCHILL, Winston, (1922), *House of Commons Speech*, 4th July, http://hansard.millbanksystems.com/commons/1922/jul/04/colonial-office#S5CV0156P0_19220704_HOC_338 retrieved 25/09/2017

DAVIES, Lord, *House of Lords Speech*, 10/3/1942, http://hansard.millbanksystems.com/lords/1942/mar/10/palestine#S5LV0122P0_19420310_HOL_59, retrieved 29/9/2017

DEVER, William, (2011), *Interview with NOVA Bible's Buried Secrets*, Documentary 08/18/2011

DUBNOW, S. M., (1916), *History of the Jews in Russia and Poland from the earliest times until the present day Vol 1*, The Jewish Publication Society of America, Philadelphia

FINKELSTEIN, I., (1996), *The Archaeology of the United Monarchy: an Alternative View*, Levant 28, pp177–187

FINKELSTEIN, Israel, (Nadav Na'aman Ed.), (1994), *From Nomadism to Monarchy: Archaeological and Historical Aspects of Early Israel*, Biblical Archaeology Society, Jerusalem

FINKELSTEIN, Israel, (2003), *Is the Philistine Paradigm Still Viable? The Synchronisation of civilisations in the Eastern Mediterranean in the Second Millennium BC. III Proceedings of the SCIEM 2000 – 2nd Euro Conference Vienna*, 28th May – 1st of June

FIRESTONE, Reuven, (2016), *Muslim-Jewish Relations, Islamic Studies, Judaism and Jewish Studies*, Religion and Politics Online Publication, http://religion.oxfordre.com/view/10.1093/acrefore/9780199340378.001.0001/acrefore-9780199340378-e-17?rskey=o40Z88&result=1 Retrieved 21/06/2017

FREDERICK II, (1236) Holy Roman Emperor, *Refuting Ritual Murder Accusations*, retrieved from http://www.ccjr.us/dialogika-resources/primary-texts-from-the-history-of-the-relationship/265-frederick-ii, 18/07/2017

GARFINKEL, Yosef, and **GANOR**, S., (2012), *Khirbet Qeiyafa - a Fortified City on the Philistia-Judah Border in the Early Iron II*. http://www.jhsonline.org/cocoon/JHS/a099.html, retrieved 15/05/2017

GOLAN, David, (1986), *Hadrian's Decision to Supplant 'Jerusalem' by 'Aelia Capitolina.'* Historia: Zeitschrift Für Alte Geschichte, vol. 35, no. 2, 1986, www.jstor.org/stable/4435963. Retrieved 14/6/2017

Human Genome Research Institute. https://www.genome.gov/19016904/faq-about-genetic-and-genomic-science/ retrieved 08/05/2017

KLEIN, Dr Eitan, *Israel Antiquities Authority*, October 26 2016, http://mfa.gov.il/MFA/IsraelExperience/History/Pages/Rare-First-Temple-period-document-mentioning-Jerusalem-uncovered-26-October-2016.aspx, Retrieved 20/7/2017

LEMAIRE, A., (1994), *House of David Restored in Moabite Inscription*, Biblical Archaeology Review, Washington, 20/3

LEMAIRE, André, (1994), *House of David Restored in Moabite Inscription -* Biblical Archaeology Review 20:03, May/June

LUCKENBILL, Daniel David, (1911), *Benhadad and Hadadezer*, The American Journal of Semitic Languages and Literatures 27, no. 3

Mandates *Palestine Report of the Palestine Royal Commission* presented by the Secretary of State for the Colonies to the United Kingdom Parliament by Command of His Britannic Majesty (July 1937),Series of League of Nations Publications VI. A. Mandates 1937. VI A. 5

MAZAR, Eilat, (2008), *Did I Find King David's Palace?*, Biblical Archaeology Review, 70, Preliminary Report on The City of David Excavations, Shalem Press, Jerusalem

MICHALOWSKI, Piotr, (1983), *Cuneiform Texts* in the National Geographic Society, Oriens Antiquus 22

MICHALOWSKI, Piotr, (1998), *Cuneiform Texts from Kazane Höyük I*, (with Adnan Misir), Journal of Cuneiform Studies 50

MICHALOWSKI, Piotr, (2008), *On Ur III Times: Studies in Honor of X*, Journal of Cuneiform Studies Supplementary Series 1

MORGENSTERN, Dr. Arie, (2002), in *Azure: Ideas for the Jewish Nation*; No. 12 Winter 5762/2002 (Polisar, Daniel (Ed.), The Shalem Centre, Jerusalem

POLKEHN, Klaus, (1976), *The Secret Contacts: Zionism and Nazi Germany, 1933-1941*, Journal of Palestine Studies, vol. 5, no. 3/4, 1976, pp. 54–82. JSTOR, www.jstor.org/stable/2536016

POPE JOHN PAUL II, (2001), *To his beatitude Christodoulos, Archbishop of Athens and Primate of Greec*, 4th May 2001, retrieved from https:// w2.vatican.va/content/john-paul-ii/en/speeches/2001/may/documents/ hf_jp-ii_spe_20010504_archbishop-athens.html, 17/07/2017

POPE PAUL IV, (1555), *Cum Nimis Absurdum* ["Since it is completely senseless ..."], 14 July

POPE PIUS VI, (1775), *Editto sopra gli ebrei* (Edict concerning the Jews), Vatican Archives

POPKIN, Jeremy D., (1981), *Zionism and the Enlightenment: The 'Letter of a Jew to His Brethren.'*, Jewish Social Studies, vol. 43, no. 2, JSTOR, www.jstor.org/stable/4467125, retrieved 25\08\2017

RHL, (1938), *Chancellor Papers*, 22:MF40, ff., 20 Dec. 1937 and FO 371/20035 E3483 and Policy in Palestine on the Outbreak of War, FO 371/21865 E56C/G, 26 Sept

SZULC, Tad, (2001), *Journey of Faith, National Geographic Magazine*, Dec, retrieved 24/03/2017 from http://ngm.nationalgeographic.com/print/features/world/asia/israel/abraham-text

SKA, J, L., (1978), *Les decouvertes de Tell Mardikh-Elba et la Bible*, Nouvelle Revue Theologique 100

The Lessons for CI of the Dreyfus Affair. (2011), 22. Studies in Intelligence Vol. 55, No. 1 (Extracts, March)

Index